Practical Reason and Norms

Practical Reason
and Norms

Joseph Raz

OXFORD
UNIVERSITY PRESS

This book has been printed digitally and produced in a standard specification
in order to ensure its continuing availability

OXFORD
UNIVERSITY PRESS

Great Clarendon Street, Oxford OX2 6DP

Oxford University Press is a department of the University of Oxford.
It furthers the University's objective of excellence in research, scholarship,
and education by publishing worldwide in

Oxford New York

Auckland Bangkok Buenos Aires Cape Town Chennai
Dar es Salaam Delhi Hong Kong Istanbul Karachi Kolkata
Kuala Lumpur Madrid Melbourne Mexico City Mumbai Nairobi
São Paulo Shanghai Singapore Taipei Tokyo Toronto

with an associated company in Berlin

Oxford is a registered trade mark of Oxford University Press
in the UK and in certain other countries

Published in the United States
by Oxford University Press Inc., New York

Originally published in 1975 by Hutchinson & Co. (Publishers) Ltd.,
and reprinted in 1990 by Princeton University Press
by arrangement with the author.
© 1975 Joseph Raz
© 1990 (with new postscript) Joseph Raz
This edition © 1999 Joseph Raz

Cover photograph: 'Underneath the arches', by Joseph Raz

Acknowledgements

I owe a debt of gratitude to H. L. A. Hart, A. J. P. Kenny and H. Oberdiek, who read and commented on earlier drafts of several sections. I am particularly bound to H. Frankfurt who did much to clear both my thoughts and my language of many obscurities. Most of all I benefited from the advice of P. M. S. Hacker who with unlimited patience mixed encouragement with criticism and from whom I learned a great deal and could have learned more.

I am grateful to the editors of *The American Philosophical Quarterly, Mind* and *The Modern Law Review* for permission to include material from the following articles:

'Permissions and Supererogation', *A.P.Q.* (1975), parts of which are incorporated in section 3.1.

'Reasons for Action, Decisions and Norms', *Mind* (1975), parts of which are incorporated in sections 1.2. and 2.2.

'The Institutionalized Nature of Law', *M.L.R.*, **38** (1975), on which parts of sections 4.3 and 5.1 are based.

JOSEPH RAZ

Contents

Introduction

This is a study in the theory of norms. The expression 'norm' is used as a term of art. The nearest English equivalent is 'rule'. Rules, however, are of a variety of logical types and the present study is concerned with only some of them, which I shall call 'norms'. These include some of the more important kinds of rules such as those which are sometimes called categorical rules, i.e. rules which require that a certain action be performed, as well as rules granting permissions. In Chapters 2 and 3 I shall offer an analysis of the different types of norms and their main logical features. Chapters 4 and 5 are concerned with an analysis of normative systems, that is of systems of norms. We regard the rules of a game or of a language, the laws of a country or the regulations and rules of a social club as forming a system. We say that 'this is a rule of soccer but it is not a rule of rugby' or that 'it is a rule of English but not of French' or that 'this is part of English law but there is no such law in the American legal system'. Such statements testify to a conception by which certain groups of norms are more than haphazard assemblages of norms. Normative systems are understood to have some kind of unity. I shall explore a few kinds of normative system and show how their unity consists in certain patterns of logical relations among their norms. One of the most important type of normative system in the modern world is the legal system and Chapter 5 is exclusively concerned with the analysis of legal systems.

The key concept for the explanation of norms is that of reasons for action. To my mind the main difficulty in explaining rules is to understand their relations to reasons for action. The central thesis of the book is that some kinds of rules (categorical and permissive rules) are reasons for action of a special type, and that other rules (power-conferring rules) are logically related to such reasons. The first chapter of the book deals with some of the general features of reasons for action and with the special features of reasons of the kind which those rules are.

The fact that norms are explained in terms of reasons for action establishes connections between them and many other normative concepts which also presuppose the notion of a reason for action. It is not possible to explore these connections in full in the present study. I have tried to show how norms and reasons contribute to the explanation of prescriptions such as commands and orders (cf. section 2.3), of authority (cf. sections 2.2 and 3.2) and of supererogation (cf. section 3.1). I have also stated rather dogmatically my view as to the way the concepts explored here are essential to the explanation of voluntary obligations such as promises (cf. section 3.2). But a full and adequate treatment of these topics would take us beyond the bounds of the present study and has not been attempted here. For the same reason I have had to resist the temptation to discuss rights and duties, despite the obvious conceptual ties between them and the concepts discussed.

The preceding remarks indicate that here and there I have included remarks which go beyond the strict analysis of norms and normative systems. I have allowed myself this luxury in order to convey my belief that practical philosophy is in many ways a unified philosophical field. The study of rules should not be viewed as an isolated investigation but as part of a larger enterprise. The success of any theory of norms depends in part on its contribution to the clarification of the other main concepts of the philosophy of practical reason (or practical philosophy for short). It will help in understanding the general tenor of the present study, and its underlying presuppositions, if I sketch in brief the relation between its subject and other problems of practical philosophy.

Practical philosophy includes both a substantive or 'evaluative' part and a formal part concerned with conceptual analysis. Substantive practical philosophy includes all the arguments designed to show which values we should pursue, what reasons for action should guide our behaviour, which norms are binding, etc. The conceptual analysis concerns the logical features of concepts like value, reason for action or norm and the nature of the rules of inference governing practical reasoning. I am not assuming that these parts of practical philosophy are entirely independent of each other. But there is no doubt that they are relatively independent: various works can emphasize one part or the other. The present study is primarily an essay in conceptual analysis.

Practical philosophy can also be thought of in terms of the spheres of activity or nature of human relationships with which it is concerned. In this sense, moral philosophy, political philosophy and legal philosophy are branches of practical philosophy each dealing with a different aspect of human life.[1] There is little point in arguing at length about the relations among different philosophical disciplines. But it is not futile to point out the many concepts which are used in all these philosophical disciplines. Rights, duties and justice, power and authority, rules and principles—these are but a few of the concepts which are extensively used both in ethics and in political and legal philosophy. There are also many problems common to all. The problem of rationality in action and that of responsibility for actions and their consequences are only two examples of common problems the solution to which consists in formulating critical or 'evaluative' principles which apply to all these disciplines. The considerable overlap between these and other related philosophical disciplines creates the need to study these concepts and problems, not within the narrow and confined bounds of each discipline, but generally, with a mind open to all their applications and consequences as part of general practical philosophy. Since the concepts of rule and normative system are important to law, morals and politics as well as to other philosophical disciplines, the study of these two concepts forms an important part of the general philosophy of practical reason. The last chapter, which deals with legal systems, is in fact an essay in legal philosophy which shows how it is grounded in practical philosophy.

A different way of dividing practical philosophy into branches is not by the sphere of activity or aspect of life which is dealt with but by the sort of practical problems discussed. By this criterion the most important branches of practical philosophy are value theory, normative theory[2] and ascriptive theory. The theory of value is primarily concerned with comparing various actual or possible situations to determine which is better than the other and to identify their good- or bad-making features. The most important concepts of value theory are value, good, bad and better or worse than. Normative theory is primarily concerned with establishing what people ought to do. It presupposes some value theory and derives from it the requirements which it imposes on the behaviour of individuals.* Who ought to realize which values and how is the main problem of normative theory. Its most important concepts are ought, reasons for action, rules, duties and rights. I shall argue below that of these a reason for

---

* Throughout this book I use 'individuals', 'persons' and 'agents' to include 'corporate persons' such as committees, parliaments and states.

action is the most fundamental. The theory of ascription is concerned with the conditions in which blame or guilt can be ascribed to people. I prefer the term 'theory of ascription' to the more familiar 'theory of responsibility' since 'responsibility' may be a slightly misleading term here.[3] It is the job of normative theory to determine whose responsibility it is to realize this or that value, whose responsibility it is to look after the sick, etc. The theory of ascription deals with the ascription of blame and praise to people who fulfilled or failed to fulfil their responsibilities. It presupposes that we have a normative theory and studies the normative consequences of failure to conform to the requirements of normative theory. The problems it studies include the relevance of mistaken moral beliefs or weakness of will or mistake of fact or clumsiness, etc., on the attribution of responsibility or blame. It also studies the features which render right behaviour praiseworthy.

The fact that this is a study in normative theory has enabled me to disregard the very difficult epistemological problems which have dominated much of the literature concerning practical philosophy during the present century. The epistemological problems of practical philosophy concern the conditions which must obtain if the making of a practical statement or utterance is to be justified. A variety of arguments against intuitionism of the kind espoused, for example, by G. E. Moore and W. D. Ross, and many different attempts to expose 'the naturalistic fallacy', have raised doubts concerning the possibility of establishing the validity of ultimate values, that is of those values whose validity cannot be derived from other values. These arguments do not pose a similar threat to the possibility of relative justification of practical statements or utterances, in which the justification of a practical statement or utterance relies on the assumption of certain ultimate values. There is nothing in the arguments referred to which suggests that given a certain set of values it is impossible to use them to justify the validity of derivative values or of rules or other reasons for action. Since the present book is not concerned in any way with ultimate values, it has been possible to disregard the sceptical arguments mentioned and related epistemological problems. All that is here presupposed is the possibility of relative justification of practical statements.

It is true that the very possibility of relative justification in practical philosophy has also been challenged. Some have expressed the view that only utterances the meaning of which can be explained by a truth-functional analysis are capable of logical relations. This view has since been disproved. R. M. Hare (*The Language of Morals*, Oxford, 1952) and G. H. von Wright ('Deontic Logic', *Mind*, lx, 1951) have led the revival of interest in the logical study of practical discourse,[4] and a growing number of works have been published dedicated to the study of the logical properties of many key practical concepts. But with very few exceptions most logical studies are confined to the logic of 'ought', 'may' and 'prohibited'. There have also been many useful studies of isolated concepts like rules, justice, duty, authority, responsibility, rights, virtue, etc. But on the whole these are studied in isolation and we are still a long way from having anything like a clear picture of the logical relations between these and similar concepts. Whatever the truth concerning the epistemological problems about ultimate values, the present work is based on the belief that it is possible and necessary to develop a unified logic of all the concepts belonging to normative theory and that the most fundamental part of such a logic is not deontic logic but the logic of reasons for action.

1 On reasons for action

1.1 ON THE STRUCTURE OF REASONS

In the following chapters norms will be analysed by explaining their relations to reasons for action. The purpose of the present section is to introduce some distinctions which will be used later on. I shall try to say enough to show that these distinctions are plausible and useful, but it will not be possible to justify them fully, or to compare them with other views of reasons to be found in philosophical writings. Many important problems concerning reasons which are not relevant for the questions discussed in this book will go unmentioned. It is my belief that in the main my conclusions concerning norms and the law do not depend on the correctness in detail of the views here expressed about reasons in general. The following remarks may be taken, therefore, as indicating just one view of reasons which makes it possible to relate norms to reasons, though I, of course, believe this view to be the correct one.

The role of reasons

As well as reasons for actions, there are reasons for beliefs, for desires and emotions, for attitudes, for norms and institutions, and many others. Of these, reasons for action and for belief are the most fundamental types of reasons, the others being derived from or dependent on them. I shall be concerned exclusively with reasons for action and by 'reasons' I shall normally refer to reasons for action only. This does not imply a belief in a fundamental difference between reasons for action and for belief. Though they differ in some important respects they share their main logical features. But although much of what will be said applies, if true at all, both to reasons for action and for belief, it will neither be possible nor necessary to comment directly on reasons for belief.

Reasons are referred to in explaining, in evaluating, and in guiding people's behaviour.[1] The concept of a reason is used for various other purposes as well, but these three are primary and the rest are derived from or dependent on them. For example, we say on the appropriate occasion that John married Mary for her money, that people should marry for love only and that therefore since John acted for the wrong reasons he behaved badly and Derek should not do the same. The explanation of the concept of a reason for action must show how it serves these purposes, how they interrelate, and why one concept serves all three purposes. The combination of the theoretical task of explaining action with the practical ones of evaluating and guiding action is the source of many of the difficulties in the explanation of reasons for action. An adequate explanation will show not only that one concept can be used for these widely differing purposes, but also that they are interdependent. Reasons can be used for guiding and evaluating only because they can also be used in explanation, and their unique feature as a type of explanation is that they explain behaviour by reference to considerations which guided the agent's behaviour.

The expression 'a reason for' and related expressions appear in a variety of types of sentences, some of which are characteristically used for explanation, others for guidance or evaluation, and others for all these purposes. Five types of sentences are of particular importance:

(1) '— is a reason for —' (For example, 'The devaluation is a reason for imposing exchange controls.')
(2) 'There is a reason for —' ('There is a reason for punishing him.')
(3) 'x has a reason for —' ('John has a reason for refusing the job.')
(4) 'x believes that — is a reason for —' ('John believes that his mother's illness is a reason for postponing the trip.' 'John believes that the approaching election is a reason for the President to go on a tour abroad.')
(5) 'x's reason for ϕ-ing is —' ('His reason for staying late in the office is the enormous amount of work which accumulated during his absence.')

The discussion that follows will revolve around the use of 'reasons' in these contexts.

Reasons, facts and persons

That which is a reason has been variously identified with statements, beliefs and facts. The main ground for regarding only statements as being reasons is that they have a logical structure. Reasons must, of course, be subject to logical analysis since they figure in practical reasoning, but both beliefs and facts are capable of logical analysis. In any case it is enough that logical analysis applies to statements of the facts or of the content of the beliefs which are the reasons. Language and our intuitions lend little support to the idea that all reasons are statements. It does not seem natural to say that the statement that it will rain is a reason for me to take an umbrella. It is either the fact that it will rain or my belief that it will which would be cited as the reason.*

The choice between facts and beliefs is more difficult. Beliefs are sometimes reasons, but it would be wrong to regard all reasons as beliefs. It should be remembered that reasons are used to guide behaviour, and people are to be guided by what is the case, not by what they believe to be the case. To be sure, in order to be guided by what is the case a person must come to believe that it is the case. Nevertheless it is the fact and not his belief in it which should guide him and which is a reason. If p is the case, then the fact that I do not believe that p does not establish that p is not a reason for me to perform some action. The fact that I am not aware of any reason does not show that there is none. If reasons are to serve for guiding and evaluating behaviour then not all reasons are beliefs. It may seem that reasons which are neither the beliefs nor the desires of the agent cannot be used in explaining his behaviour, but this is a mistake. The explanation depends on his belief that the reasons obtain, but again this does not establish that his belief is the reason. All it shows is that this type of explanation of a person's behaviour turns on his beliefs that certain reasons apply rather than on the fact that they do apply. We can understand his behaviour even if we think he was wrong in believing that there were good reasons for him to do what he did.

The view that that which is a reason is a fact is not free of difficulties. To a certain extent, I hope, the discussion in the rest of this section will suggest ways of overcoming them. But a few remarks are in order here. When saying that facts are reasons I am using the term 'fact' in an extended sense to designate that in virtue of which true or justified statements are true or justified. By 'fact' is meant simply that

---

* I shall argue below that facts are reasons. Both 'the fact that . . .' and 'the statement that . . .' are designator-forming operators on sentences. They share many but not all of their logical properties. My point is that they differ *inter alia* in that 'is a reason for' can always be predicated of 'the fact that . . .', but only exceptionally of 'the statement that . . .'

which can be designated by the use of the operator 'the fact that . . .'
A fact is that of which we talk when making a statement by the use
of sentences of the form 'it is a fact that . . .' In this sense facts are
not contrasted with values, but include them ('It is a fact that human
life is the supreme value', 'The fact that human life is an important
value has long been recognized in all human societies'). Similarly
facts include the occurrence of events, processes, performances and
activities. Given this wide use of 'fact', beliefs, though not their
contents, are also facts. The fact that John believes that p can be a
reason for action both for him and for others. This way of regarding
beliefs as reasons does not, however, explain most of the contexts in
which the agent's beliefs and not facts are normally cited as reasons.
Some ways of dealing with such contexts will be suggested below but
it must be admitted that the analysis here offered sounds odd when
applied to some contexts. Philosophical systematization of a sphere
of discourse inevitably involves a certain degree of regimentation, and
the acceptance of unidiomatic expressions.

There is no denying that we use locutions of the form 'his reason
for ϕ-ing was his belief that p'; 'the reason he ϕ-ed was that he thought
that p', etc. These can be used even when p is not the case (as in 'his
reason for not coming was that he thought you would not be here').
What is cited as a reason in such cases is of course a fact; for though
p is not the case, that he thought that p is. But it is not a fact which
is a reason for the action explained. That one's friend will not be here
may be a reason for not coming here. But that one believes this is not
such a reason. When asked why he did not come the person concerned will normally reply: because my friend was not there. It is
mostly when we come to believe that the reason on which we relied
does not obtain that we cite our belief in it as a reason. We could, on
such occasions, say, in conformity with the proposed analysis, that
we had no reason for not coming but we had a reason for thinking
that we had a reason.

We should admit that we use reasons in both ways. We could even
distinguish between two notions of reason. But they should not be
regarded as of equal significance. Only reasons understood as facts
are normatively significant; only they determine what ought to be
done. To decide what we should do we must find what the world is
like, and not what our thoughts are like. The other notion of reasons
is relevant exclusively for explanatory purposes and not at all for
guiding purposes. It is precisely this which shows that this purely
explanatory notion is the secondary one presupposing the other and

not being presupposed by it. It is not only that the purely explanatory notion can, as we saw, be eliminated in favour of belief in reasons (of the first kind). It is rather that the special feature of explanations of behaviour in terms of reasons is that they explain the agent's behaviour in terms of his beliefs as to what he should do, in terms of his own assessment of the relevant reasons (in the primary, normative, sense) which apply to him.

We usually think of reasons for action as being reasons for a person to perform an action when certain conditions obtain. The performance of an action by an agent in certain circumstances can be regarded as a fact, and it may be thought that reasons are relations between facts. This suggestion is plausible in so far as we are concerned with explaining or evaluating actions which are actually performed ('His reasons for ϕ-ing were . . .', 'he had [or has] good reasons to ϕ', etc.). It fails, however, to account for the use of reasons to assess hypothetical cases ('Everyone in this situation has reason to ϕ', etc.), or in guiding behaviour when the action is not actually performed. To account for such cases it may be tempting to regard reasons as relations between facts, actual or possible. I should like, however, to avoid having to refer to possible facts and will, therefore, regard reasons as being reasons for persons. Consequently, the action-specification is to be regarded as part of the specification of the reason. Sentences of the form 'x has a reason to ϕ' are to be regarded as predicating 'has a reason to ϕ' of 'x'. The expression 'a reason for action' is not itself an operator but a variable taking special kinds of operators as its values. It is used as a (usually bound) variable ranging over reasons for performing specific actions, both generic and individual. (For example, 'a reason to kill Caesar', 'a reason to have dinner or to go to bed', 'a reason to promote human happiness'.) These are operators. Reasons, on this view, are relations between facts and persons.* In other words, expressions of the form '. . . is a reason for . . . to ϕ' are sentence-forming operators on ordered pairs of fact-designators and singular expressions designating persons.

These last comments should, however, be qualified. The variety of contexts in which reason-expressions are used and the variety of

---

* It is of course true that fact-designators are not names but pseudo-names, and that facts are not individuals but logical constructs. Hence in a strict sense of 'relation' reasons are not relations, since relations obtain between individuals. However, for the purposes of the present study no harm comes from using 'relation' in a wider sense.

purposes which they serve give rise to a considerable logical complexity. Consequently reason-expressions must be interpreted somewhat differently according to the context in which they occur. For the purpose of analysis I shall use operators of the form '$R(\phi)$' to be read as 'a reason for ϕ-ing'. These are sentence-forming operators on fact-designators ('that p', 'the fact that p') and singular expressions designating persons, that is to say, they designate relations between a fact and a person. Any sentence in which this reason-operator appears will be called an R-sentence.

On the logical structure of reason-sentences

A complete analysis of the concept of a reason for action consists of (a) providing a semantic interpretation and a logical analysis of the '$R(\phi)$' operators, (b) showing how every reason-giving statement (regardless of whether or not it is standardly made by the use of the expression 'a reason') can be made by sentences of the canonical form, and (c) providing an analysis of sentences of the canonical form by the use of the '$R(\phi)$' operators.

I shall say nothing on (b), and confine myself to some scattered and rudimentary comments on (a). First, however, I wish to outline the way in which reason sentences of the canonical form can be analysed by the use of the '$R(\phi)$' operators. Again my purpose is to make a few suggestions, rather than to provide a complete analysis.

(1) 'The fact that p is a reason for x to ϕ'. Sentences of this form are atomic R-sentences. Their symbolic formulation is '$R(\phi)p,x$'.* Such sentences are true only if both p is the case and it is a reason for x to ϕ. In sentences like 'The devaluation is a reason for the Chancellor to impose exchange controls', the phrase 'the devaluation' refers to the fact that there was a devaluation. Statements made using the sentence in the normal way are true only if the devaluation referred to occurred. Sentences like 'A devaluation is a reason for the Chancellor to impose exchange controls' do not presuppose that a devaluation occurred. They can be rephrased as: 'Whenever a devaluation occurs, its occurrence is a reason for the Chancellor to impose exchange controls'.

---

* I shall use 'p' in such contexts as short for 'the fact that p'. Here and elsewhere in the book I use symbols for two purposes only: to facilitate the exposition through abbreviation and to indicate a measure of indifference to mere stylistic variations in the use of the analysed expressions in English.

(2) 'There is a reason for x to ϕ'. Sentences of this form are equivalent to 'There is a fact p such that R(ϕ)p,x'.

(3) 'x has a reason to ϕ'. The analysis of such sentences is far from clear. On many occasions they are used in a way which suggests that they are equivalent to 'There is a reason for x to ϕ' type of sentences. On other occasions they are used to assert that there is a reason for x to ϕ and x knows it.

(4) 'x believes that p is a reason for y to ϕ'. Sentences of this form carry with them the ambiguity noted in (1). Sometimes they are used in a way which ascribes to x the belief that p and sometimes in a way which does not.

(5) 'x's reason for ϕ-ing was p' is used to assert that either (a) if 'p' does not include a desire of x, x believed both that p and that p is a reason for him to ϕ, and x ϕ-ed intentionally because of these beliefs of his, or (b) if 'p' is of the form 'x desired s, and q' then 'the reason x ϕ-ed is p' is used to assert that x desired s and believed that q and x ϕ-ed intentionally because of these beliefs and desires of his. Much has been written in recent years on the force of the 'because' in this formulation. The problem is, however, both too complex and of too little relevance to our main concern with the guiding function of reason to be discussed here.[2]

There is one type of reason which does not easily fit the outlined analysis. Often we cite as reasons 'the probability that p', 'the prospect that p', 'the danger that p', and so on. These are not in themselves the facts that are the reasons. The analysis of statements containing such phrases may vary according to context. The feature common to all of them is that they combine assertion or presupposition of a reason for belief with the assertion of a reason for action. Consider the following two cases: (a) 'The probability that it will rain is a reason for taking an umbrella.' This is to be analysed as asserting: 'There is a reason to believe that it will rain and that it will rain is a reason for taking an umbrella.' In such cases 'the probability that p is a reason for x to ϕ' is analysed into 'There is reason to believe that p and R(ϕ)p,x'. (b) 'The danger of an accident in this fog is a reason for driving very slowly.' This example cannot be analysed in the same way. That an accident will occur is a reason to take out an insurance policy but it is not a reason to drive slowly. But it is not difficult to see how the statement should be analysed. It states that the fog is a reason to believe that unless one drives slowly an accident will occur. The fact that unless one drives slowly an accident will

occur is a reason for driving slowly. Similar statements can be analysed in similar ways. A complete analysis of such cases requires a
further probing of 'a reason to believe' which cannot be undertaken
here. The juxtaposition of reasons to believe and reasons for action
is common to many contexts. Consider the following: 'The reason
I am going to the station is that I have received a letter from my
friend saying that he will arrive today.' In this case, that I have
received such a letter is a reason for believing that my friend will
arrive today, which in turn is the reason for my going to the station.
In such a case 'p is a reason for x to ϕ' is elliptical for 'p, and p is a
reason to believe that q and $R(\phi)q,x$'. A similar interpretation will
apply to statements in the other canonical forms.

It seems to me that most of the difficulties in regarding reasons as
relations between facts and persons turn on examination to be the
same as the difficulties concerning probabilities or, at any rate,
amenable to treatment in a similar way. The analysis sketched here
combines insistence on regarding only facts as reasons with ways of
explaining behaviour in terms of one's beliefs in reasons. The same
is true of the evaluation or assessment of behaviour. A person's
action can be judged as being well grounded in reason or not according to whether there actually are reasons for performing the action.
It can also be assessed as reasonable or rational according to whether
the person had reasons to believe that there were reasons for his
action. It is the world which guides our action, but since it inevitably
does so through our awareness of it, our beliefs are important for the
explanation and assessment of our behaviour.

Complete reasons

In ordinary conversation we almost never make a full and complete
statement of our reasons. We state only a part of them, our choice of
which part to state being determined by pragmatic considerations.
What we say and how much we say depends on our assessment of how
much the hearer already knows, what he wants to know, to what
extent we are willing to take him into our confidence, what it would
not be polite to say, etc. When asked why he goes to the station,
John may say that (a) James will be arriving there, or that (b) James
will be pleased to be met at the station, or that (c) he would like to
please James. Which of these statements he will make in reply to the
question depends on a variety of considerations. It is rather unlikely
that he will make all three statements in his first reply, though he

may very well make all of them and more in reply to a persistent friend. And yet we feel that the three belong together, that only in combination do they come anywhere near to being a statement of a complete reason. Each one in isolation is a statement of only a part of a reason. If we feel we understand a person's reason when given a statement of only a part of the reason, this is because we know the other parts of the reason, or because we are not interested in all the details.

The idea of a complete reason is not the invention of philosophers with excessive zeal for logical tidiness. It underlies our understanding of reasons and is indispensable in any logical explication of reasons. Imagine that in response to successive questions we are first given (a), then (b), then (c); and that then John says that (d) he has promised James that he will meet him at the station, that (e) one ought to keep one's promise, and that (f) one ought to please one's friends. I think we all feel that there are different logical relations among these statements, and between them and John's action of going to the station. (a) to (c) state parts of a reason which John has for going to the station. (d) states not a further part of the same reason but a part of a second reason for the same action. (a) may well be a statement of part of the second reason as well, but not (b) or (c). (e) and (f) are quite different again. They are not parts of reasons which John has for going to the station. They are reasons for the reasons for going to the station. They explain in two different ways why John has or regards himself as having two reasons for going to the station.

A terminological point should be established here. The word 'reason', like 'father', can occur in both relational expressions and predicative ones. The predicate 'is a reason to ϕ' is true of a fact if, and only if, there is some person such that the relation holds between the fact and the person. Just as a is a father if, and only if, there is an x such that a is the father of x, so p is a reason to ϕ if, and only if, there is an x such that $R(\phi)p,x$. I shall also refer occasionally to objects as reasons: when the fact that x exists is a reason for action I shall often abbreviate and refer to x itself as a reason.

The problem of explaining what is one complete reason is that of explaining the difference between completing the statement of a reason and either stating a second reason for the performance of the same action by the same person or providing a reason for the reason. The problem is not to explain what it means for there to be a reason. We assume that that is understood, and on the basis of this understanding we propose a definition of 'a complete reason'. This means that we assume that sentences of the canonical forms (2) and (3) are understood, and we are concerned with sentences of type (1), and of types (4) and (5) which are constructed on the basis of (1). These sentences say not only that there is a reason but also state what it is. When do they state a complete reason?

The fact that p is a complete reason to ϕ for a person x if, and only if, either (a) necessarily, for any person y who understands both the statement that p and the statement that x ϕ's, if y believes that p he believes that there is a reason for x to ϕ, regardless of what other beliefs y has, or (b) $R(\phi)p,x$ entails $R(\phi)q,y$ which is a complete reason. However, the fact that p is not a complete reason if the statement that p trivially satisfies the definition only because it entails that some person knows some fact s, and s satisfies the definition.[3]

This definition assumes that the truth of statements of the form $R(\phi)p,x$ is partly a matter of logic. Whether or not p is true is a contingent factual matter or a problem of moral or practical philosophy. But if p is a complete reason then whether 'wherever p, $R(\phi)p,x$' is true is a matter of logic. Such statements are either logically true or logically false.

In crude form the intuitive idea behind this definition is that the fact stated by any set of premises which entail that there is a reason to perform a certain action is a complete reason for performing it. This intuitive idea has, however, to be refined. The proposed definition does so in several ways. It makes clear, for example, that the fact that x knows that p is not a reason to ϕ even if p is such a reason. It also entails that an analytic statement is not part of a statement of a complete reason even if it is a necessary premise for the entailment that there is a reason to ϕ.

Suppose John says: wherever ϕ-ing would increase human happiness one has a reason to ϕ. Let us assume that Jack denies this. How are we to understand Jack's position? Is he guilty of a mistake in logic? Not necessarily. John does not state a complete reason, though it is easy to see which complete reason he is invoking. It is that human happiness is a value and that under certain conditions ϕ-ing increases human happiness. This is his complete reason for ϕ-ing when those conditions obtain. In denying this Jack probably intends to deny that human happiness is a value. If this is the reason for his denial then his mistake is not a logical mistake but a moral one. But if the reason for his denial is that values do not always constitute reasons, or that sometimes there will be stronger reasons for not ϕ-ing despite the fact that it contributes to happiness, then his mistake is one of logic. For it is a matter of logic that values are reasons and that a reason is a reason even if outweighed by other conflicting reasons.

As has already been mentioned, on most occasions when reasons are given they are not the complete reasons. I see no reason to deviate from this practice. A fact is a reason only if it belongs to a complex fact which is a complete reason, and yet not only the complete reason but its constituent facts as well are reasons.

By definition two complete reasons are a complete reason. We can define an atomic complete reason as a complete reason which would cease being complete if any one of its constituent parts were omitted. To be precise and correct much more needs to be said about the structure of reasons. For present purposes the above characterization will suffice. Most of the interesting philosophical problems concern the analysis of atomic complete reasons, and much of the rest of this section is about them. Unless otherwise indicated by 'a reason' I shall henceforth refer to a complete reason.

The strength of reasons

Reasons have a dimension of strength. Some reasons are stronger or more weighty than others. In cases of conflict the stronger reason overrides the weaker. This feature of strong reasons is their defining characteristic. The strength of reasons with which we are concerned is their logical strength. It differs from their phenomenological strength as measured by the degree to which the thought of the reason preoccupies a person and dominates his consciousness. The two may go together in the sense that sometimes the more the thought of a reason dominates the consciousness of a person the more likely he is to think that it is a strong reason. But this is not always the case; often the reverse is true. The logical and phenomenological notions of strength are not logically related and a person may believe that a reason is weak and not act on it in conflict even though he is aware that it fills his mental horizon.

Since the logical strength of reasons depends on which conflicting reasons they override we have first to define 'conflicts of reasons' and 'overriding'.

(1)   p strictly conflicts with q relative to x and ϕ if, and only if, $R(\phi)$p,x and $R(\bar{\phi})$q,x, i.e. that p is a reason for x to ϕ and that q is a reason to refrain from ϕ-ing.

If p is a reason to ϕ and q is a reason to perform another action, ϕ', and it is logically impossible both to ϕ and to ϕ', then q is also a reason to refrain from ϕ-ing and it strictly conflicts with p. If, however, it is merely physically impossible both to ϕ and to ϕ', then q, in conjunction with the facts which make it impossible to perform both actions, is a reason to refrain from ϕ-ing. Similarly if r is a reason to refrain from both ϕ-ing and ϕ'-ing but not a reason to refrain from either of these actions so long as the other is not performed, then p and r is a reason for $\bar{\phi}$-ing. Other cases can be dealt with in similar ways.

(2) p and q logically conflict relative to x and ϕ if, and only if, p entails p' and q entails q' and p' and q' conflict in the strict sense relative to x and ϕ.[4]

(3) p overrides q relative to x and ϕ if, and only if, p and q are conflicting reasons in the strict sense relative to x and ϕ and $R(\phi)p\&q,x$, and not $R(\bar{\phi})p\&q,x$.*

(4) Of two conflicting reasons one is stronger than the other if, and only if, all the reasons entailed by it override all the strictly conflicting reasons entailed by the other.†

The relation of strength can be extended beyond conflicting reasons. If p and q are reasons for ϕ-ing then p is a stronger reason for ϕ-ing than q if, and only if, there is a reason to refrain from ϕ-ing which is overridden by p and not by q and there is no such reason which is overridden by q and not by p. Finally, if p and q are reasons for action (not necessarily for the same action) then p is stronger than q if, and only if, there is a reason r such that p is and q is not stronger than r, by this or one of the previous definitions, and there is no reason s such that q is and p is not stronger than s.[5]

The notion of strength thus defined relates the strength of a reason to those reasons which actually obtain. It can be said to indicate the actual strength of a reason in the actual world. One can define other notions of strength relative to all possible reasons which may but do not actually obtain. But we need not explore these possibilities here. These definitions may look a trifle too technical and complicated but their aim is merely to express in a relatively precise way the two most important features of our common conception of the strength of

* I am not assuming that of every two strictly conflicting reasons one overrides the other. It may be that a conflict of reasons cannot be resolved.

† I have introduced relativized definitions of conflict and of overriding and a non-relativized definition of strength. But all these notions are used both in a relativized and a non-relativized sense.

reasons. These can be expressed crudely as follows. Firstly, of two conflicting reasons the one which overrides the other is the stronger. Secondly, if one reason overrides all the reasons which are overridden by another reason, and if it overrides other reasons as well, then it is stronger than that second reason.

The relative strength of a reason has been explained in terms of its power to override other reasons. The notion of one reason overriding another should be carefully distinguished from that of a reason being cancelled by a cancelling condition. A reason can be overridden only by a fact which is itself a reason for contradictory action. But sometimes we find that $R(\phi)p,x$ and not $R(\phi)p \& q,x$, and yet not $R(\bar{\phi})q,x$. Indeed q itself may not be a reason for any action at all. The need to take an injured man to hospital at the time I promised to meet a friend at Carfax is a reason for not keeping the appointment which overrides the promise which is a reason for keeping it. The fact that my friend has released me from my promise is a reason for nothing at all and yet it cancels the reason to go to Carfax created by the promise.[6]

The analysis of cancelling conditions is of great importance to the study of reasons for action. Whether a reason can be subject to cancellation and in what conditions are questions which reflect on the nature of the reason concerned. But we need not inquire into these questions here. The only point I am concerned to make is that since cancellation by a cancelling condition does not involve a conflict of reasons it does not reflect on the strength of reasons. The fact that one reason would be cancelled by a certain condition whereas another reason would not does not tend to establish that the second is stronger than the first. It implies nothing of the relative strength of these reasons. This, it seems to me, is in accord with our normal way of assessing the strength of reasons.

On the basis of the concepts of complete reasons and of the strength of reasons several useful additional concepts can be introduced.

(1) A conclusive reason: p is a conclusive reason for x to ϕ if, and only if, p is a reason for x to ϕ (which has not been cancelled) and there is no q such that q overrides p.
(2) An absolute reason: p is an absolute reason for x to ϕ if, and only if, there cannot be a fact which would override it; that is to say, for all q it is never the case that when q, q overrides p.
(3) A *prima facie* reason is one which is neither conclusive nor absolute.

The following hypothetical case illustrates the difference between conclusive and absolute reasons. The fact that my son has been injured is a reason for me to drive him to the hospital at 45 m.p.h. It is not an absolute reason. It is possible for a pedestrian to step suddenly into the road. If this were the case it would override my reason to drive so fast. But since in fact no pedestrian does step suddenly into the road my reason is a conclusive one. It overrides the only conflicting reason present: the legally imposed 30 m.p.h. speed limit.

To be complete the example has to be filled in. In particular it should be noticed that I have specified only parts of the reasons involved. I have also disregarded the problems arising from partial ignorance of the facts. It is possible that, for all I know, a pedestrian may step into the road. In that case, following the analysis offered above, for all I know my reason is not conclusive.

Not every conclusive reason is absolute. A reason may be conclusive because it overrides all the existing reasons which conflict with it and yet not be absolute because it would not override a certain possible reason, had it been the case. Not every absolute reason is conclusive for p may be an absolute reason even though it is cancelled by q. In this case it would not be a conclusive reason. A reason to ϕ is conclusive only if there is reason to ϕ even when all the reasons for and against ϕ-ing and all the relevant cancelling conditions are considered. An absolute reason is not subject to the same condition. An atomic reason can be conclusive and there may be more than one conclusive reason for an agent to perform an action.

Reasons, 'ought' and practical inference

Statements of facts which are reasons for the performance of a certain action by a certain agent are the premises of an argument the conclusion of which is that there is reason for the agent to perform the action or that he ought to do it. Statements of the form 'p is a reason for x to ϕ' correspond to an inference of which 'p' is the premise and 'there is a reason for x to ϕ' the conclusion. An inference the conclusion of which is a 'There is reason to . . .' statement or an 'ought' statement is a practical inference.[7] We can now see more clearly the logical relation between the five main forms of reason-giving statements. 'x's reason for ϕ-ing was p' is analysed in terms of 'x believed that p is a reason to ϕ', and the problematic 'because'. Both 'x believes that p is a reason to ϕ' and 'x has a reason to ϕ' depend for their logical analysis on 'p is a reason for x to ϕ' and 'There is a reason for x to ϕ'. These last two statement forms are the basic forms. Of these two, 'p is a reason for x to ϕ' represents the form of a practical inference, whereas 'There is a reason for x to ϕ' is the conclusion of a practical inference.*

Given a full analysis (which I have not provided) of the logical properties of reason-giving statements and their relations we would have a theory of when 'There is reason . . .' type statements are justified, correct or well grounded (or whichever predicate we choose to serve as the corresponding one to 'truth' with regard to theoretical statements). To be complete the analysis of reasons for action must also include an account of the conditions under which one is justified in ascribing to a person the belief that there is a reason for x to ϕ. But I will say little on this problem.

As indicated above, I believe that statements of the form 'x ought to ϕ' are logically equivalent to statements of the form 'There is reason for x to ϕ'. This claim may sound odd and though I cannot fully defend it here I should like to make a few comments in its defence. In the first place I am not claiming that the two types of sentences are synonymous. My claim is merely that statements standardly made by their use are logically equivalent. The premises which would justify drawing the one conclusion would also justify drawing the other. Every conclusion which is entailed by one statement is also entailed by the other. It should be conceded right away that sentences of these types differ in various other respects. In particular, for stylistic and other pragmatical reasons they are not always interchangeable. In many contexts, for example, it will be natural to say 'you ought to see him', but not 'you have a reason to see him'. We can say 'the reason you ought to ϕ is p' but not 'the reason there is a reason for you to ϕ is p'. These stylistic and pragmatic considerations do not, however, affect the inferential powers of these statements.

Secondly, my claim seems to conform better with our use of general 'ought' statements than with our use of singular 'ought' statements. General 'ought' sentences are often used to assert that there is a case, which is not necessarily a conclusive one, for acting in a certain way.

---

* One welcome result of this approach is that practical inferences are defeasible, that is, the addition of further premises can turn a valid argument into an invalid one. There are other forms of practical inferences. For example, p is a reason for x to ϕ; q is an overriding reason for x not to ϕ; therefore x has a reason not ϕ. But these can be either reduced to or explained on the basis of the type of inference mentioned above.

Stating that 'one ought not to lie' or that 'soldiers ought to obey orders' does not commit one to the belief that one ought to behave in these ways whatever the conflicting reasons may be. It might be suggested that 'ought' statements assert the existence of strong, even if not conclusive, reasons. But even this is not true, at any rate of general 'ought' statements. Asserting that 'everyone ought to see Naples' does not commit one to the belief that there are *strong* reasons to do so. It is true that we rarely make general 'ought' statements unless we believe that the reasons are fairly strong. There is little point in asserting the existence of reasons which are likely to be overridden. But this is not a result of the meaning of 'ought'. It is a pragmatical rule for conducting conversations and it applies also to statements made by the use of 'there is a reason for x to ϕ' sentences as well.

Thirdly, since reasons can conflict so, on my interpretation, can 'ought' statements.[8] As we have already noted this creates a problem in the interpretation of singular 'ought' statements. A person may have a reason to perform an action and a reason for not performing it. It follows that it may be the case that a person ought to ϕ and that he ought not to ϕ. It must be admitted that there is an air of paradox to the statement that it may be true both that I ought to keep my promise and that I ought to break it. The apparent paradox can be explained away, however, as the product of pragmatic implicatures. Because of the pragmatic requirement that the speaker should not hold back relevant information, my saying to John, 'you ought to keep your promise', carries the pragmatic implicature that I do not believe in any reasons overriding those for keeping the promise nor in any facts cancelling them. The same, of course, is true of John. Therefore, if he tells me that on the contrary he ought to break his promise, there is a genuine conflict of opinions, for we are both stating our views on the balance of reasons. But this is so because of the pragmatic implicatures, not because of the meaning of 'ought'. If it were a result of the meaning of 'ought' then both general and singular 'ought' statements would be statements of conclusive reasons. We have already seen that this is false of general 'ought' statements. Since 'ought' has the same meaning when used in asserting either general or singular statements we are forced to conclude that the difference between general and singular 'ought' statements is due to a difference in pragmatic implicature. Because of the great variety of factors which may prevail in different circumstances we do not expect a speaker who is discussing a general situation to do more than

to point to some of the important factors which should affect decisions in all those situations. Someone who is discussing a particular
problem, on the other hand, is expected to state his view of the
conclusive reason which applies to the problem.

My suggestion is, therefore, that 'ought' statements and 'there is a
reason' statements have the same inferential powers and differ only
in other respects. One such difference is the fact that 'there is a
reason' statements do not give rise to the same pragmatic implicature
even when stated in a context in which an 'ought' statement would
have created such an implicature. The only explanation of this
difference in pragmatic implicatures which I can tentatively offer is
that the explicit existential form of the reason-statement weakens or
even negates the implication.

Fourthly, it may be said that we use 'ought' sentences of this form
to assert ultimate moral truths which do not depend on further
reasons for their support. 'Persons ought to be respected' could be
cited as an example of such a statement which cannot itself be
justified by further reasons though it provides reasons for action.
Such a moral view could be reconciled with my explanation, however, by regarding the mentioned 'ought' statement as a (trivial)
conclusion of an inference the sole premise of which is that respect
for persons is a value. The value is the reason for the 'ought' statement, which is, therefore, logically equivalent to 'there is reason to
respect persons'. This construction involves, no doubt, a degree of
systematization and regimentation of ordinary discourse. Nevertheless, I believe that the construction is justified by the need to draw a
fairly clear terminological distinction between value theory (which is
concerned to establish which state of affairs is good or valuable and
which is better than which) and normative theory (which is concerned with who should do what). Both 'reason' and 'ought' are
primarily normative terms. Both are, however, used occasionally as
value-terms. My suggestion is that they should be treated as exclusively normative.

Finally, this account of 'ought' may help to explain the use of
'ought' in theoretical contexts. For fairly obvious reasons, 'you
ought to believe that p' is not often used as a substitute for 'you have
reason to believe that p'. But 'The train ought to be here in five
minutes' time' or 'This stone ought to break the window' are logically equivalent to 'There is reason to believe that the train will be
here in five minutes' time' and 'There is reason to believe that this
stone will break the window'.

The logical equivalence between 'ought' statements and their corresponding 'there is reason' statements is sufficiently close that if a person believes in either he necessarily believes in the other. The same conditions for belief apply to both forms of statement. It might be thought that a person believes that x ought to ϕ if and only if he will try to ϕ given that he is aware of an opportunity to ϕ. This criterion will not do, however, for a person may believe that another ought to perform an action. Even if a person believes that he himself ought to perform an action, he may fail to try to perform it even if he believes that he can perform it. The best first move is to say that a belief in an 'ought' statement entails having a certain critical attitude towards behaviour which conforms to or conflicts with the statement. This in turn manifests itself in action and in other beliefs, attitudes and emotions (towards facts, persons, etc., which either facilitate or hinder conformity with the 'ought' statement).[9]

The analysis of this critical attitude cannot be undertaken here. I shall make only two points. Firstly, whenever one believes that p, one has a critical attitude to conflicting and conforming beliefs (discouraging the first and encouraging the latter) which manifests itself also in critical attitudes to persons, books, etc. (they are ignorant or knowledgeable, wise or stupid, etc.). If p is an 'ought' statement or a 'there is reason' statement one has in addition to the first critical attitude an additional critical attitude directed towards aspects of the world other than the beliefs people have. This attitude I shall call the practical critical attitude. Secondly, if a practical inference is valid then it is irrational, though in many cases possible, for a person to believe in the premises and yet not to have the critical attitude appropriate to the conclusion. Since having this critical attitude is a condition of belief in the conclusion this amounts to no more than saying that it is irrational for a person to believe in the premises and not in the conclusion. (Believing that there is a reason to ϕ entails having a practical critical attitude even if one believes in other reasons which override this one.)

A full analysis of the practical critical attitude would relate directly to belief in conclusive 'ought' statements and only through them to non-conclusive 'ought' statements. It should be clear that saying that belief in an 'ought' statement entails having the practical critical attitude is not the same as saying that the statement is about that attitude. It should further be remembered that the practical critical attitude is not necessarily the attitude of moral approval or disapproval. It is directed towards the rationality, strength of will and effectiveness of the persons concerned. Only when the reason for action is a moral reason will the critical attitude assume a moral character.

Operative reasons

One aspect of the philosophical debate concerning what is commonly known as the 'is'–'ought' question revolves around the possibility of valid inferences such that belief in their conclusions entails having a practical critical attitude while no such attitude is required for belief in their premises. Consider the following case. I promised John to buy for him all the new philosophy books published this year; this is a philosophy book and it has just been published; so I ought to buy it for John. If belief in the conclusion entails having a practical critical attitude it is only because belief in one of the premises requires such an attitude. In this case the premise is that I promised to John, etc. I shall call any reason an *operative reason* if, and only if, belief in its existence entails having the practical critical attitude. A reason which is not an operative one will be called an *auxiliary reason*.

It seems to me to be a logical truth both that every complete reason includes an operative reason and that every operative reason is a complete reason for some action or other. The following are examples of complete reasons consisting of one operative reason and of the actions for which they are reasons. If respect for persons is a value then there is reason for everyone to respect persons. If James has promised to ϕ then James has a reason to ϕ. If he desires x then there is reason for him to promote the realization of his desire, etc.

The function of the premises stating the auxiliary reasons is to justify, as it were, the transfer of the practical attitude from the statement of the operative reason to the conclusion. Imagine that John would like to offend James and that reminding James of a certain incident would offend him. Therefore, there is reason for John to remind James of the incident.* Anyone who believes that John desires to offend James believes that John has a reason to do something, namely something that will offend James. By virtue of this belief he has the practical critical attitude appropriate to it. Knowing that John will offend James by mentioning the particular incident to him binds one on pain of irrationality to have the critical attitude

---

* This is yet another case where our conviction that there are overriding reasons against John's so doing would deter us from using an 'ought' sentence to state the conclusion.

appropriate to the conclusion that there is reason for John to mention the incident.

Most operative reasons are either values or desires or interests.[10] 'Desire' is used here to designate a 'spontaneous' or 'felt' desire which is to be contrasted with a reason-based desire. In this sense a person who acts intentionally does not always do what he desires to do. He may act because he recognizes that he has a reason to act though he does not particularly want to perform the action. He may be said to have a reason-based desire but not a spontaneous or felt desire. The same applies to actions which the person intends to perform.

Desires and interests can, if this is thought illuminating, be regarded as values as well. In that case they should be distinguished from other values by being called 'subjective values', while other values are dubbed 'objective values'. Desires and interests differ from other values in that it is a logical principle that (a) if p is an (objective) value then everyone has an operative reason to promote p. If p is in a certain person's interest or something he desires then the above is not true, at least not as a logical principle. All that follows logically is that (b) there is an operative reason for the person in whose interest p is, or who desires p, to promote p. It is a matter of moral controversy whether the satisfaction of all wants or the promotion of everybody's interests are moral values. If they are then everyone has an operative reason to promote everyone's interests and the satisfaction of everyone's desires. But regardless of one's views on the moral issue it is a logical truth that a person's desires and interests are operative reasons for him.[11]

Every value is a reason for action. It is, however, an open question whether all operative reasons are either subjective or objective values. It is one of the main theses of the next chapter that norms are operative reasons, though they are not values.

Auxiliary reasons

Auxiliary reasons play a variety of roles in practical reasoning. For our present purpose it is enough to point to two such roles. Some auxiliary reasons can be called identifying reasons, for their function is to help identify the act which there is reason to perform. Consider the inference: I want to help him. Lending him £400 will help him. Therefore, I have reason to lend him £400. The first premise states an operative reason, the second states an identifying reason. It transmits, as it were, the force of the operative reason to the particular act of lending him £400. Identifying reasons can be contrasted with strength-affecting reasons (though one fact can be a reason of both types). Strength- (or weight-) affecting reasons are important only in conflict situations and their function is to help determine which reason is more weighty. I want to help Jim. There are two things, each of which I can do and which will help him, but I can only do one. What I require is knowledge of strength-affecting facts which will enable me to determine what to do. What good will doing A produce and what precisely are the results of doing B, and which will be more beneficial? These facts are not operative reasons in their own right. They presuppose that I have reason to help Jim. Nor do they simply identify an action which will help him; they may do this but they do more—they help determine the relative strengths of competing reasons. Similarly let us assume that a desire to maintain good neighbourly relations is a reason to please one's neighbours in various small ways. The strength of such a reason is affected by the way the neighbours react and the degree to which they reciprocate. These are strength-affecting reasons.

1.2 EXCLUSIONARY REASONS

The problem

Much of the previous section was taken up with an elaborate description of conflicts of reasons and their resolution. This is one of the most intricate and complex areas of practical discourse, which has led to much confused theorizing. It is also one of the most revealing, for much can be learnt about the nature of reasons from conflict situations. In particular, it is the detailed examination of conflicts of reasons which forces the recognition that different reasons belong to different levels, which fact affects their impact on conflict situations.

We have at our disposal a set of interlocking notions which we commonly employ to describe both the way in which conflicts of reasons are resolved ('He was aware of conflicting reasons but thought that the need to look after his sick child overrode all other considerations') and the way in which such conflicts should be resolved. The pervasive use of this terminology suggests that all practical conflicts conform to one logical pattern: conflicts of reasons are resolved by the relative weight or strength of the conflicting reasons which determines which of them overrides the other. So long as we are content to handle such conflicts in an impressionistic way there is nothing wrong in this suggestion. But if we are concerned to construct a logical theory of practical conflicts we have to recognize that not all conflicts are of the same type. My claim, yet to be explained and defended, is that we should distinguish between first-order and second-order reasons for action and that conflicts between first-order reasons are resolved by the relative strength of the conflicting reasons, but that this is not true of conflicts between first- and second-order reasons.

The distinction between first-order and second-order reasons for action has not been recognized or discussed by philosophers. This is no doubt due at least in part to the fact that it is not reflected in any straightforward way in our use of the expressions of ordinary language. Reasons of both kinds are referred to as 'reasons', 'considerations', 'grounds', 'factors', etc. The resolution of conflicts of reasons belonging to different levels, just like the resolution of conflicts of reasons belonging to the same level, is described in terms of one reason prevailing over, or overriding, or being stronger than the other. So long as we are content to rely on our intuitive grasp of the sense and use of such expressions the distinction between first-order and second-order reasons need not concern us. My claim is that a useful explication of the notions of strength, weight and overriding is possible but only at the cost of restricting their scope of application and that if we embark on such an explication the theory of conflict must allow for the existence of other logical types of conflicts and of conflict resolutions.

In the previous section an explanation of the notions of strength and overriding was provided which closely conforms to our intuitive conception of their nature. According to our intuitive conception of practical conflicts such conflicts are to be resolved by assessing the relative strength or weight of the conflicting reasons and determining what ought to be done on the balance of reasons. To put it another way, one ought always to do whatever one has a conclusive reason for doing. Or, which is another way of saying the same, one ought always to act on the balance of reasons. This is the intuitive conception of conflict resolution explained on the basis of the analysis in the previous section. We can formulate it in the form of a practical principle:

P1. It is always the case that one ought, all things considered,* to do whatever one ought to do on the balance of reasons.

* I am using 'ought all things considered' to indicate what ought to be done on the basis of all the reasons for action which are relevant to the question, and not only on the basis of the reasons the agent in fact considered or could have considered. Contrast D. Davidson, 'How is Weakness of the Will Possible?' in *Moral Concepts*, J. Feinberg (Ed.), Oxford, 1969.

I do not wish to challenge the validity of P1 directly. Instead I shall show that it is not normally applied to many quite common conflict situations.

Imagine the case of Ann who is looking for a good way to invest her money. Late one evening a friend tells her of a possible investment. The snag is that she has to decide that same evening for the offer to make the deal will be withdrawn at midnight. The proposed investment is a very complicated one, that much is clear to Ann. She is aware that it may be a very good investment, but there may be facts which may mean that it will not be a good bargain for her after all, and she is not certain whether it is better or worse than another proposition which was put to her a few days before and which she is still considering. All she requires is a couple of hours of thorough examination of the two propositions. All the relevant information is available in the mass of documents on her table. But Ann has had a long and strenuous day with more than the average amount of emotional upsets. She tells her friend that she cannot take a rational decision on the merits of the case since even were she to try and work out the consequences of accepting the offer she would not succeed; she is too tired and upset to trust her own judgement. He replies that she cannot avoid taking a decision. Refusing to consider the offer is tantamount to rejecting it. She admits that she rejects the offer but says that she is doing it not because she thinks the reasons against it override those in its favour but because she cannot trust her own judgement at this moment. He retorts that this violates P1 and is unreasonable. Her weariness and her emotional state are not reasons for rejecting the offer. They do not establish that it would be wrong or undesirable to accept it, or that to do so would be contrary to her interests, etc. According to P1 she should examine the offer on its merits. P1 does not entail that she should disregard her present mental condition. She must, in following P1, recognize that her judgement may be affected by her mental state and correct it to prevent this from happening. Ann, however, finds that this will only make things worse. She certainly cannot trust herself, in her present state, to work out how her mental state might taint her judgement. She insists that, though she is taking a decision against the offer, she can rationally do so not on the ground that on the merits the offer ought to be rejected but because she has a reason not to act on the merits of the case. This, she concedes, is a kind of reason not recognized in P1, but that only shows that P1 is not valid.

Ann's case is interesting because she claims to be acting for a

reason which is not taken into account in P1. It may be that she is
wrong in thinking that she has a valid reason for her action, but
since the reason she relies on is not uncommon it deserves a closer
study. The special feature of her case is, not that she regards her
mental state as a reason for action, but that she regards it as a reason
for disregarding other reasons for action. P1 allows her to take her
fatigue as a reason for going to bed. But she regards it as a reason
(or proof of a reason) for rejecting a business proposition despite the
fact that her weariness does not bear at all on the merits of the proposition. She claims to have a reason for not acting on the balance of
reasons. In my example Ann has not formed any view on the
balance of reasons. But this is immaterial. She might have formed
the opinion that the offer is a good one and refuse it all the same.
She may distrust her judgement and refuse to act on it. My analysis
of Ann's reasoning is incomplete. It shows that she believes she
ought not to act on the balance of reasons, but not why, given this
assumption, she opts for rejecting the offer rather than accepting it.
The most likely explanation is that she relies on some rule of thumb
of the kind analysed in section 2.2 below. Ann's reasoning is typical
of situations in which the agent cannot trust his judgement because
he is under pressure of time or because he is drunk or subject to a
strong temptation or to threats or because he realizes that he is
influenced by his emotions, etc. But such reasoning is not confined
to situations of such a nature.

Another example is as follows. While serving in the army Jeremy
is ordered by his commanding officer to appropriate and use a van
belonging to a certain tradesman. Therefore he has reason to appropriate the van. His friend urges him to disobey the order pointing to
weighty reasons for doing so. Jeremy does not deny that his friend
may have a case. But, he claims, it does not matter whether he is
right or not. Orders are orders and should be obeyed even if wrong,
even if no harm will come from disobeying them. That is what it
means to be a subordinate. It means that it is not for you to decide
what is best. You may see that on the balance of reasons one course
of action is right and yet be justified in not following it. The order is
a reason for doing what you were ordered regardless of the balance
of reasons. He admits that if he were ordered to commit an atrocity
he should refuse. But his is an ordinary case, he thinks, and the order
should prevail. It may be that Jeremy is wrong in accepting the
authority of his commander in this case. But is he not right on the
nature of authority?

Finally, consider the case of Colin who promised his wife that in all decisions affecting the education of his son he will act only for his son's interests and disregard all other reasons. Suppose Colin has now to decide whether or not to send his son to a public school. Among the relevant reasons are the fact that if he does he will be unable to resign his job in order to write the book he so much wants to write, and the fact that given his prominent position in his community his decision will affect the decisions of quite a few other parents, including some who could ill afford the expense. However, he believes that because of his promise he should disregard such considerations altogether (unless, that is, they have indirect consequences affecting his son's welfare). Again, some will think that his promise is not binding, but that is beside the point. Our aim is simply to understand the reasoning of those who believe in such reasons, and it must be admitted that they are numerous. Colin's promise, like Ann's fatigue, does not affect the balance of reasons. It is not itself either a reason for sending his son to a public school or against doing so. Nor does it change whatever reasons there are. It does not mean that the consequences of Colin's decision on his chances of writing his book or on the decisions of other parents are no longer relevant reasons. They are, but Colin has, or believes he has, a reason to disregard them and not to act on them. Colin, like Ann and Jeremy, believes that he has a reason for not acting on certain reasons and that means that he believes that he may be justified in not acting on the balance of reasons.

Second-order reasons

To explain the form of reasoning in the above three cases several new concepts have to be introduced. Let us say that a person ϕ-s for the reason that p if, and only if, he ϕ-s because he believes that p is a reason for him to ϕ. A person refrains from ϕ-ing for the reason that p if, and only if, it is not the case that he ϕ-s for the reason that p. In other words, a person refrains from acting for a reason if he does not do the act or does it but not for this reason. 'Refrains' is used here in an extended sense which does not imply that the agent intentionally avoids acting for the reason. A *second-order reason* is any reason to act for a reason or to refrain from acting for a reason. An *exclusionary reason* is a second-order reason to refrain from acting for some reason. Colin, Jeremy and Ann believe that their reasoning is sound because they believe that they have valid exclusionary reasons on which their decisions are partly based. They reject P1 because it does not take account of exclusionary reasons. Exclusionary reasons are the only type of second-order reasons with which we will be concerned here.

If p is a reason for x to ϕ and q is an exclusionary reason for him not to act on p then p and q are not strictly conflicting reasons. q is not a reason for not ϕ-ing. It is a reason for not ϕ-ing for the reason that p. The conflict between p and q is a conflict between a first-order reason and a second-order exclusionary reason. Such conflicts are resolved not by the strength of the competing reasons but by a general principle of practical reasoning which determines that exclusionary reasons always prevail, when in conflict with first-order reasons. It should be remembered that exclusionary reasons may vary in scope; they may exclude all or only some of the reasons which apply to certain practical problems. There may, for example, be some scope-affecting considerations to the effect that though Colin's promise apparently purports to exclude all the reasons not affecting his son's interests it does not in fact validly exclude consideration of justice to other people. Furthermore, as will be explained below, an exclusionary reason may also conflict with and be overridden by another second-order reason. Only undefeated exclusionary reasons succeed in excluding. If exclusionary reasons are ever valid then the following principle is valid:

P2. One ought not to act on the balance of reasons if the reasons tipping the balance are excluded by an undefeated exclusionary reason.

P2 contradicts P1 and if valid should lead to the modification of P1. The introduction of exclusionary reasons entails that there are two ways in which reasons can be defeated. They can be overridden by strictly conflicting reasons or excluded by exclusionary reasons. (They may, of course, also be cancelled by cancelling conditions, cf. p. 27.) It follows that if P2 is valid then P1 should be replaced with P3.

P3. It is always the case that one ought, all things considered, to act for an undefeated reason.

Strong and exclusionary reasons

So far we have been concerned to show firstly, through the examples, that exclusionary reasons are frequently used in ordinary practical reasoning and secondly, through the analysis above, that the notion of an exclusionary reason is coherent and can easily be integrated with first-order reasons to form a coherent logic of practical reasoning. Most of the analysis of the previous section applies to second-order reasons. They differ only in their effect in conflict situations.

To understand the meaning of 'exclusionary reason' we must also have a test by which to distinguish between the two ways in which a reason can be defeated. If a person's reason to perform an action is defeated by a certain fact, is that fact an overriding first-order reason or an exclusionary second-order reason? How is one to tell?

In many cases the difference is obvious. One has only to look at the content of a promise (like Colin's in the last example) to see whether it is an exclusionary reason. In other cases a conceptual link can be established between some practical concepts and the notion of an exclusionary reason. Thus it will be claimed in the next chapter that both decisions and mandatory norms can only be explained by reference to exclusionary reasons. But there is also need for a general test applicable to these and all other cases, by which exclusionary reasons can be distinguished from strong first-order reasons. It is this question that we must now address.

The presence of an exclusionary reason may imply that one ought not to act on the balance of reasons. The exclusionary reason may exclude a reason which would have been overridden anyway, but it may also exclude a reason which would have tipped the balance of reasons. When the application of an exclusionary reason leads to the result that one should not act on the balance of reasons, that one should act for the weaker rather than the stronger reason which is excluded, we are faced with two incompatible assessments of what ought to be done. This leads normally to a peculiar feeling of unease, which will show itself when we wish to censure a person who acted on the balance of reasons for disregarding the exclusionary reason and when we have to justify someone's acting on an exclusionary reason against claims that the person concerned should have acted on the balance of reasons. These two types of situation provide the test case for the presence of exclusionary reasons precisely because it is in these situations that their presence makes a difference to the practical conclusion.

The examples at the beginning of the section can be used to illustrate the peculiar impact of exclusionary reasons in the type of situations envisaged. Consider the case of Jeremy, who was ordered by his commanding officer to appropriate a van belonging to a civilian. Let us assume that before reaching his decision Jeremy becomes convinced that the balance of reasons clearly indicates that he should disobey the order. He can carry out the mission for which the van

was required in another and better way. His disobedience will not
be discovered either by his superiors or by anybody else and will not
lead to any harmful consequences either to himself or to others. On
the balance of reasons he should, therefore, disobey the order and he
knows this. Yet he persists in thinking that it is not for him to judge
the merits of the case. This is the responsibility of his commanding
officer. He interprets his position in the army as entailing that he has
to obey lawful orders regardless of their merits, except when given
authority to deviate from them in certain unusual circumstances.
Some may feel that Jeremy is wrong, but we are not trying to judge
him, only to understand his line of reasoning; and it cannot be
denied that it is a relatively common way of reasoning. The best way
to explain Jeremy's argument is by saying that he regards his commander's order as both a first-order and an exclusionary reason. It
is for him a reason for appropriating the van and for not acting on
certain first-order reasons which apply to the case and which but for
the exclusionary reason would have entailed that he ought not to
appropriate the van. But must we really interpret Jeremy's reason in
this way? Can we not say that he regards his commander's order
solely as a (first-order) reason to which he assigns a weight sufficient
to override the other conflicting reasons? I think that the interpretation of Jeremy's reasoning as involving exclusionary reasons is forced
on us by two considerations.

In the first place we would be disregarding Jeremy's own conception of the situation if we were to say that he regards the order only
as an overriding first-order reason. Another person in his place
might have regarded the situation in this light, but this is not the way
Jeremy (according to our example) conceives of his problem. He does
not claim that the order is a conclusive reason for appropriating the
van. Moreover (and this is the important point) his reaction is by no
means untypical. His claim is that the order is a reason for him not to
act on the merits of the case. Had the decision been left to his judgement, he says, he would not appropriate the van. The fact that he
was ordered to do so does not in his view merely mean that yet
another factor is added to the balance of reasons. A different person
might have regarded it in this way. But Jeremy interprets the order
as meaning that it is not for him to act on a complete assessment of
the pros and cons, that whatever his view of the case it should not
affect his action, that all or most of the other considerations are to
be excluded from the range of facts determining his action.

To see the second reason for regarding Jeremy as acting on an exclusionary, rather than on an overriding first-order, reason, let us continue a little further with the story. Jeremy, acting on his convictions, instructs Dick, one of his subordinates, to appropriate the van. Dick becomes convinced that on the merits this should not be done, and he disobeys. Now Jeremy finds himself in the second test situation described above. He is faced with conduct which is right on the merits but wrong in disregarding the exclusionary reason. His reaction is characteristic. He is torn between conflicting feelings. On the one hand he is convinced that Dick did the right thing. On the other hand he thinks he acted wrongly. He wants to praise and blame him at the same time. What he will actually do, which public action he will take, will depend on further, and to our purpose irrelevant, considerations. His predicament is, however, not uncommon. It is familiar to parents whose children have disobeyed them and yet proved to be correct, if one disregards the fact that they were told otherwise. In more heroic circumstances armies have been known to solve such problems by both decorating and court martialling the individual concerned for the same action.

The importance of these cases is that they can hardly be interpreted as ordinary first-order conflicts. When a person having full knowledge of all the relevant factors acts on the weaker reason, either because he does not appreciate the full weight of the stronger reason or for some other motive, we may find various mitigating circumstances but we do not feel torn in the same way. The peculiarity of the situations we are concerned with is that we are aware that the action can be assessed in two ways which lead to contradictory results. It is not that we are uncertain which assessment should prevail. It is rather that since the two assessments are on different levels we are not always quite happy to say merely that the subordinate one has been outweighed and that this is the end of the matter.

To deal with these situations we must distinguish between various types of reasons so that one assessment concerns reasons of one type while the other involves reasons of a different type. Then we can both admit that one assessment is subordinate to the other and still regard it as having a certain autonomy so that it is not merely cancelled by the other. The problem is to reconcile a theory of types of reason with the principle that all reasons are comparable with regard to strength (i.e. that the relation stronger than or of equal strength to is connected in the domain of first-order reasons), and that this is their only feature relevant to the outcome of practical inferences. We require the latter principle if the logic of practical reasoning is to be strong enough to provide ways of representing all practical problems. There-fore, though it is possible that in the end the principle will have to be abandoned or weakened, we should try to adhere to it as long as we can. But if a theory of types of first-order reasons is not reflected in a view that there are various dimensions of strength it does not establish the existence of different types of assessments. That is the ground for introducing exclusionary reasons to deal with the problem. Here we have a theory of types of reasons which regards 'stronger than or equal to' as connected over first-order reasons and as the only factor determining the validity of inferences involving first-order reasons. At the same time the theory introduces a second type of reasons, second-order reasons, which among themselves are again governed by the relation of strength. So we have the two types of assessment which we required. By interpreting the second-order exclusionary reasons in the way we did, one type of assessment is subordinated to the other without the separateness of the two types being destroyed, which would have been the case had we regarded the commander's order merely as a strong first-order reason.

The distinction between first-order and exclusionary reasons derives its usefulness from the need to present practical reasoning as ranging over a field of commensurable reasons despite the inability of the relation of overriding to do justice to the complexity of the relations between reasons. We often express our realization of this complexity by referring to different points of view according to which there are different and incompatible things which ought to be done. But the expression 'different points of view' and related expressions are loosely used to indicate a great variety of practical phenomena and such expressions betray little more than an awareness of complexity. (Points of view are further discussed in sections 4.3 and 5.4.) Our discussion of exclusionary reasons can, therefore, by no means be regarded as an explanation of such expressions, though some cases thus described, as well as many other cases, can be explained as involving exclusionary reasons. No claim is made that the use of the distinction is sufficient to account for the complexity of the relations between reasons. Indeed in section 3.1 a further element will be added to the map of practical reasoning. The introduction of the concept of an exclusionary reason does, however, go some way towards explaining important practical concepts, as will be seen in the next chapter.[12]

Exclusionary reasons are used to explain cases in which, though there may be no doubt what ought, all things considered, to be done, we believe that the defeated reason is not merely overridden. It represents a different way of assessing what ought to be done. An assessment which should not be acted upon in the present situation, but which has some autonomy manifests itself in the two test situations:

(1) If we do wrong when we act contrary to what we ought, all things considered, to do, then our judgement that someone did wrong because he acted on a reason which is overridden by another is more complete and unequivocal than our condemnation of a man who acted on reasons which, though not overridden, are excluded by second-order reasons such as the presence of authority or facts indicating that he should not trust his judgement on the merits.

(2) Conversely, though we approve of people acting as they ought, all things considered, to do, our approval is more complete and unreserved when the reasons for which they acted prevail on balance than when these are reasons which entail overruling, as it were, an autonomous practical assessment.

When people react to actual or hypothetical test situations with these 'mixed' reactions, with all the consequences they entail to the theory of ascription, they provide the evidence required to ascribe to them belief in exclusionary reasons. When we judge that such mixed reactions are appropriate we indicate our belief in the validity of exclusionary reasons. As these remarks make clear, the difference between the two ways of acting rightly or wrongly has practical consequences in the ascription of praise and blame. This is no more than one would expect of all the consequences of normative theory. The detailed examination of these differences is, however, a matter which requires a comprehensive survey of the principles of ascription and cannot be undertaken here.

Practical conflicts

It may be useful to recapitulate and summarize the emerging picture of practical conflict. The simplest non-trivial form of practical inference has one premise stating an operative reason, one or more premises stating auxiliary identifying reasons and a conclusion stating that there is reason for a certain person to perform a certain action. For example: I want to please Joan. Buying her this record will please her. Therefore I have reason to buy her the record. More complex practical inferences contain statements of cancelling conditions. But cancelling conditions are, as already noted, very different from conflicting reasons. Practical inferences involving statements of conflicting reasons are much more complicated in several respects. As well as including statements of several operative reasons and of various identifying reasons related to them, they may include statements of strength-affecting reasons, and assumptions or intermediate conclusions concerning the relative weight of the various reasons involved. Without pretending to explain the structure and rules of practical inferences involving conflicts, I wish to distinguish briefly between three types of practical conflicts, a distinction made necessary by the introduction of second-order reasons.

(1)   First-order conflicts. Conflicts of this type were considered in the last section. They are resolved by considering the intrinsic weights of the conflicting reasons involved and the way they are affected by various strength-affecting considerations.

(2)   Conflicts between exclusionary and first-order reasons. This is the type of case considered in the present section. It involves a first-order reason for action and an exclusionary second-order reason to the effect that the first-order reason should not be acted on. In such conflicts the exclusionary reason always prevails. But this does not mean that these conflicts are easy to resolve. It is true that the strength of the exclusionary reason is not put to the test in these cases. It prevails in virtue of being a reason of a higher order. It can, however, be cancelled by cancelling conditions. Furthermore the scope of the exclusionary reason can be affected by auxiliary reasons of a type which has not yet been mentioned. I shall call reasons of this type 'scope-affecting reasons'.

An exclusionary reason may exclude all or only a certain class of first-order reasons. The scope of an exclusionary reason is the class of reasons it excludes. Just as any reason has an intrinsic strength which can be affected by strength-affecting reasons so every second-order reason has, as well as a strength, an intrinsic scope which can be affected by scope-affecting reasons.

If for Jeremy any order by one of his superiors in the army is an exclusionary reason then it can be assumed that all their orders *qua* orders are equal in scope. Any argument which shows that one order should have a certain scope just because it is an order by a legitimate military authority, would establish the same scope to any order by a legitimate military authority. There may be, however, other auxiliary reasons leading Jeremy to conclude that the orders of one officer should be assigned a different scope than those of another. He may assign a greater scope to the orders of an officer of a higher rank.

There will be fewer cases in which he would rely and act on his own judgement when it conflicts with instructions given by a high-ranking officer, and relatively more cases where he will be willing to do this when the order was given by an officer of a lower rank. For Jeremy, we must conclude, the rank of an officer is a scope-affecting auxiliary reason. It is not in itself an operative reason: that John is a Major is not an operative reason for anything. Given the operative reason 'I was ordered by a superior to ϕ', the fact that the superior is a Major affects the scope of the reason. Similarly it may be that John would regard the fact that the officer has been serving with an armoured unit or that he is an RAF man, etc., as scope-affecting auxiliary reasons. He may regard the quality of his own personal relations with the officer in a similar way and so on.

The main problem in cases in which an exclusionary reason conflicts with a first-order reason which it excludes is to establish whether there are scope-affecting considerations which would lead to such a narrowing of the scope of the exclusionary reason that it would not exclude the conflicting first-order reason.

(3) Conflicts between second-order reasons. Only one type of such conflicts will be mentioned here.[13] These involve conflicts between a reason to act for a certain reason and an exclusionary reason to refrain from acting for it. These turn, like first-order conflicts, on the strength of the conflicting reasons involved and on the presence of any strength-affecting auxiliary reasons. They also involve problems of scope. I have said little on second-order reasons to act for reasons, and they are not going to be discussed in this book. We have introduced second-order reasons because they explain the nature of exclusionary reasons, which are in turn important for our understanding of norms. We need not be concerned here with other types of second-order reasons. Nor need we be concerned with the reasons, if any, which may lead one to assert reasons of higher orders.[14]

Two types of exclusionary reasons

A complete analysis of exclusionary reasons would have to include a survey of the variety of these reasons. This task cannot be undertaken here and I shall confine myself to contrasting two kinds of exclusionary reasons, exemplified by the examples narrated at the beginning of this section.

In some cases, as in the example of Ann's decision, the exclusionary reason is based on the agent's temporary incapacity to form a balanced judgement. This may be a result of temptation, or of a threat or of drink and so on. When this is the basis of the exclusionary reason then it applies only if the merits of the case were not examined before the incapacity arose. If, for example, Ann had an opportunity to consider the offer before it was actually made and had then formed an opinion on its merits then there is no reason why she should not act on the merits. The exclusionary reason arises only if the agent has to assess the merits while he is temporarily incapable of doing so.

Incapacity-based exclusionary reasons differ from all others (for example, authority-based reasons) in that they depend on the circumstances of the agent at the time he decides what to do. This may incline people to think that such reasons are not exclusionary reasons at all. Some may feel that they are ordinary (first-order) reasons not to consider the merits of the case (i.e. not to perform a certain mental act). But this is obviously wrong. There is no reason to prevent a person in such circumstances from going through the arguments to amuse himself or as an exercise, etc., so long as he does not trust his judgement enough to act on it.

Alternatively, some may claim that incapacity is a reason for not acting on one's judgement (because it is likely to go wrong). It is not a reason for not acting on valid reasons. It is obvious that the fact that one's judgement may be wrong is in such circumstances the ground for the reason.[15] But is it also true that the reason is a reason for mistrusting one's judgement rather than for not acting on certain reasons? One cannot act for a reason unless one believes in its validity. The practical relevance of a reason not to act for the reason that p is, therefore, the same as the practical relevance of a reason not to act for p if one believes that p is a valid reason. In an obvious sense the latter is a reason not to act on one's beliefs. But in this sense every second-order reason is also a reason to act on or to refrain from acting on one's beliefs in reasons. There is no independent argument which I can see which shows that only reasons grounded in temporary incapacity are reasons not to act on one's beliefs or that they are not reasons not to act on reasons.

One final comment. There is one thing which the arguments presented in this section do not do. They do not, and do not purport to, prove that one cannot explain what an order is, or explain the nature of any other normative institution except by resorting to the notion of exclusionary reasons. All that has been argued is that some people regard some orders as exclusionary reasons, not that all orders must be so regarded. The case for this latter conclusion will be presented in the following chapters.

2 Mandatory norms

2.1 THE PRACTICE THEORY OF NORMS

The purpose of this chapter is to single out and explain one important type of rule and principle. Rules and principles of this type are normally stated by saying that a certain person ought to, should, must, etc., perform a certain action. This marks them out as practical principles and rules. It also distinguishes them from permissive rules and from power-conferring rules. Technical rules (such as instructions how to bake a cake or operate a computer), though often stated by the use of sentences of the same types, do not belong to the type of rules we are concerned with. Only 'categorical' rules and principles will be examined.

'Principles' and 'rules' are often used interchangeably, though the word 'principles' usually carries an implication of greater generality and greater importance than the word 'rules'. Many of the features which mark the distinction between rules and principles in common discourse are devoid of philosophical importance. Some philosophers have suggested ways of drawing a distinction between the two which is philosophically significant.[1] For the most part I shall not be concerned with the distinction between rules and principles. It should be mentioned, however, that the word 'principle' is sometimes used to assert an ultimate value or to assert that such a value is a reason for action ('the principle of the supreme value of human life' or 'the principle that human life should always be respected'). As will presently become clear we shall not be concerned with this use of 'principle'.

I shall use the term 'mandatory norm' to designate the rules and principles with which we are concerned. I prefer 'mandatory' to the more common 'prescriptive' for several reasons. 'Prescriptive' is often used to characterize a type of meaning or a type of speech act; rules and principles are neither. 'Prescriptive' also connotes the presence of someone prescribing. Rules and principles need not be enacted, laid down or issued by anyone. Rules and principles are necessarily general. 'Mandatory norms' will be used in a wider sense to include particular norms. Hence not all mandatory norms are rules or principles. This use of the term is justified since our interest is in the role of norms in practical reasoning, which does not significantly depend on the generality of the norms. In other words, some other normative phenomena resemble rules and principles in all respects except in being particular, and it is advantageous to treat them together.[2]

For convenience I shall, following von Wright (in *Norm and Action*, ch. v), distinguish four elements in every mandatory norm: the deontic operator; the norm subjects, namely the persons required to behave in a certain way; the norm act, namely the action which is required of them; and the conditions of application, namely the circumstances in which they are required to perform the norm action. Endorsing this distinction means that what was regarded above as an act is now analysed into an act and the circumstances in which it is performed. This does not imply belief in the possibility of determining on some good grounds for every factor whether it is part of the act or of the circumstances in which the act was performed.

The practice theory explained

The content of a rule can be stated by the use of an elementary 'ought' sentence to the effect that some person ought to perform a certain action. When a person makes such a statement and is asked what he means, he may reply that he meant that there is a rule that those persons ought to perform that action, or that it is a rule that etc. Such a reply is sometimes appropriate, but not always. Not every time a person ought to behave in a certain way is there a rule to that effect. This means that either we can say that elementary 'ought' sentences are standardly used either to assert that there is a reason or to assert that there is a rule, or, alternatively, we can remain faithful to the analysis given in the previous chapter and regard them as standardly used only to assert that there is a reason. On this interpretation, when, in answer to further questions, one goes on to say that there is a rule that . . ., one is spelling out the reason the existence of which was asserted by the use of the 'ought' sentence. I say, 'People ought to ϕ.' You ask, 'How do you mean?' and I reply, 'It is a rule that they ought to ϕ.' On the first interpretation I have made the same statement twice using different sentences. On the second interpretation I have first said that there is a reason and then I have spelled out what the reason is. To keep the analysis of 'ought' simple I shall endorse the second interpretation. Whichever interpretation one adopts it is clear that rules are reasons for action.* This is a straightforward result of the second interpretation, but it also follows on the first interpretation. For the use of 'ought' sentences to state rules must be regarded as sufficiently close to other uses of 'ought' to entail that what is stated is a reason. The main problem of understanding rules is to see what sort of reasons rules are, and how they differ from other reasons.[3]

Since any action and any person can be subjected to regulation by norms we cannot distinguish norms from other reasons by the character of the norm subjects or of the norm acts. Similarly, it would be futile to distinguish between norms and other reasons by their strength. We are all familiar with norms of widely differing strength. Some relate to fundamental features of human societies and human life and are to be regarded as very strong reasons. Others, like many rules of etiquette, are of little importance and carry little weight. One is thus forced to look to content-independent features of rules to distinguish rules from reasons which are not rules.

One early attempt which still has some following was to look to the mode of origination of norms. Norms, we were told, are imperatives. They are laid down by an individual or groups of individuals with the intention of guiding human behaviour. This is the imperative theory of norms.[4] Objectors were quick to point out that though this may be true of some norms, it is by no means true of all, as every customary rule will prove. But the proponents of the imperative theory were not to be so easily converted. The simplicity of the imperative theory with its attractive central image of a person imposing his will on others was such that many tried by various ingenious means to explain how customary rules can be regarded as imperatives issued by a society to itself and to meet in similar ways other objections to the theory. The futility of the imperative theory has been amply proved in recent writings and there is no need to repeat here the arguments against it.

As the defects of the imperative theory became clearer another theory gained in popularity: the practice theory. The most thorough and successful analysis of rules as practices was made by H. L. A. Hart in *The Concept of Law.*[5] I shall first present a summary of his views and then comment on them. But my aim is not to criticize

---

* Since rules are objects and only facts are reasons rules are not, strictly speaking, reasons. The fact that there is a rule that p is a reason and not the rule that p itself. For brevity I shall, however, refer to rules as reasons, just as I shall continue to refer to values and desires as reasons.

Professor Hart's particular version of the practice theory. It is to show that rules cannot be analysed as practices and that the whole conception of rules underlying the various practice theories is misguided.

If rules are construed as practices the first question that springs to mind is, whose practice are they? We must distinguish between three types of rules: personal rules, social rules and institutionalized rules. A personal rule is referred to whenever we say that John or Ralph or Judy acts on the rule, or the principle, that . . ., that he or she accepts or follows a rule, or has a rule, etc. Personal rules are personal practices. They are the practices of those who have the rule.

A social rule is a rule of a certain society or community. These terms are very elastic, they may include the members of a college, of a dramatic society, of a profession, the residents of a village, town or region or the inhabitants of a country, etc. We refer to social rules when talking of the rules of some specified group. Often no explicit reference to the group is made, it being assumed that the context makes it sufficiently clear which group is referred to. Social rules are the practices of the groups whose rules they are.

Institutionalized rules are really a subclass of social rules except that they exist only when there are institutions designed to ensure conformity to the rules or to deal with deviations from them. (Institutionalized rules will be discussed at some length in Chapter 4.) When referring to social rules, institutionalized rules will usually be excluded. Hart examines at length both social rules and legal rules, which are a type of institutionalized rules. His analysis can be modified to apply to personal rules and to other types of institutionalized rules. Since we are concerned only with the main features of the practice theory, we can use his analysis of social rules as an example on which to base our comments.

According to Hart a rule that x ought to ϕ when conditions C obtain exists in (the society) S if, and only if, the following conditions obtain:

(1)   Most x's who are members of S regularly ϕ when C. In other words, the rule is regularly complied with by members of the society to whom it applies.

(2)   On most occasions when an x does not ϕ when C, he encounters some critical reaction from other members of S. In other words, deviations from the rule are the occasion for a critical reaction.

(3)   Such critical reactions do not themselves attract further criticism from members of S. Those who manifest critical reactions to deviations from the rule are not in turn subjected to criticism for doing so, by members of S.

(4)   Members of S use expressions such as 'an x ought to ϕ when C' and 'it is a rule that an x ought to ϕ when C' to justify their own actions and to justify demands made of others or criticism of their behaviour.[6]

Oversimplifying a little, it can be said that the first condition ensures that the rule is widely followed, that it is more than a mere aspiration of a few people. The second and third conditions are designed to guarantee that what is complied with is really a rule; that it is not merely the case that many do the same thing at the same time (like going to the coast during the summer Bank Holidays), but that they regard it as something which ought to be done by the relevant group of people. The fourth condition makes doubly sure of this. It also ensures that it is one rule which is endorsed by the society. It rules out the possibility that different people accept several different rules none of which is identical with the rule under examination, but all of which together cover all cases of an x doing ϕ when C. If this were the case people, though agreeing that x's ought to ϕ when C, would not invoke this generalization when making demands or criticizing or justifying behaviour.

A major feature of the practice theory is that it allows for every form of human behaviour to be regulated by rules. It also allows for all possible justifications of rules. Moreover, that a rule is accepted and followed by a society does not mean that the members of the society are agreed on the justification for the rule. They may all think that one should not lie and that this is a rule, while disagreeing on the reasons for the prohibition.

Criticism of the practice theory

The practice theory suffers from three fatal defects. It does not explain rules which are not practices; it fails to distinguish between social rules and widely accepted reasons; and it deprives rules of their normative character.[7] Let us consider these points one by one.

Rules need not be practised in order to be rules. It may be true that certain types of rules must be practised. A legal rule is not a legal rule unless it is part of a legal system which is practised by a certain community. But this is necessary because it is a *legal* rule, and not because it is a rule. Likewise a rule is not a social rule unless it is practised by a certain community, but it may still be a rule. Moral rules are perhaps the clearest example of rules which are not practices. For example, many believe that it is a rule that promises ought to be kept. It may be true that this rule is practised in their communities, but what they believe when they believe that this is a rule is not that it is a practice. Nor is it a necessary condition for the correctness of their belief that the rule is practised. For one may believe that it is a rule that promises ought to be kept even if one is not, and has never been, a member of a community which practised the rule. Similarly, a person may believe in the validity of a rule that one ought to be a vegetarian even though he knows no other vegetarians.

One may be tempted to regard the cases I have referred to as cases of personal rules, but this is unlikely to solve our problem. We have not considered what the explanation of personal rules might be. It seems fairly clear, however, that to be useful at all the notion of a personal rule must mean more than simply a rule in the validity of which a person believes. If the conditions which must be satisfied before a person can be said to have a personal rule are more stringent than those on the basis of which a belief in the validity of a rule can be ascribed to him, then it is possible for a person to believe in the validity of a rule which is not his personal rule. A person may believe that a rule is valid even though he does not observe it. If so then on many occasions when a person believes in the validity of a moral rule the rule he believes in may not actually be his personal rule. Moreover, a man who follows a rule normally regards this fact as irrelevant to the correctness of his belief in the validity of the rule. We would not be surprised to hear him explain that he believes that it is a rule that such and such or that he believes that there is such a moral rule and therefore he has decided to try and follow it, or to make it his practice to follow it. Nor would we be surprised to hear him apologize and explain that despite his belief that there is such a moral rule he has never succeeded in behaving accordingly. We cannot refute him by saying that, since he is not actually following the rule, since it is not his personal rule, he must be wrong in thinking that it is a moral rule. Nor can we say that he is mistaken if it is neither his rule nor a social rule. He may admit to that and confess that neither he nor anybody he knows follows the rule, but regard this as proof of human imperfection and still believe in the validity of the moral rule. This argument does not imply that avowal of belief by a person is a sufficient condition for ascribing the belief to him. A person may sincerely declare that he believes in the validity of a rule and be mistaken. All I am arguing for is that the condition for ascribing the belief may not depend on his following the rule in practice. His belief may manifest itself, for example, in feelings of guilt and regret, and these may exist even though he invariably fails to follow the rule.

Nor can we escape from the problem by equating the holding of a personal rule with belief in the validity of the rule. If we do this it will be true, at the cost of trivializing the notion of a personal rule, that whenever a person believes in the validity of a rule it is his personal rule. Yet when he asserts that there is a rule he is not asserting that he believes in its validity. This view is no more plausible than the thesis that when a person asserts that it is raining what he is stating is that he believes it is raining.

These arguments do not, and are not designed to, prove that there are rules which are not practised. It may be that the person in my example is mistaken in believing that there are such rules, and he may be mistaken because the rules are not practised. He may be mistaken in thinking that there can be rules which are not practised. But even if he is wrong his belief is intelligible. He may be mistaken but he is not perverse or irrational or misusing language. This means that even if we believe that there can be a rule only if it is practised the word 'rule' does not mean 'a practice', and hence the explanation of what a rule is cannot be in terms of the practice theory. At best the practice theory is part of a substantive moral theory explaining when rules are valid or binding. It forms no part of the analysis of the concept of a rule.

The second major defect of the practice theory is its failure to distinguish between practised rules and accepted reasons. According to the practice theory, whenever a reason is believed in, followed and acted on by the relevant person or group, then they have a rule. If my first argument against the practice theory is sound, it follows that we can distinguish between a rule and a reason (which is not a rule) regardless of whether they are acted on and followed in practice. This suggests that there must be a distinction between the practice of acting on a general reason and that of following a rule. This distinction is in fact reflected in the way we interpret our practices. We do not regard every practice of acting on a general reason as acting on a rule. The practice theory fails to draw this distinction and it thereby fails to capture the essential feature of rules.

Consider the case of Jack. Jack believes that he ought to read all of Iris Murdoch's novels and he does usually read them not long after publication. If he fails to read one of her novels within a year of its publication he tends to reproach himself for the omission. Yet he does not think of himself as having a rule that he should read all her novels. He does have other rules. He is a vegetarian and he cleans his teeth every evening. He does this because he believes that these are good rules to have. But he does not read Murdoch because of a belief in any rule.

Consider a community in which almost everybody believes that babies should be breast-fed or that children should be encouraged to learn to read when they are three years of age. This is generally done and people tend to reproach mothers who do not breast-feed or parents who do not teach their three-year-old children to read. Yet people in the community do not regard these as rules. They merely think that they are good things to do. They do regard it as a rule, for example, that people should go to church on Sunday. Somehow they think differently of this, though the difference is not reflected in their practice (except that they would talk of a rule only in the latter case). Warnock in *The Object of Morality* makes the same point using the following example: 'Consider the situation of the spectator of a cricket match, ignorant of the game, and trying to work out what rules the players are following. He will find for instance that, when six balls have been bowled from one end, the players regularly move round and six balls are then bowled from the other end; deviations from this, he will observe, are adversely criticized. He will probably find also that, when a fast bowler is replaced by a slow one, some persons who were previously stationed quite close to the batsman are moved further away, some, probably, a lot further away; and he will find that, if this is not done, there is adverse criticism. But if he concludes that, in so acting, the players are following rules, he will of course be right in the first case, and wrong in the second. There is *no* rule that a slow bowler should not operate with exactly the same field setting as a fast one; this is indeed scarcely ever done, and it would nearly always be regarded as wrong to do it, but that is because, quite independently of any rules, it is something which there is nearly always good reason not to do' (pp. 45–6). The practice theory is at fault for failing to recognize and explain this distinction.

The third major defect of the practice theory is that it deprives rules of their normative character. We have already mentioned that a rule is a reason for action. The fact that rules are normally stated by using normative terms (and in trying to refute the practice theory I am arguing, among other things, that it can only be stated in such terms) indicates that they are operative reasons. A practice as such is not necessarily a reason for action. It may be, provided that there is reason for all to behave as everyone does (to drive on the left, or follow the common rules of etiquette, etc.) or if a certain person has, generally or in particular circumstances, reason to conform to the practice (in order not to be rejected by his neighbours or not to lose his job, etc.). But the practice theory fails to account generally for the normative character of rules. At best it could claim to explain conventional rules, namely those social rules which are maintained because people believe that all have a reason to behave as everyone does.[8] Ultimately it fails to explain even those.

To appreciate this point we should return to Hart's analysis of social rules. His fourth condition is that members of the relevant community use expressions such as 'it is a rule that one ought to . . .' to justify their own actions, and to justify demands and criticisms addressed to others. But what is it that they are actually saying when stating that one should have behaved in a certain way because it is a rule that. . . ? There are three possible interpretations. According to the first they are not stating anything; they are acting. They are performing the speech act of criticizing (or demanding or justifying). The way Hart presents his analysis suggests that he does not accept this explanation, and surely he is right. For on this interpretation citing a rule does nothing to explain the demand or criticism, a view which is clearly wrong. Moreover, this interpretation does not apply at all to those cases in which one explains one's own or another person's action by saying that it was done because of a rule.

According to the second interpretation the statements under consideration invoke the practice as (an incomplete) reason for action. 'I did it because of the rule' means I did it because everybody does. 'Do it because of the rule' means do it because everybody does. There is no denying that sometimes this is what one intends to convey by making such a statement. This is the case when the rule is a conventional rule or when the speaker intends to appeal to reasons which his hearers may have for conforming to the rule, of the kind mentioned above (fear of public disapproval, etc.). But rules are invoked in other circumstances as well. When one explains a demand by reference to the rule that promises ought to be kept, one may intend to intimate that the hearer had better keep his promise or else he will have to take the consequences. But more often than not this is not the speaker's intention. And since at least sometimes this second interpretation fails, it always fails to explain what is stated, because what is stated is the same on all normal occasions on which such sentences are used. Though of course the speaker may have on occasion an additional point which he intends to convey, this cannot be part of what is stated. It is merely what is intimated or implied by the fact that he made the statement.

The third interpretation seems to be the one Hart has in mind. According to this interpretation, sentences of the form 'it is a rule that x ought to ϕ' and of the form 'x ought to ϕ' are standardly used to make the same statement. In other words, to state that it is a rule that one ought to ϕ is to state that one ought to ϕ. One can use either sentence to make this statement except that one can properly use the 'it is a rule' formulation only if the appropriate practice exists. To state that it is a rule . . ., is not to state that there is a practice. It is to assert that one ought to behave in this way, but one is entitled to use this sentence to make the assertion only if the practice exists. Both sentences are used to make the same statement with the use of the 'it is a rule' sentence presupposing that the practice exists. This seems to me to be Hart's interpretation of the use of these sentences to make statements 'from the internal point of view'. They can, according to his theory, also be used to make statements 'from the external point of view' which means statements that the practice exists.

On this interpretation rule sentences are used to make normative statements. They are not, however, statements of a reason. They are merely statements that there is a reason. But there is a more serious drawback to this view. According to it the fact that there is a rule is irrelevant to the normative import of the statement. Saying 'it is a rule that one ought, etc.' is rather like saying 'one ought, etc., and besides, though this is irrelevant from the point of view of practical reason, there is a practice of a certain kind'. To be sure, mentioning the rule is not entirely irrelevant. In so far as it implies the existence of a practice it indicates that the speaker is not alone in his view; it is, therefore, an important rhetorical device. But it is irrelevant for practical reasoning. We must, therefore, reject the practice theory and look for an alternative.

2.2   REASONS AND RULES—THE BASIC MODEL

Rules, and mandatory norms generally, must be distinguishable from other reasons, independently of whether or not they are believed in, followed or practised. Once we know the distinction between mandatory norms and other reasons we are in a position to know whether what is practised or believed in is a mandatory norm or not. We cannot reverse the order and establish the nature of mandatory norms by examining the practice itself.

I shall argue that a mandatory norm is either an exclusionary reason or, more commonly, both a first-order reason to perform the norm act and an exclusionary reason not to act for certain conflicting reasons. The analysis will be completed in the next section. The purpose of the present section is to advance some persuasive, though non-conclusive, arguments in support of the conclusion that mandatory norms are exclusionary reasons. In the first half of the section it will be argued that two types of rules, rules of thumb and rules issued by authority, are exclusionary reasons. The second half of the section contains an analysis of decisions and advances the claim that the analogy between rules and decisions provides an invaluable clue to an understanding of the notion of a rule.

'Rules of thumb'

It may be of some help to examine the sort of reasons usually given for having rules. Our aim in doing this is not to survey comprehensively the possible ways of justifying rules. It is to look at some common ways of doing so in order to gain some insight into the nature of mandatory norms generally. Mill admirably summarizes two very common reasons for having rules: 'By a wise practitioner, therefore, rules of conduct will only be considered as provisional. Being made for the most numerous cases, or for those of most ordinary occurrence, they point out the manner in which it will be least perilous to act, where time 'or means do not exist for analysing the actual circumstances of the case, or where we cannot trust our judgement in estimating them' (*A System of Logic*, 6, 12, 3). Rules are thus justified as time-saving devices and as devices to reduce the risk of error in deciding what ought to be done. We may add to these features the related justification of rules as labour-saving devices. A rule can be examined in tranquillity on the basis of the best information available concerning the factors likely to be present in the situations to which it applies. The rule states what is to be done in these situations on the balance of foreseeable reasons. When a situation to which it applies actually occurs the norm subjects can rely on the rule, thus saving much time and labour and reducing the risks of a mistaken calculation which is involved in examining afresh every situation on its merits.

These reasons for having rules determine the nature of the rules themselves. There is no use for them when one has all the time in the world on hand, can call on the advice of the best experts, and when using up time, and the time of experts, has no other undesirable results. This will be reflected in the specification of the conditions of application of the rules. Rules which are justified along such lines specify that they are to apply only when a decision is required in a hurry, when the norm subject is drunk or subject to great pressure or temptation, or that they are to apply always except if the norm subject has the free use of a computer, and so on, depending on the nature of the rule and the situation to which it applies. It has often been said that such rules are required only because of human imperfection. Under conditions of complete rationality and complete information there will be no use for such rules. This is a mistake. Though human fallibility is a major reason for having such rules it is not the only one. Fact-finding and evaluating the different reasons for action consume time and effort and these are costs which even under conditions of infallibility will often outweigh the marginal benefits which in many cases ensue from engaging in a complete assessment of the situation on its merits. Even under ideal conditions, accordingly, we will still be in need of rules of this type.

Modern philosophers tend not to take rules of this kind very seriously. This reflects their preoccupation with ultimate values and ultimate principles of action to the neglect of the logic of the practical reasoning that is necessary for their application. Some philosophers, however, have gone further and suggested that such rules are not rules at all. This seems to me wrong. But to show why it is wrong the idea of a rule as a labour-saving device has to be further explored.

Imagine a person who finds himself in a situation to which a labour-saving maxim applies. He knows what is required of him by the maxim, but he knows enough of the calculations on which the maxim is based to realize that the situation with which he is confronted is somewhat irregular. Certain facts not taken into account in the calculations on which the maxim is based are present in it. He does not know their nature precisely and he has no idea whether they tip the balance of reasons against the solution given by the maxim. The agent's reaction in such circumstances will show whether he believes that the maxim is a rule or not. If he believes that whenever it is not certain whether on the balance of reasons the solution given by the maxim is right he should find the solution required on the balance of reasons, then the maxim is not for him a rule. It is still a labour-saving device. It serves like a logarithmic table to which one resorts to avoid the full calculation; it is like a map which simplifies navigation, but on which one relies only if it can be trusted not to mislead in the particular situation in which it is used. A man regards such a maxim as a rule only if he believes that at least in some cases the maxim ought to be followed even if in doubt whether its solution is the best on the balance of reasons, even if, were he to consider the case on its merits, he might find that the maxim should not be followed in this case. It may be that some readers will feel that even a man who has the first kind of attitude to the maxim can be said to regard it as a rule. All I can say is that this is not the type of rule that I call a norm, whereas a man who has the second sort of attitude regards the maxim as a rule of the type which I regard as a norm. There is no need to legislate on usage or to present a picture of usage more tidy than it is. The important fact is that the two types of attitude are clearly distinguishable and that this distinction is familiar and common.

This way of drawing the distinction between a rule and a maxim which is not a rule is quite familiar. Indeed, I am relying in part on its intuitive appeal. Our problem is to interpret the distinction, and if we examine carefully the characterization of the distinction as drawn above we shall see that there is only one interpretation open to us. Both the rule and the maxim indicate to us what action we have reason to take. But only the rule, and not the maxim, indicates that we also have an exclusionary reason not to act for other reasons. Following a rule entails its acceptance as an exclusionary reason for not acting on conflicting reasons even though they may tip the balance of reasons.

This interpretation may sound paradoxical. We assume that it is sometimes justified to have rules of this nature. Therefore, an agent who is justified in acting according to such a rule has reason on his side. How can it be said that he refrains from acting for reasons which are not overridden? Suppose that a man argues along the following lines: If I examine each case on its merits, disregarding the costs of engaging in the examination, then I will do better than I would by following the rule, because following the rule would occasionally lead me to perform the wrong action. But if I bring into my reckoning the costs of examining each case on its merits I find that they are greater than the harm done by following the rule. Since by following the rule I avoid the costs at the expense of a lesser evil, I should follow the rule. Surely, the imaginary objector would conclude, that is a straightforward piece of reasoning by way of weighing the reasons for and against the action.

The objection is not so much wrong as misdirected. It derives whatever persuasive force it may have from a misconceived idea that to believe that there are exclusionary reasons is to be irrational, or arbitrary, to choose against reason. But we should not confuse an arbitrary decision to disregard reasons and not to act for them with a *reason* to exclude reasons and not to act for them. Whenever one acts for a valid reason which is a reason for not acting for some other reason, one is acting in accordance with reason and not at all in an arbitrary or unjustifiable way. Therefore, if a rule is justified, its norm subject acts in accordance with reason when he relies on it. Rules can be justified by considerations such as those described by my imaginary objector. But saying that a person acts in accordance with reason does nothing to explain the logical character of the practical inferences involved in reaching this conclusion. This is, however, the only problem with which I am concerned. The only point I was making is that since the rule requires that its subjects shall perform the prescribed act, disregarding other relevant considerations, it is an exclusionary reason. The justification suggested by the imaginary objector is indeed the right justification, except that it is the justification for having an exclusionary reason, that is, for regarding the maxim as a rule, as a mandatory norm.

Norms issued by authority

It is time to review the overall scheme of our discussion. In trying to explain the nature of mandatory norms, I have suggested that they are to be understood as being exclusionary reasons. This can be seen by examining possible justifications of norms, because the nature of the justification shows that the justified norm will fail to achieve its purpose if it were not regarded as an exclusionary reason. Not being able to examine every possible method of justification, I have chosen the justification of rules as labour- and time-saving devices and as error-eliminating devices, since rules based on such grounds are regarded as the least controversial type of rule. The argument has been that these rules would not serve their purpose unless they were treated as exclusionary reasons. Therefore, if we have such rules at all they are exclusionary reasons. In this subsection I shall show that the same is true of the instructions of authorities. Later on I shall argue that all mandatory norms are exclusionary reasons.

Norms issued by authority are another very important kind of norm. Their analysis is an integral part of the explanation of the nature of authority, at least of that of practical authority (to be distinguished from theoretical authority, such as scientific authority). To understand what it is for a person to have authority one must understand what it is for another person to regard him as having authority. A person has authority either if he is regarded by others as having authority or if he should be so regarded. To regard a person as having authority is to regard at least some of his orders or other expressions of views as to what is to be done (e.g., his advice) as authoritative instructions, and therefore as exclusionary reasons.

To show that this is indeed so, we must once more examine the ways in which authority can be justified. Since there are many methods of justifying authority I shall pick two of the most common and important: practical authority based on knowledge and experience, and practical authority based on the requirements of social co-operation.

It is frequently important to be able to be helped by the advice of someone with greater knowledge or of someone whose judgement we trust. But respect for someone's views and advice does not necessarily mean that he is regarded as having authority or as being in authority. Perhaps more often than not the point of seeking advice is simply to acquire information which may bear on the practical problem one faces. In such cases the adviser is perhaps being regarded as an authority on the facts, but not as an authority on what is to be done. Sometimes the purpose of seeking advice is to see how someone else assesses the various relevant considerations and to use this as a check on one's own assessment. If the reasoning of the adviser differs from his own, the person who seeks the advice is not going to defer to the judgement of the adviser. He will simply regard this as an inductive indication that he may have erred, and he will double-check his own arguments. Again the adviser is not being regarded as an authority.

A piece of advice or an expression of opinion as to what is to be done is regarded as authoritative only if it is regarded as a view which ought to be followed despite one's inability to assess its soundness. This is the case when the advice is based on information or experience which the adviser cannot or will not share with us. Then we lack the means necessary for establishing whether the advice is correct on the balance of reasons. In such cases we are forced either to disregard the advice or to follow it without checking its correctness. We take the latter course if we are certain of the adviser's motives and if we trust his knowledge and judgement better than our own. We are not acting arbitrarily. We have reasons for regarding him as an authority, but the reasons we have are reasons for treating his advice as an exclusionary reason. That is, the fact that he advised us to ϕ is an exclusionary reason for disregarding other reasons as well as a first-order reason for ϕ-ing.

Since we are unable to assess his advice we must, if we are to follow it, disregard various conflicting reasons of which we are aware, not because we can see that they are overridden, but simply because we are substituting the adviser's judgement for our own. We do not surrender our judgement altogether. But our deliberations are not about what is right on the balance of reasons. They concern the second-order question of whose judgement regarding the balance of reasons to trust. Our problem becomes a problem of justifying an exclusionary reason. So it seems that in many cases we must either forgo the advantages of relying on the knowledge and judgement of others or regard their views as exclusionary reasons.

A similar line of reasoning will apply to authority based on the need to co-ordinate the action of several people. All political authority rests on this foundation (though not only on it). Many of the classical political philosophers (for example, Hobbes and Locke) regarded authority as established by the citizens' surrender of their right to determine for themselves what to do in all or in some areas. Citizens were conceived as delegating this right to an authority or as entrusting it to him. Much of the classical analysis of authority is vitiated by a failure to distinguish clearly between three problems: (a) What is it to be an authority? (b) How is authority to be justified? (c) How does one acquire authority? Its proponents also held very naive views about the third question. Modern discussions of authority concentrate on the second and third problems and often erroneously assume that their solution is also the solution to the first. We are concerned with the first question only. Our purpose is to show that if authority is to be justified by the requirements of co-ordination we must regard authoritative utterances as exclusionary reasons. The proof is contained in the classical analysis of authority. Authority can secure co-ordination only if the individuals concerned defer to its judgement and do not act on the balance of reasons, but on the authority's instructions. This guarantees that all will participate in one plan of action, that action will be co-ordinated. But it requires that people should regard authoritative utterances as exclusionary reasons, as reasons for not acting on the balance of reasons as they see it even when they are right. To accept an authority on these grounds is not to act irrationally or arbitrarily. The need for an authority may be well founded in reason. But the reasons are of a special kind. They establish the need to regard authoritative utterances as exclusionary reasons.

We have briefly examined two methods of justifying authority. There are others. But we may perhaps generalize on the basis of the cases examined and conclude that to regard somebody as an authority is to regard some of his utterances as authoritative even if wrong on the balance of reasons. It means, in other words, that an authoritative utterance is regarded as an exclusionary reason. To say that a person is an authority is to say that his word is taken as an exclusionary reason, or just that it is an exclusionary reason, namely that one ought, that there are reasons, to regard it as such.

Not all authoritative utterances are norms, but some of them are. And since all authoritative utterances are exclusionary reasons, so are norms issued by authority. The next section will explain which exclusionary reasons are norms and which are not.

Decisions and reasons

Decisions are not norms nor are norms decisions. Yet there are certain analogies between decisions and norms the exploration of which can help to illuminate the nature of norms. But the notion of a decision has to be explained first.

Decisions have not been much discussed in recent philosophical literature, and then usually in the context of questions such as 'Can decisions be caused?', 'Can the agent predict his own decisions?', 'Does the fact that an agent made a decision entail that he has non-inductive knowledge that he will try to carry out his decision and does it entail that he believes that he can succeed in doing so?' Whatever the answers to such questions it seems safe to assume that in all these respects a decision to do A is similar to an intention to do A. But in what ways does a decision to perform an action differ from an intention to perform it? It is quite clear that often there is little difference. On many occasions 'he intends to' and 'he has decided to' are used interchangeably. Yet the central cases of decision differ from mere intentions in important respects and it is to these that we must turn.

Four features[9] characterize fully fledged decisions:

(1) To decide is to form an intention. A decision may or may not involve a mental act of deciding. But even in those cases in which the decision is not crystallized in a mental act it is true that if a person decides at time t to do A then for some time immediately before t he did not intend to do A and for some time after t he does intend to do A.
(2) Decisions are reached as a result of deliberation. x decides to do A only if he forms the intention to do A as a result of a process of deliberation whether to do A or how to solve a practical problem, where the doing of A is regarded by the agent as a solution to the

problem. In most cases a decision results from deliberating on the reasons for or against the action. But a person may decide to perform an action without having first considered the reasons for it, if he has considered some alternative solutions to a practical problem and if the moment the thought of the action occurs to him it appears to him as the appropriate solution to that problem.

'Decision' is sometimes used to apply to an intention formed without deliberation, usually when the agent is aware of conflicting pulls. One may even talk of an unconscious decision. But the central cases are those of intentions formed on the basis of deliberation. Not every intention to perform an action is a result of a decision. It is the process of deliberation as well as the fourth condition discussed below which distinguishes decision-based intentions from other intentions.

(3) Decisions are taken some time before the action. Occasionally we speak of a decision which is immediately carried out. But normally one decides to perform an action some time in advance. It is characteristic of decisions that one can change one's mind about them. In this respect decisions are similar to intentions and differ from straightforward cases of choosing. If Jones is offered a tray of different kinds of drinks and takes a martini it would be correct to say that he chose the martini but not that he decided to take the martini. The salient point is perspicuously made in a recent article: 'If Jones decided to take a martini, then we expect that prior to the action there was deliberation, or at least some preference and resolution, and *that between the time he decided and the time he acted we could correctly say that he intended to take the martini.'*

(4) Decisions are reasons. The three features of decisions discussed above fail to account for some aspects of decisions. They do not explain why a decision is normally regarded as a stronger indication that the act will be done than an intention to do it which is not based on a decision. Nor do they explain why people often refuse to consider reasons for or against the action they have decided to take on the ground that the matter has already been settled by their decision. The explanation lies in the fourth feature of decisions: a decision is always, for the agent, a reason for performing the act he has decided to perform and for disregarding further reasons and arguments. It is always both a first-order and an exclusionary reason. I shall first argue that decisions are exclusionary reasons and then that they are first-order reasons.

* A. Oldenquist, 'Choosing, Deciding and Doing', *Encyclopaedia of Philosophy*, P. Edwards (Ed.-in-chief) (New York, 1967), 2, p. 98 (italics added).

It should be remembered that a decision is reached only when the agent *both* reaches a conclusion as to what he ought to do *and* forms the belief that it is time to terminate his deliberations. The first condition is not enough. Imagine a person who considers a problem for a while and then postpones the decision to the next day. At the time he concludes his deliberations for the day he may be as much in the dark as to which decision to take as when he began his deliberations. But it is also possible that he has already formed the view that the proper decision is to do A. That he has not yet decided to do A is not due to any hesitation or uncertainty on his part. He simply wants to consider another argument which he has no time to examine today, or he may want to hear the view of a friend whom he will meet tomorrow. He may be quite certain that the further argument or any facts to which his friend may draw his attention will make no difference to his decision. The reason for which we say that he has not yet reached a decision (and therefore also that he has not yet formed an intention) is not any uncertainty about what to decide or what to do, but only that he genuinely believes that he should consider some further reasons or facts or re-examine his reasoning—just in case. Indeed the following day he may decide that it would be futile to re-examine his reasoning, or that there is no point in waiting for the advice of his friend, etc., and decide without further deliberation to do A. His decision consists simply in bringing the readiness to continue deliberation to an end.

To make a decision is to put an end to deliberation. It is also to refuse to go on looking for more information and arguments and to decline to listen to them when they crop up in one's mind or are suggested by other people. No doubt in most cases the refusal to reopen the case is not absolute. Usually it is accompanied by some unspecified rider: provided no new information becomes available, or, more strongly, provided no major change occurs, etc. Not all decisions are of the same strength, not all of them are subject to the same escape clause. But all of them are exclusionary reasons and it is this which distinguishes between them and mere intentions to act. An intention may often be less liable to change than a decision. But it is always (unless based on a decision) open to the competing claims of other reasons. To decide what to do is to rule out such a competition or at least to limit it.

Similarly, though a decision is completely abandoned only when the agent abandons his decision-based intention, it is partly abandoned the moment the agent, still intending to perform the action, is ready to reconsider the case for doing it.* That explains why a person may refuse to discuss a problem with another on the grounds that he has already made his decision. That one has taken a decision means that one regards oneself as having an exclusionary reason to disregard further reasons or arguments. To convince another that we hold ourselves open to argument we have to make it clear that we are ready to change our mind and to do so is already partly to abandon the decision.

So far I have tried to show that decisions are exclusionary reasons in the sense that it is logically true that if x has decided to do A then x *believes* that his decision is a reason for him to disregard further reasons for or against doing A. It is not part of my claim that all decisions are valid exclusionary reasons, but only that whoever makes a decision regards it as such. A decision is a valid exclusionary reason only if the agent is justified in treating it as such. Often he is not. However, few would deny that sometimes there must rationally be an end to deliberation and indecisiveness even before the time for action. Hence it is clear that some decisions are valid exclusionary reasons. Paradoxical as this may seem reason sometimes requires disregarding reasons for action.

It could be claimed that though it is a necessary truth that whenever a person makes a decision he believes that he has exclusionary reasons to disregard further reasons, it is not the case that he regards the decision itself as an exclusionary reason. This seems to me wrong. To believe that one has a reason not to consider the matter any further is to believe that one ought to decide. One may of course believe that one ought to decide without being able to do so either because one does not know what to decide or because one cannot stop one's deliberations and form a firm intention. The interesting point is that having taken a decision a person may come to the view that it was a premature decision. He may become convinced not that the decision was wrong but rather that it was wrong to decide at that time. Nevertheless, since he has taken a decision, he now has an exclusionary reason not to reconsider the matter. That the decision was premature is a consideration which may lead the agent to reopen the matter for further consideration but this is never an automatic result. A decision to disregard a decision is itself a new step which should be based on reasons.

* A person may change his mind either in accordance with some rider implied by his original decision, or by going back on his original decision. It is only when considering the problem in contemplation of the possibility that he may go back on his original decision that he has already partly abandoned his decision.

Furthermore a decision, like any other action, can be taken for a reason or for no reason. A person may take a decision even while believing that there is no reason for him to take a decision now. He may not believe that he has a reason to exclude other reasons from consideration and to bring his deliberation to an end and yet do so and make his decision. Once the decision is made it is a reason for him to avoid further consideration. If this were not the case it would have been impossible to make a decision without believing that one should decide. These facts show that the decision itself is an exclusionary reason.

The status of decisions as exclusionary reasons may be clarified by comparing them to promises. That a person promised to do A is a reason for him to do so. One should make a promise only if there are sufficient reasons to do so. But once a promise is made it is a reason for action even though it is a promise which should not have been made. Moreover, a person can promise knowing that he should not. Once the promise is made he has a reason to perform the promised act despite the fact that he made the promise knowing that he should not make it. The same is true of decisions. That a person has made a decision is an exclusionary reason for him not to consider further reasons. One should make a decision only if there are sufficient reasons to do so. But once a decision is made it is an exclusionary reason even though it is a decision which should not have been made. Moreover, a person can decide knowing that he should not. Once he has made his decision he has an exclusionary reason despite the fact that he decided while knowing that he should not do so.

A promise is a reason which can be defeated by other reasons and the fact that it should not have been made may be relevant to whether or not it is defeated. This is true also of decisions. Some will think that a promise is a reason only in virtue of a general principle that promises ought to be kept.[10] We could similarly regard decisions as exclusionary reasons in virtue of a general principle that decisions ought to be respected. Both principles need to be spelt out. Both are based on the idea that people should have a way of binding themselves by intentionally creating reasons for action. The Promise Keeping Principle states that a person creates a reason to do A if he expresses an intention to another person to be bound to do A. The Decision Principle states that people can create an exclusionary reason to exclude further consideration by deciding, i.e. by meeting the first three conditions of a decision and forming an intention to stop deliberation. Both principles are sound practical principles, though both can be abused by making a promise or a decision which should not be made.

It should be remembered that the analogy I am discussing is between the formal features of promises and decisions. Materially they differ. Promises are designed to increase trust and predictability in interpersonal relations; decisions are designed to enable people to settle matters in their own mind and put an end to deliberation. The reasons justifying them and determining their strength are entirely different. The formal analogy is, however, considerable. Its most important feature is that a person cannot make a promise without regarding it as a reason for him to behave in a certain way, nor can he make a decision without regarding himself as having an exclusionary reason.

That the analogy between decisions and promises is really a close one can be seen by comparing both with oaths and vows. These are often regarded as promises one makes to oneself. They can also be regarded as a kind of decision: a solemn and formal decision with very few escape clauses. I believe that the analogy between decisions and promises can be further explored. For example, both are content-independent reasons: regardless what you promise or decide to do you have a reason to do it because you have promised or decided. To examine the full scope of the analogy would involve establishing that a promise is not only a first-order reason to perform the promised act but also an exclusionary reason not to act for other, conflicting, reasons. This investigation cannot be undertaken here. It is worth noticing, however, that decisions are not only exclusionary reasons but also first-order reasons for performing the act decided upon.

The main argument for regarding decisions as first-order reasons for performing the act decided upon must establish that since they are exclusionary reasons of a certain kind, it is preferable, in developing a general theory of practical reason, to regard them also as first-order reasons. The same argument also provides the main support for the contention that mandatory norms are reasons for the act they prescribe. The argument will be described in some detail in the next section when discussing the complexity and completeness of mandatory norms. For the present let us merely notice that ordinary language does not in itself settle the question, and leaves room for theoretical considerations.

Normally one decides to perform an action because one thinks that, all things considered, it ought to be done. In such circumstances it makes little difference whether the reasons for the decision are also regarded as the reasons for the action or whether the decision itself is regarded as the reason for the action and the reasons for it are only the reasons for the reason, so to speak, i.e. they are the grounds for which the reason is considered to be a valid one. Even in these circumstances the agent, when asked for his reasons for performing or for intending to perform the action, may refer to his decision. But more often than not he will refer to the reasons for his decision. It is tempting to regard such references to the decision as refusals to reveal the reasons or as assurances that the action was taken after serious consideration of the reasons. But an alternative interpretation is also available. We can regard the decision as the reason for the action and maintain that when the agent refers not to it but rather to the reasons for the decision this is because he knows that the purpose of the inquiry will be better served by stating the grounds on which his reason is based. My reason for not stealing may be that stealing is wrong but when asked why I did not steal I may say that God's commands must be observed—which is, I am assuming, my reason for believing that stealing is wrong.

Furthermore, a man may decide to do A even though he does not believe that, all things considered, he ought to do A. He may, for example, believe that he ought to decide and that it does not matter what he decides or he may believe that he ought to decide and not know what to decide. In such cases it is clear that the decision is regarded by the agent as a reason for action. Before he decided he saw no reason why he should do A rather than not-A. Having decided he has a reason to do A: namely, his decision.

These considerations suggest that at the very least we sometimes cite decisions as reasons for performing the action decided upon. The argument that we should always regard decisions as such reasons will be presented in the next section.

Decisions and norms

The role mandatory norms play in affecting the behaviour of a person who believes in them is analogous to that of decisions. This analogy provides a key to an understanding of the nature of mandatory norms.

Suppose I discover a mechanical fault in my car. I decide to take it to the garage the next morning, but to drive in it to a very important meeting today. It occurs to me that at the meeting some acquaintances of mine are likely to ask for a lift home. I do not want to take the risk of giving them a lift, even if they are ready to take it when told of the condition of the car. I know that if asked I will find it difficult to refuse. I therefore decide now not to take anybody in the car that day. I am taking a decision in advance, hoping that this will help me not to yield to requests when I am faced with them.

I may go further. I may, reflecting on the matter, decide on this occasion to make it a rule never to take anyone in my car when I suspect it has some mechanical fault. If so I am simply making a general decision. Of course even if I adopt the rule now I may have to decide again in the future what to do in particular cases, but my problem then will be different from what it would have been had I not adopted the rule. Having adopted the rule, what I have to decide is whether to act on it in this particular case. What I am not doing is assessing the merits of the case taking all the relevant facts into consideration. I am not doing this because I have decided on a rule, that is, I have accepted an exclusionary reason, to guide my behaviour in such cases. I may occasionally, of course, examine the justification for the rule itself. If I re-examine the rule on every occasion to which it applies, however, then it is not a rule which I have adopted. I may on the other hand examine the rule occasionally even when not confronted with a case to which it applies. This is the test by which to determine whether a person follows a rule.

Given our analysis of decisions there is little surprise that if a person decides to follow a rule he has an exclusionary reason to behave in accordance with the rule; the decision is his exclusionary reason. A person may, however, come to follow a rule without having decided to do so. He may have been brought up from early childhood to believe in the validity of the rule and to respect it. He may have drifted into following the rule as an adult gradually over a period of time without ever really making up his mind to do so. It is quite clear that the role a rule plays in the deliberations and behaviour of a person who follows it does not depend on whether he came to follow it one way or the other. A person who follows a rule without having decided to do so may one day critically examine his practice and decide to continue to follow the rule. But the role of the rule in his practical reasoning will not change, now that he has decided to follow it, from what it was before. Indeed this is precisely the purport of the decision, that he should continue to follow the rule as before.

The conclusion to which we are driven is that mandatory norms in general play the same role as decisions in the practical reasoning of those who follow them. A person follows a mandatory norm only if he believes that the norm is a valid reason for him to do the norm act when the conditions for application obtain and that it is a valid reason for disregarding conflicting reasons, and if he acts on those beliefs. Having a rule is like having decided in advance what to do. When the occasion for action arises one does not have to reconsider the matter for one's mind is already made up. The rule is taken not merely as a reason for performing its norm act but also as resolving practical conflicts by excluding conflicting reasons. This is the benefit of having rules and that is the difference between mandatory norms and other reasons for action.

Not every rule is a valid reason. The point I am concerned to argue is that a person follows a rule only if he believes it to be both a valid first-order and an exclusionary reason. He may be wrong, but for him the rule is a rule only in being such a combination of reasons in the validity of which he believes. To explain what rules are one must do more than explain what it is to follow a rule. One must first of all explain what it means for a mandatory norm to be valid. But the analysis of following a rule provides the clue to the analysis of 'a valid norm'. For a norm is valid if, and only if, it ought to be followed (see further on the validity of norms in the next section). Thus if our analysis of following a rule is correct it follows that a rule is valid only if it is a valid exclusionary reason.

The analogy with decisions, it must be stressed, extends only to the indicated similarity in their role in practical reasoning. Both decisions and norms are, if valid, exclusionary reasons. One should not be led to the conclusion that decisions are norms or *vice versa*. A decision, whether good or bad, must be taken by a person, and is personal to him; it is and can only be his decision. A rule can apply to more than one person and can be valid even if nobody believes in it. It is true that there could be rules with only one norm subject which are valid only if their norm subject accepts them and follows them (see further in sections 2.3 and 4.1 below). But a stranger can (mistakenly) believe that such a norm is valid despite the fact that its only norm subject neither believes in it nor follows it. No one can believe that a decision is binding on someone who has not taken it.

2.3 THE ANALYSIS OF MANDATORY NORMS

Norms as exclusionary reasons

I have suggested that the notion of exclusionary reasons is essential to the explanation of mandatory norms, especially in order to understand the ways in which their role in practical reasoning differs from that of ordinary reasons for action. In the preceding section I argued that norms justified as labour- and time-saving devices, those justified as error—minimizing devices, and those issued by authority and justified by the wisdom of the authority or by the need to secure coordination must be regarded as exclusionary reasons. An argument from the justification of norms cannot, however, establish that all norms are exclusionary reasons. There are many different methods of justifying norms and I know of no general argument which would show that all possible justifications require the norm to be an exclusionary reason. Furthermore, many people endorse many norms without having any clear view as to how they are to be justified. Therefore we used the analogy with decisions. This was an argument based, not on the ways in which rules can be justified, but on their role in the practical reasoning of those who believe in their validity. If, as was claimed, they function like decisions and if decisions are exclusionary reasons then so are norms.[11]

There is yet another argument to show that mandatory norms are exclusionary reasons, an argument based on the test suggested in section 1.2.

The test is meant to establish whether a person regards a reason as exclusionary by attending to certain of his reactions in actual or hypothetical conflicts, and whether a reason is a valid exclusionary reason by establishing whether these reactions are justified. A person regards a reason as exclusionary if in certain cases in which he is faced with incompatible reasons his reaction differs from the one appropriate to conflicts in which one reason overrides another because it is stronger or more weighty. The difference is that the person concerned regards the incompatible reasons as belonging to two different types or levels of reasoning. He thinks that reasons belonging to one level preclude action for reasons of the other level and yet the two levels are not directly comparable so that if one acts for the reasons of the inferior level one deserves not outright criticism, as is the case when a person acts for the less weighty reason, but a mixture of praise and criticism; for one has done the right thing according to one assessment of the situation which, though it should not have been acted on, is not simply overridden. The explanation of this complex reaction is that the person concerned regards himself as faced with incompatible first-order and exclusionary reasons and that though he is required by the exclusionary reasons not to act for some first-order reasons he is aware that were he to act on the balance of first-order reasons he would have performed a different action.

It seems to me that if we examine the characteristic reaction to the test situation of people who endorse a mandatory norm we will find that they do regard it as an exclusionary reason. Everyone who follows a rule may find himself in a situation in which he knows that he ought to perform the norm act and yet he has the characteristic mixed reaction to the effect that doing so is not all right, i.e. that there is a different calculation according to which he ought not to perform the action. As suggested above this is evidence that he does indeed follow the rule as a mandatory norm, i.e. regards it as an exclusionary reason which may on occasion require action contrary to the balance of reasons. When we find ourselves in such a situation we normally believe that we are justified in following the rule. To this extent we regard the rule as a decisive and important reason. But the mixed reaction leads us to deny that the rule or the reasons for the rule always override conflicting reasons. We rather feel that they exclude them, they justify action despite those other reasons even though on the particular occasion concerned they do not override them.[12]

To turn to the other type of test case we find again that the mixed reaction typical of an exclusionary reason is often to be found in cases of deviation from norms. We are always aware of the fact that deviation from a rule can be beneficial in its particular circumstances. Sometimes we conclude that the deviation was justified and that the rule should not have been followed on this occasion. But this is not always the case. Often we feel that the rule should have been followed even though it was known in advance and proved after the event that deviating from it would have been beneficial, and even if it is established that it would not have undermined the chances that the rule would be followed on other occasions. This reaction is conclusive proof that the rule is regarded as a rule, that is, as an exclusionary reason. There are some, no doubt, who think that such a reaction is never justified. But this is beside the point. The crucial fact is that such reactions are fairly common and that they are the test for determining whether a person really regards the rule as a rule, or merely as a statement of a first-order reason for action. This last point is conceded by those who challenge the justification of such reactions, for they are the very same people who challenge the validity of rules and claim that all action should be governed by the direct application of ultimate values. (The arguments put forward in the previous section suggest that those who think it impossible to justify rules because it is impossible to justify not acting on the balance of reasons may be wrong after all.)

To endorse a norm entails, as we have seen, belief that it is an exclusionary reason. A norm which is practised is an exclusionary reason for those who practise it. What of moral rules which are not generally followed? Are they exclusionary reasons as well? If the rule is justified it should be practised as one practises a rule, that is as an exclusionary reason. Hence, to establish that it is justified is to establish that it is an exclusionary reason. The case of the two types of rules discussed in the last section can be used as an example for arguments concerning the validity of mandatory norms. But any other types of moral rule or other valid rule would illustrate the same point.

It has often been said that rules are not important for moral philosophy because they are not ultimate principles of action. Rules, it seems to me, are very important for practical reasoning, which includes much besides moral reasoning. They are also important for moral reasoning. It is true, however, that rules are not ultimate reasons. They have always to be justified on the basis of fundamental values. This is a result of the fact that norms are exclusionary reasons. A reason not to act for reasons cannot be ultimate. It must be justified by more basic considerations. Furthermore, rules, as has often been noted, normally represent the result of considering the application of a variety of conflicting considerations to a generic situation. This explains why they are not ultimate. It also explains why the reasons for the norm are not always obvious from the formulation of the norm. As has been noted (in section 1.1) every complete reason includes an operative reason which is itself a complete reason for another action, namely the action that would promote the goal set by the operative reason, be it the realization of a value or conformity to a norm. Every act required by any complete reason is also an instance of the act required by the operative reason alone. When the operative reason is a value this enables one to characterize the act required as the promotion of that value, thus making the grounds for the desirability of the act obvious. Since a norm is the outcome of the requirements of various conflicting values it does not carry its desirability on its face. It simply states what is required, of whom and when, but it does not always do so in a way which makes obvious the reasons for the requirements.

The complexity and completeness of mandatory norms

I have argued at length that mandatory norms are exclusionary reasons, because this fact has not received sufficient attention and because it is the key to understanding the role of norms in practical reasoning and of the problems involved in justifying them. We must not forget, however, that most norms are also first-order reasons—a reason not only to disregard other reasons but also to perform the norm act when the conditions of application apply. In a case to which a reason incompatible with the norm, but not excluded by it, applies one must determine what one ought to do on the balance of reasons, comparing the weight of the norm as a first-order reason with the weight of the competing reason.

The first-order strength of a norm depends on the values it serves; it depends on the strength of the reasons for the norm which are reasons for doing what is required by the norm. These are all the reasons for the norm except those which justify its character as an exclusionary reason. The first-order strength of the norm also depends on the likelihood that deviating from it in a case where this is otherwise justified will increase the risk that it will be disregarded in cases in which it should be followed. Facts affecting this risk are best regarded as strength-affecting auxiliary reasons.

Not all norms are, however, first-order reasons. One can think of a mildly rebellious youth who endorses a rule to disregard all considerations of etiquette—not to violate them, but simply to disregard them. We are also familiar with mild ascetic principles, e.g., that a person should disregard those of his desires frustration of which will not endanger health. These norms are only exclusionary reasons. It is a mistake to think that those who endorse them either deny that the excluded considerations are reasons at all, or that they are always overridden. They need do neither. They may simply believe that there are good reasons to exclude those considerations. Such a line of argument makes it more difficult to show that such purely exclusionary norms cannot be consistently endorsed. They may be misguided and mistaken, but they are not necessarily irrational.

Not all exclusionary reasons are norms. We have noted that all authoritative utterances are exclusionary reasons, and yet they are not all norms. Let us suppose that being completely ignorant in the matter I always invest my money according to the advice of a friend who is an expert on the Stock Exchange. His advice is an exclusionary reason for me and I regard him as my authority. And yet he is not issuing norms when he gives me advice. It will be argued below that all orders are, in a sense, exclusionary reasons. But they are not always norms. It seems that norms and other exclusionary reasons do not differ in any way which is relevant to practical reasoning. The difference is primarily ontological. We talk of norms as entities. It may be that this mode of speech can in many cases be eliminated in favour of other expressions which do not refer to a norm as an entity. But this is beside the point, for we do in common discourse use 'norm', 'rule' and 'principle' as components of singular expressions referring to objects. Therefore, we talk of norms when we have and expect to have occasions to refer to the content of the norm, rule or order, disregarding the particular circumstances which gave rise to the norm: the act of giving an order, the fact that the norm is practised or the circumstances which justify it. When we do not expect to have occasion to refer to the content of the reason, irrespective of the circumstances on which its existence depends, we do not talk of it as a norm. In such cases we refer directly to the act of giving the order, or to the social practice or to the drought (which is a reason for cutting down water consumption) as a reason.

That is why we normally refer only to general norms, to rules and principles, and not to particular norms. General norms apply to many situations and we may have many occasions to refer to them. Particular norms apply only to one case, and normally will be discussed with reference to the circumstances which generate them. So they will not be discussed as norms at all. But we have occasion to refer to them in institutional settings, when they form part of an institutionalized normative system. A club may lay down a rule which applies to one occasion only (for example, that on its tenth anniversary there will be a general meeting) and it may adopt the rule years in advance. In such settings we can and do refer to particular norms as norms.

When discussing the dimensions of mandatory norms below, we shall notice other conventions which govern the use of 'norm' and 'rule'. For the present we have to face one important consequence of the fact that norms are treated as 'entities', namely that they are complete reasons. We have seen that when a person states that one ought to ϕ he is not giving a reason for ϕ-ing, but is merely stating that there are such reasons. Stating that it is a norm or a rule that one ought to ϕ is giving a reason. Why the difference? Why not say that statements of the 'it is a rule that . . .' variety are also merely statements that there is a reason, in this case an exclusionary reason. First let us note that the fact that rules and norms are treated as entities indicates that the difference exists. Even the most cursory survey of practical discourse will reveal that rules are frequently cited as reasons (for example, when asked why I ought, many will respond that I ought because it is a rule). Since norms are treated as objects this could hardly be otherwise. But why is it that we regard norms as complete reasons? Must this fact be accepted as a brute fact of our use of language or does it reflect an aspect of practical reasoning? It seems to me that there is an explanation of the fact that norms are regarded as complete reasons which is both simple and instructive. It also helps to explain why they are treated as objects.

We have emphasized the flexibility and complexity of practical reasoning involving norms. The presence of a norm does not automatically settle practical problems. There may be other conflicting reasons not excluded by the norm. There may be scope-affecting considerations, etc. But it must be admitted that for the most part the presence of a norm is decisive. The complicating factors apply only in a minority of cases. The whole purpose of having norms is to achieve this simplification. The fact that norms are exclusionary reasons enables them to achieve this purpose. Since a norm is an exclusionary reason it does not have to compete with most of the other reasons which are likely to apply to situations governed by the norm, for it excludes them. In this way norms simplify practical reasoning. Once it is established that a norm applies to the case at hand we need not be concerned with the weight of the conflicting reasons affecting the case. They are in most cases excluded and their exclusion is not a matter of weight. It is determined by the fact that the norm is a second-order reason. Thus norms have a relative independence from the reasons which justify them. In order to know that the norm is valid we must know that there are reasons which justify it. But we need not know what these reasons are in order to apply the norm correctly to the majority of cases. The reasons for the norm determine its weight both as a first-order and as an exclusionary reason. But in most situations its weight is not in question. It prevails in virtue of being an exclusionary reason.

This relative independence of norms from their justifying reasons explains why they are regarded as complete reasons in their own right and why we hypostatize them and treat them as objects. It also explains the difference between 'ought' statements and statements of the 'it is a rule that one ought . . .' variety. Assume that somebody tells me that I ought to perform a certain action but that he does not tell me what the reasons are. Assume further that I believe him, that is, I believe he knows of certain reasons for the action which escaped me. I am aware only of some reasons against that action. In such a situation I am at a loss. I can make no use of his advice since, though I take his word that there are reasons for the action, every-thing turns on whether they are stronger than the reasons against it of which I am aware. This I cannot know without knowing what the reasons for the action are.* Compare this situation with the follow-ing one which is identical in all respects except that the advice my friend offers is that there is a valid rule that I ought to perform the action. Again I believe him; I believe, that is, that there is a reason to perform the action and a reason to exclude other considerations. Again he does not tell me what the reasons for the rule are. But this time this does not matter. Unless the conflicting reasons of which I am aware are of an exceptional nature, the question of the weight of the reason of which he advised me does not arise. The rule prevails because it excludes the conflicting considerations. It is only in excep-tional circumstances that I must know the precise reasons for the rule in order to know what to do. And this explains why 'ought' statements are merely statements that there is a reason, whereas statements that there is a rule are statements of a reason—the rule being the reason.

The dimensions of mandatory norms

Throughout this chapter I have on occasion been using expressions such as 'a norm is justified', 'it ought to be endorsed', 'it is endorsed', etc., and I have been wary of saying that a norm exists or that there is a norm. Existential sentences about norms are used for a variety of purposes, among which three are the most important. In saying that there is a norm one may state either that it is valid (that is, justified), or that it is practised, or that it has been prescribed by a certain person or body. These are the three dimensions of norms, and we shall briefly survey them.

A norm is valid if, and only if, the norm subjects are justified in guiding their behaviour by it whenever it applies; that is, whenever its conditions of application obtain. The question of the validity of a norm should be clearly distinguished from other questions of justification. A norm may be valid and yet a norm subject may not be justified in performing the norm act in certain circumstances, for there may be present in these circumstances some other conflicting reasons not excluded by the norm, which should prevail. Similarly a legislated norm may be valid even though the legislative authority

---

* I can, of course, trust his judgement because I believe he knows how to handle such cases better than I do. But this would be to regard him as an authority and his advice as an exclusionary reason.

was not justified in enacting it. Once enacted the norm subjects may have ample reason to regard the norm as binding despite the fact that the norm should not have been enacted in the first place. By talking of the validity of norms we isolate one problem of justification: should the norm subjects guide their behaviour by the norm? We have already provided examples of ways in which the validity of norms can be established.

A valid norm can either be practised or not. It can be followed and endorsed by a person or a society or it can be disregarded by them. A norm which is not valid can, of course, also be practised. That a norm is practised entails that at least some believe that it is valid, but it does in no way entail that the norm is valid. The practice theory of norms is mistaken in thinking that by explaining what it is for a norm to be practised it explains what a norm is. Nevertheless, H. L. A. Hart and other proponents of this theory have contributed much to our understanding of social, institutional and personal practices. We have already explained Hart's analysis of social norms and we will have occasion to examine some aspects of institutionalized norms in the next chapters. The analysis of social practices and of what constitute following a rule offered by Hart and other philosophers can no doubt be further refined and improved. For our purpose, however, only one point should be added: a person follows a norm only if he regards it as an exclusionary reason as well as a first-order reason to perform the norm act. The tests suggested in section 1.2 to determine whether a man regards a fact as an exclusionary reason must be applied to determine whether he is following a norm. A norm is practised by a society only if the bulk of the society follow the rule and hence the same tests apply in determining whether a norm is a social norm.

Whether or not a norm is practised is, sometimes, relevant to its validity. There are social rules which it would not be right to adopt but which it would do more harm than good to change, so that once we have them we should stick to them. In such cases the practice turns an invalid norm into a valid one. Similarly, there are conventional rules, namely those we have reason to follow because everyone does. These are rules which are good rules to have, and yet they are valid rules only if actually practised. It is good to have a rule determining which car has precedence on the road—the one coming from the right or from the left. It is good to have such a rule regardless of whether or not it is practised. But the rule is valid, namely people ought to be guided by it, only if it is practised. In a society in which no such rule of precedence is recognized it would be extremely dangerous and foolish to try and act on one oneself. These cases bring out the importance of clearly distinguishing between the question of validity and other problems of justification. In particular it shows the difference between there being reasons for having a rule and there being a valid rule. There are very good reasons for having a rule prohibiting travel to a certain country. But since no such rule is practised and since its being followed by all is a condition of its validity (no good will come if just one person follows it) it is not a valid rule that I am bound to observe. (I may, of course, have other reasons for not going to that country. I may think that this will contribute to a campaign to establish the rule. Or I may think that it will prevent a possible misunderstanding of my motives in advocating acceptance of the rule.)

It may well be that one of the reasons for the apparent plausibility of the practice theory of norms is the fact that there are many norms whose validity depends on their being practised. In the case of these norms it is true to say that there is a norm only if it is practised. If it is not there is no valid norm and all one can say is that we ought to have such a norm. However, not every norm depends for its validity on the fact that it is practised. This is one, but only one, of the reasons for the failure of the practice theory.

A norm is prescribed if it is set by an individual or a group as a norm to guide the behaviour of some other person or persons. A prescribed norm is one set by a speech-act intended to be taken by the norm subjects as an exclusionary reason for action. Not all prescriptions are norms (see p. 77), but all prescriptions are in a sense exclusionary reasons. A prescriptive situation is by its very nature asymmetric. It involves a person who lays down the rule, or gives an order, etc., and another to whom the rule or order is addressed. The addressee of a prescription may regard it in any possible way. His reaction is irrelevant to the nature of the prescription. This depends on the intentions of the one who issues the prescription. It has often been noted that he must intend that his act of issuing the prescription with the intention that it be taken as a reason will be recognized and taken as a reason for action by the addressee.[13] This condition is, however, too weak. What the prescriber intends is that his prescription shall be regarded as an exclusionary reason.

It is interesting to compare a prescription with a request and with a threatening warning (for example, 'if you continue using your electric lawn mower on Sunday mornings I will not let you use my garage'). A person who makes a request intends his making the request to be a reason for the addressee to comply with it. He hopes no doubt that his request will be a conclusive reason, but he does not intend it to be an exclusionary reason. If his request is turned down and he is shown that there were sufficiently strong reasons to refuse his request he may be disappointed but he has nothing to complain about. Admittedly, his request was not complied with but it was considered in precisely the way he intended it to be. Similarly a person making a threatening warning intends the threat to be taken seriously and the prospect of the threat being carried out to be sufficient to tip the balance in favour of the action he desires. If his adversary persists in his ways, the person who gave the warning may be disappointed and he may think that his adversary is a fool. But he also has nothing to complain about; and if he is convinced that his adversary has sufficiently strong reasons to persist despite the threat, he will have to agree that he was right to do so. By giving a threatening warning one offers one's opponent a choice with the intention that he will choose in a certain way, but one cannot complain if the threatened person chooses otherwise.

The situation is completely different in the case of an order or any other prescription. The prescriber intends his order to be taken as an exclusionary reason. If the person to whom the order is addressed does not perform the act he was ordered to perform because he finds, correctly, that on the balance of reasons he should not perform it, he may still be disobeying the order and acting contrary to the intention of the prescriber. This is the case even though he considered as a reason for performing the action the fact that the prescriber intends him to perform the act. In other words, the addressee may act contrary to the prescriber's intention even if he regards his prescription as a request and accords it the full weight he would give to a request. This shows that in issuing an order a person has an additional intention which he does not have when he makes a request. He intends not merely that his act be taken as a reason to perform the prescribed act but also that it should be taken as an exclusionary reason to disregard some or all conflicting reasons for action.

In general, since an order is meant to be taken as an exclusionary reason, it is disregarded if it is not obeyed. The fact that on the balance of reasons, taking into account the reason for performing the act which the order is, the prescribed act should not be performed is no good reply to the charge of disobeying an order (though it is to an accusation of disregarding a request). Sometimes, however, an order is not meant to exclude all other considerations. If the addressee did not perform the prescribed act because of the presence of an overriding reason not meant to be excluded by the order he is not regarded as having disobeyed the order (though he did not obey it either), since he did not act contrary to the intention of the prescriber. He will have a justification for his action which will be regarded as valid by the man who issued the order.

If the order is accompanied with a threat one is not offering the addressee a choice. Rather, one is reinforcing the reason which is the order itself with a further reason. It should be remembered that, because of the basic asymmetry of the situation, the decisive question concerns the attitude implied by the act of giving the order. The validity of the prescription is irrelevant to its characterization.

It is because a prescription is intended as an exclusionary reason that it is more presumptuous than a request or a threatening warning. One cannot interpret a prescription as issued with an intention that it be taken as a very strong or even as an absolute reason. The prescriber's attitude will normally be that he is not saying that his saying so is the most weighty consideration in the world, but rather that because he gave the order the addressee should forget all other considerations. If the addressee disobeys, the prescriber may admit that on one assessment he has done well, and yet he may maintain that though aware of this it was his intention that the addressee will obey the order and disregard conflicting reasons. Thus the test for identifying exclusionary reasons applies to prescriptions.

Normally we are interested in norms either because they are prescriptive, practised, or valid, or possess some combination of these properties. When asserting the existence of norms we mean that they have one or more of these properties. Normally the context clarifies the exact meaning of such utterances. If it does not it is always proper to require a clarification. (For a more detailed discussion of normative statements see section 5.4.) Of the three dimensions, that of validity is beyond doubt the primary one. Only valid norms are valid or good reasons. Practised norms or prescribed norms can be called reasons only in the sense in which we refer to the reason for which a person performed some action: it is a reason simply because he believed it to be a reason. When using reasons in this sense we distinguish between good and bad reasons. An enacted or a practised norm is a reason in this sense. But it may be a bad reason. To put it another way, it may not be a reason at all but some people believe that it is or intend others to take it as a reason.

3 Non-mandatory norms

3.1 PERMISSIONS

The variety of permissions

In this chapter I shall examine the nature of two types of non-mandatory norms: permissive and power-conferring norms. The purpose of the present section is to clarify the sense in which permissions can be regarded as norms. 'Permission', like so many other normative terms, is used in a variety of contexts to make a variety of points. It is best to begin by distinguishing some of the main uses of 'permission' in order to isolate the type of permission which is a norm.

That a person is permitted to perform an act does not necessarily imply that anyone has given him permission to do it. We shall discuss the granting of permissions below. That an act is permitted might mean no more than that the reasons against performing it are not sufficient to determine that it ought not to be done. In this sense a person is permitted to perform an action if, and only if, it is not the case that he ought, all things considered, to refrain from it. Used in this sense, being permitted to perform an action is compatible with having to perform it. Indeed in this sense, if one ought all things considered to perform an action, it follows that one is permitted to perform it. Often, however, when saying that an action is permitted we mean that one is at liberty to perform it, that one may either perform the action or refrain from performing it. In this use a permission entails that there are no reasons either for or against performing it or that these reasons are evenly balanced.

More often than not, however, permission sentences are used to make more restricted statements. In particular, in saying that a person is permitted to perform an act one normally means that he has no reason other than his own desires not to perform it. Such sentences are also used to state that one has no duty not to do it. It may be that there are good reasons for not doing the act, that on the whole he should not do it, but he is permitted to do it since he is not under an obligation not to do it. There are other ways in which the scope of a statement of a permission may be restricted. It may be restricted to a particular type of reason. For example, in saying that you are permitted to engage in some action one may mean that you are legally permitted or that you are morally permitted, that is that there are no sufficient legal reasons or moral reasons which require you to refrain from it. This use is compatible with a belief that there are reasons of a different kind for refraining from this action.

Permission sentences are also used to assert that in so far as one's obligations are concerned, or from the moral or the legal point of view, one is at liberty to perform the act or to refrain from doing so. These statements are equivalent to saying that one has no obligation either to perform it or to refrain from it, or that one is required by law, or by morality, neither to perform nor to refrain from that action.

Many philosophers have characterized permissions of all the kinds so far mentioned as weak permissions. It is often said that an act is strongly permitted only if its being permitted is entailed by a norm. It is permitted in the weak sense if the permission is not entailed by any existing norm but is simply a consequence of there being no norms prohibiting the performance of the action. It seems to me that this distinction is of great importance.[1] But both the meaning and relevance of the distinction have not been made very clear by existing discussions of the subject.

It is often said that the distinction between strong and weak permissions applies to prescribed, i.e. enacted, norms and that it applies to normative systems, for example to the law. It should be remembered that normative systems contain customary norms which are not prescribed, but which may be permissive norms, so that it seems that we are faced with two distinctions, that between permissions granted by prescriptions and those which one has in the absence of a prescription to the contrary, and that between a permission given by a norm of a system and a permission one has in the absence of a norm to the contrary.

It may seem that the first of these distinctions is identical with the distinction between a permission one has because somebody has given one permission to do the act, and a permission which was not granted by anyone. These distinctions are not identical, however, since a permission can be granted by the repeal of a norm and not only by making a norm. The railway board, let us assume, has laid down a rule that smoking in its coaches is prohibited. Five years later it repeals the rule. It has, thereby, granted permission to smoke in coaches, but it has not created any new norm; it has merely repealed an old one. Its book of regulations will not include a rule that smoking is permitted; the only change is the omission of the old rule prohibiting smoking. This is the correct interpretation of its action regardless of whether the repeal was effected by passing a resolution to repeal the prohibiting rule, or by resolving that henceforward smoking is permitted. The analysis of the granting of permissions is interesting, but the distinction between permissions granted by an enacted norm and other permissions does not seem to me to lead anywhere.

What is the sense or importance of the distinction between permissions entailed by norms and those entailed by the absence of norms to the contrary? Here again, it is not clear that there is one purpose the distinction is meant to serve. It is sometimes said that a weak permission indicates the existence of a gap in the law (or whichever normative system), whereas a strong permission does not. It is also said that a strong permission entails that an authority inferior to the one which made the permissive law cannot repeal the permission, even in cases in which it is entitled to impose a duty and thus to reverse weak permissions. There is a grain of truth in both allegations except that the distinctions on which they rely need not coincide. For example, if a duty-imposing norm is repealed this presumably does not entail that the law now contains an additional gap, but it may mean that a subordinate legislator may step in and regulate the conduct which was the subject of the repealed law. In general, the law concerning gaps in the law and the powers of subordinate authorities is contingent on the details of different systems. There is no reason to believe that one conceptual distinction will meet the varying needs of different societies. It is rather likely that a variety of much more complex distinctions are drawn by different normative systems and by each one of them for different purposes.

It is not only the purpose but also the very sense of the distinction which is troublesome. Every general mandatory norm of the form 'Every x ought to ϕ in C' can be formulated in a universal sentence: 'Everyone is required to ϕ in C except one who is not an x'. It can also be formulated by a pair of sentences: 'All are required to ϕ in C', 'Everyone who is not an x is permitted not to ϕ in C'. How is one to decide whether a permission is a strong one or not? Bentham correctly observed that all the laws of a country can be represented as one prohibition against performing any action, with a long string of exceptions, limitations, etc. Does the fact that a permission is a strong one depend on the actual way in which the authoritative text of the law is formulated? But what of customary laws for which there is no authoritative formulation? Why assign such importance to the stylistic inclination of the legislator anyway? Does anything turn on whether an obligation is imposed on people over thirty or on all with an exemption for those under thirty? Are we to say that if the law is formulated in the first way then those under thirty have a weak permission to refrain from the action required of their elders, whereas if it is formulated in the second way they have a strong permission?

It seems to me that the distinction between strong and weak permissions as it is commonly drawn makes little sense. It is rather foolhardy to speculate about people's philosophical motivations. It seems reasonable to surmise, however, that at least some of the philosophers interested in the distinction have been motivated by the feeling that permissions based on permissive norms are a different type of permission from 'weak' permissions, and in particular that they have a greater normative force. (This is very clear in the case of von Wright in *Norm and Action*, pp. 85–9.) But these philosophers have failed to identify the way in which a strong permission differs from a weak one in its normative force. In the final analysis strong and weak permissions are permissions in precisely the same sense differing only in their source. Attempts to find the difference in the law on gaps or in the powers of subordinate authorities are bound to fail since they turn on the contingent existence of various norms which distinguish between various permissions. But these are additional norms, the conditions of whose application depend on the existence of permissions of one kind or another. They do not affect the normative character of the permissions themselves.

It is partly because no substantive distinction between strong and weak permissions has been established, that it is difficult to know which law establishes a strong permission and which does not. Since there is no difference in the normative force of the permissions one is forced, in order to draw the distinction, to rely on linguistic and formalistic criteria lacking any rationale. Once one establishes the different sense of different types of permission the question of whether a norm establishes the one or the other becomes an ordinary problem of interpretation; that is, whether there are reasons to regard the law as intending to achieve the result secured by a weak permission or by a strong permission. Often it will be hard to decide. But at least one would know what the problem is, and why it matters.

Exclusionary permissions

I shall suggest a sense in which one can regard some permissions as based on permission-granting norms, and which is different from the sense of all the weak permissions mentioned above. This sense of permission is very different from the one commonly assigned to strong permissions, but it may be that it explains one of the fundamental intuitions behind much of the writings on strong permissions, namely, that there are permissive norms (i.e. permission-granting norms) and that permissions based on such norms differ in their normative force from other permissions.

Permissions play a special role in practical reasoning. Reasons for action impose practical constraints, constitute requirements to act in a certain way and not in others. Permissions indicate the absence of constraints. To state that one is permitted to act in a certain way is to say that one will not be acting contrary to reason in doing so. There are various grounds on which a permission may be based. A person may be permitted to ϕ because the reasons for not ϕ-ing do not outweigh the reasons for ϕ-ing (and this includes the case in which there are no reasons for not ϕ-ing). But a person may be permitted to ϕ, despite the existence of a strong reason for not ϕ-ing, if there are reasons to exclude the reasons for not ϕ-ing, or at least to exclude some of them so that those not excluded do not outweigh the reasons for ϕ-ing. A permission based on exclusionary reasons can be regarded as a strong permission because it is based on reasons and not merely on their absence. It requires, therefore, a positive justification. It is not justified simply by the absence of reasons to the contrary.

Permissions based on exclusionary reasons do not, however, play an important role in practical discourse. Exclusionary reasons are almost invariably tied to first-order reasons and their combined application normally leads to a certain action being required. Since it is required it is also permitted, but that it is permitted is less interesting compared with the fact that it is an action one ought to perform. Here we should again remember the prevalence of pragmatic conventions. It would be correct but highly misleading to state, in normal circumstances, that an act which in fact one ought to perform is permitted. This conversationally implies that it is merely permitted, and not required. Whether it is required is relevant to almost all purposes for which it is relevant to know whether it is permitted. To be told that an act is required is more informative than to be told that it is permitted since, if correct, it solves the practical problem. Hence one is expected to state that an act is required, rather than merely permitted, if one believes this to be the case. For this reason, and since normally an act which is permitted on the basis of an exclusionary reason is also one which one ought to perform, the notion of a permission based on an exclusionary reason is not an important one.

There is yet a third way of justifying permissions. I am permitted to perform an act despite the fact that there are conclusive reasons for not performing it if I *may* disregard those reasons. A permission of this kind differs from a weak permission which is based on the absence of conclusive reasons for not performing the act. It also differs from a permission based on an exclusionary reason in that I do not have a reason requiring that I shall disregard conflicting reasons. I merely *may* do so. I shall call such permissions exclusionary permissions. Exclusionary permissions differ from exclusionary reasons in that they do not entail that one ought to disregard the excluded reasons. They merely entitle one to do so. I act against reason if I do not disregard reasons excluded by an exclusionary reason, whereas I am not acting against reason when I act on reasons which I am merely permitted to disregard.

Exclusionary permissions are strong permissions. They are not merely the result of the absence of reasons to the contrary. Since they allow disregarding conclusive reasons for refraining from an action, they cannot be taken for granted. They always require a justification. They are, however, permissions. They do not impose constraints on action, they do not in themselves determine what one ought to do. Being permitted to perform an action means being free from constraints. In the case of exclusionary permissions, however, this is not a result of the absence of reasons to the contrary; it is the result of considerations which establish that one may disregard conflicting reasons. At the same time, since exclusionary permissions counteract reasons, they are relevant to practical reasoning in a way in which weak permissions are not. Weak permissions contribute nothing to practical reasoning. They may be the conclusion of a practical inference, but they never affect its outcome. Exclusionary permissions, because they counteract the power of reasons, do affect the outcome of practical inferences. Despite the fact that they do not directly guide behaviour and are not reasons for actions, they have a normative force which is manifested in their contribution to practical inferences.

We have seen that weak permissions can be relativized to certain kinds of considerations. That one is permitted to perform an action may mean, not that there is no conclusive reason against it, but that there is no conclusive moral or legal reason against it or that there is no duty to refrain from it. Exclusionary permissions can be similarly relativized. One can say that a person has an exclusionary permission to perform an action, meaning by this, not that he is entitled to disregard all reasons against it, but only certain kinds of considerations. Exclusionary permissions, like exclusionary reasons, can be restricted in their scope.

Exclusionary permissions and supererogation

The analysis of exclusionary permissions given above does nothing to show that they have an important role in ordinary practical reasoning. This I shall now try to do, using as an example the problem of understanding the nature of supererogation.[2]

One important characteristic of supererogatory acts (though not only of them) is that their performance is praiseworthy while their omission is not blameworthy. This creates a problem. If to do a supererogatory act is praiseworthy there must be reasons for doing it, and the reasons must outweigh any conflicting reasons for not doing it. But if there are conclusive reasons for performing the act then not to perform it is to act against the balance of reasons. If reason requires that the act be done then surely one ought to do it, and the 'ought', being based on all the reasons which apply to the case, is a conclusive ought. But this entails that failing to perform the act is failing to do what one ought (conclusively) to do, so why is it not blameworthy not to perform a supererogatory act? One way out of the problem is to concede that it is blameworthy not to perform such acts and to maintain that there are no supererogatory acts. This answer may be correct, but even if correct it fails to solve the problem. Even if those who believe that there are supererogatory acts are mistaken, they are not incoherent. Those who criticize their views are exposing a moral mistake, not a logical inconsistency. How, therefore, is supererogation to be explained?

Consider the following case. Michael has reason to use all his earnings for the benefit of his family. He also has reason to donate half of it to Oxfam. Assume that he does not donate the money. Some will say that he acts wrongly, for the money would produce much better results if donated to Oxfam. Others will maintain that he did nothing wrong in not donating the money. The latter may be mistaken, but it would be odd to maintain that they have committed either a factual mistake or a contradiction. Is their position coherent? Assume that they accept that donating the money to Oxfam will do more good than spending it on one's family. They maintain that the donation would have been a praiseworthy act of supererogation and yet that Michael did nothing wrong. They are precluded from saying that the extra benefits to Michael's family are more weighty reasons than the more pressing needs of other people, for this would mean that had Michael donated the money he would have acted on the lesser reason. Yet they are equally precluded from saying that the reasons for the donation are more weighty, for they maintain that Michael did not act against reason.

It might be thought that there is an easy way to solve this problem. A supererogatory act, it is often said, is one which one ought to do but which people are not expected to perform. It is because their performance is rare that one is praised for doing it. It is because their omission is frequent that it is not criticized. It may be a correct observation that we do tend to praise people for doing the right thing when it is known that most people fail to do it. It may also be true that we tend not to criticize people for common failings. In many cases there are indeed good reasons for not doing so. But this does not turn any act required by strong reasons into a supererogatory act. A person who drives carefully in a country of careless drivers is not performing supererogatory acts every time he drives his car. There is often no point in criticizing careless drivers in such a country, but their behaviour is, nevertheless, blameworthy and wrong.

To have any plausibility the proposed solution to our problem must be reinterpreted. A supererogatory act must be construed as an act which ought to be done but which people are not in a normative sense expected to do. It is not just that we know that in fact the act is rarely performed, but that there are normative considerations explaining why performance need not be expected in many cases. I have no quarrel with this very vague formulation. It is, however, commonly taken to mean that people are normally excused for not doing what they ought to have done if it is a supererogatory act. Supererogatory acts, it is often said, call for rare qualities: great courage or self-sacrifice, or great presence of mind, or some other rare skill or character trait. Therefore, though these are acts which ought to be done, one can be excused for not doing them. One is not to be blamed for lack of a measure of greatness in some aspect of one's character.

There are two defects to this explanation. In the first place it does not apply to all the acts which are commonly regarded as supererogatory. Many such acts do not call on any exceptional qualities. Consider, for example, the case of Michael above. Donating the money to Oxfam will not, let us assume, deprive his family of the necessities of decent life. They will have to forgo only some of the luxuries of life. To go to the theatre or to concerts once every two months instead of once a month, to have an ordinary family saloon instead of a Rolls-Royce, to serve expensive French wines less frequently. Many of Michael's friends are doing just this because they do not have the money to spend on the extra luxuries of which Michael will be deprived if he gives the money to Oxfam. There is nothing unusual about this form of deprivation. Giving money to Oxfam does not require great courage or self-sacrifice or any other exceptional qualities. Yet some still maintain that it is a supererogatory act, even though they concede that it does not call for exceptional personal qualities.

The objection cannot be met by saying that if the case is indeed as described then those who maintain that Michael's act of giving the money is supererogatory are simply wrong. They may be, but we still want to understand what it is that they are saying and to avoid accusing them of inconsistency. Nor can the objection be met by saying that the excuse in Michael's case is weakness of will. We may assume that Michael himself regards donating the money as something which though praiseworthy is not strictly required of him.* Finally it cannot be claimed that Michael's excuse is his ignorance of what is morally required of him. Our problem is to understand how the action is conceived as supererogatory according to the moral theory of Michael himself and of those others who agree with him and think that he has committed no mistake in his practical reasoning.

There is a second objection to the explanation we are considering. This explanation implies that determining which act is supererogatory belongs to the theory of excuses and not to the normative theory.

---

* Even if Michael regards himself as failing in his duty, it would be difficult to find a satisfactory theory of excuses which would justify regarding weakness of will of such a nature as an excuse.

Failing to perform an act of supererogation is, according to this explanation, wrong but excusable. This is not, however, the way we normally think of supererogation. Failing to perform a supererogatory act is not a matter of doing something wrong. One is normally thought to be permitted to refrain from supererogation. Hence there is no room for an excuse for not doing such actions.

But if the non-performance of a supererogatory act is not a wrong excused but a permissible course of action, we are back with our original problem: how can one be permitted to refrain from action which is required by reason? The solution is to be found in the notion of an exclusionary permission. The permission to refrain from performing an act supererogation is an exclusionary permission, a permission not to act on certain reasons. An act is a supererogatory act only if it is an act which one ought to do on the balance of reasons and yet one is permitted not to act on the balance of reasons.[3] To say this is not to explain which acts, if any, are supererogatory. But it does help to clarify what it is to say that an act is supererogatory and what has to be proved if the supererogatory character of an action is to be established.

Since exclusionary permissions are required to explain the nature of supererogation there can be no doubt of their importance to practical reasoning. The use of exclusionary permissions in the analysis of supererogation also helps to bring out their role in practical reasoning. They are second-order permissions in the sense in which exclusionary reasons are second-order reasons. They are permissions not to act on reasons, whereas exclusionary reasons are reasons for not acting on reasons. Just as we require the concept of an exclusionary reason to explain some cases in which we are faced with two practical assessments belonging to different levels of argument, so we require the concept of an exclusionary permission in order to explain other cases of practical reasoning on two different levels.

Philosophers have tended too often to avoid facing the complexities of practical reasoning with its multi-level assessments. They have either overlooked these complexities, or denounced them as irrational and inconsistent, or just given up the attempt to explain them by saying that different considerations belong to different points of views, to reasoning starting from incomparable and irreconcilable bases. There may be some truth in that. I have certainly said nothing which completely refutes such views. But it has been a large part of my aim to show that this pessimism is premature. Many of the pessimistic conclusions are based on a confusion between the epistemological difficulties in establishing the validity of ultimate values and the logical difficulties in explaining the considerations often found in practical reasoning. None of the arguments in this book bears on epistemological difficulties of the philosophy of practical reason. But some of them may help to disentangle these difficulties from the logical problems and to show that the latter are amenable to rational analysis.

Permissive norms

Little needs to be said about permissive norms. It is evident that the very same considerations which make it possible to talk of mandatory norms, and on which the need for this mode of expression is based, apply to permissive norms as the basis of many exclusionary permissions. The fact that we often have occasion to refer to the content of an exclusionary permission abstracted from the circumstances which establish the permission, creates a need to refer to permissive norms as abstract entities. The fact that exclusionary permissions are relatively independent of the considerations establishing them both partially explains this need and makes it possible to talk of a permission being based on a norm or 'granted' by a norm. The relative independence of exclusionary permissions means the same as the relative independence of exclusionary reasons, namely that, because their normative force for most purposes does not depend on their strength, they can be relied upon and used in practical reasoning even by those not familiar with the considerations on which they are based. Because of this we often have occasion to refer to the fact that we have an exclusionary permission, without reference to the considerations which justify or give rise to it. Because of this relative independence we can hypostatize a norm which is regarded as directly granting the permission. The considerations justifying the permission or creating it are regarded as justifying or creating the norm.

Not every exclusionary permission is based on a permissive norm. It is only when the ontological considerations mentioned above obtain that one can talk of an exclusionary permission as based on a norm. In all this the considerations are the exact analogue of those which apply to exclusionary reasons and mandatory norms. In both cases we are interposing a norm between the facts requiring or permitting the action and the action itself.

Permissive norms have the same structure as mandatory norms. A statement of a permissive norm states that certain norm subjects have an exclusionary permission to perform the norm act when the conditions of application obtain. They differ from mandatory norms only in the deontic operator: the exclusionary permission operator replaces that of the exclusionary 'ought' coupled with a first-order 'ought' which figure in statements of mandatory norms.

Permissive norms also have the same three dimensions of mandatory norms. They are valid if it is right that their norm subjects should rely on them, if they are entitled to disregard certain reasons. They are practised if people believe in them or rely on them. We have seen that to establish whether a mandatory norm is followed we have to pay equal attention to people's behaviour and to their own conception and explanation of it. People's conception and explanation of their behaviour is even more important in establishing that a permissive norm is followed. Since the norm permits action and does not entail any restrictions on one's choice the norm act may either be performed or not in conformity with the norm. If the norm subjects generally refrain from performing the norm act when the conditions of application obtain this may be an indication that they think that they are not permitted to perform the act, but this need not be the case. Everything depends on people's attitudes to their own and to other people's behaviour.

Permissions have also a third dimension. Just as mandatory norms can be prescribed so permissions can be given or granted. Giving a permission differs from stating that an act is permitted. Giving a permission turns an act which is not permitted into one which is permitted.[4] Stating that an act is permitted is true only if the act is permitted; the assertion does not in itself make it so. Both weak and exclusionary permissions can be granted. One grants a weak permission if one can and does change the reasons against an action so that its omission is no longer required. If a person owes money to another and his creditor waives his right to the debt he thereby gives his debtor a weak permission not to pay the debt. An exclusionary permission is granted if a person can and does act in a way which does not change the reasons for refraining from an act but entitles a person to disregard them. The simplest case of giving an exclusionary permission is a case of a man who consents that another shall perform an act harmful to his interests. The permission does not alter the reasons against the action. It will still harm the person's interests. The intention and import of the permission is to allow the man who contemplates the action to disregard the interests of the person who granted the permission. The permission, it should be noted, is no reason for disregarding the interests of the person who gave it. It merely allows one to disregard them. We are all familiar with cases in which such permissions are given in the hope that the person who receives them will not disregard the interests he was given permission to disregard. This fact demonstrates that the reasons for refraining from the action are not removed by the permission. All it does is to allow one to disregard them. I am assuming that the person who gives the permission has power to give it (cf. section 3.2). If he lacks the power he cannot give the permission. Many moral theories deny that a person has complete power to allow harm to himself. They maintain that there are some ways of harming a person which are wrong even if he purports to permit them.

Not every act resulting in another's becoming permitted (in either sense of the term) is the granting of a permission. A permission is granted only by an act intended to have this result through being recognized as being so intended.

We have discussed the possibility of permissive norms granting exclusionary permissions. Can there be norms granting weak permissions? A negative answer is implied by all our deliberations.[5] A weak permission' has no normative force. It is a negative notion indicating the absence of reasons to the contrary. It is therefore based on the absence of norms to the contrary, not on any norms granting it. It requires no separate justification, fulfils no independent role in practical reasoning and therefore there is no use for talk of norms establishing such permissions. Moreover, to postulate such norms would be positively confusing and misleading. There are no criteria of identity for such norms, and besides, to talk of a norm granting a weak permission is to obscure the difference between weak and exclusionary permissions. It creates the impression that weak permissions too contribute to the practical reasonings which guide human behaviour, whereas in fact they do not.

3.2 POWER-CONFERRING NORMS

Lawyers and legal philosophers have long been discussing the nature and importance of legal powers. Powers to make contracts and wills, to sell property and to vote in elections, to make laws and to repeal them, are all standard cases of legal powers. Some of the institutions in the regulation of which powers are involved are unique to the law. Others are analogous to non-legal institutions governed by rules of games or of voluntary associations, etc., perhaps even by moral rules. It seems reasonable, therefore, to regard legal powers as just one type of normative powers in general. Philosophers have been surprisingly slow in recognizing the importance of normative powers. The purpose of this section is to examine the way in which normative powers can be distinguished from other types of powers, and to explain the nature of power-conferring norms.

Normative powers

Normative power is a distinct type of power.[6] It differs both from power as the ability to perform an action (ability to speak French, to drive, etc.) and from power as influence, that is, the ability to affect people's fortunes and behaviour. Power in all its forms is related to the idea of the possibility of realizing one's wishes. But none of the forms of power can be defined by equating statements that 'a person has a power to . . .' with statements that 'it is possible that he will realize . . .' Each form of power requires a much more complex analysis.

It has been suggested that normative power can be defined as the ability to perform a normative act, and legal power (which is a species of normative power) as ability to perform a legal act (for example, ability to make a contract, a will or a promise). If normative or legal acts are defined as acts the performance of which is an exercise of a normative or a legal power then the definition is correct but rather uninformative. It is useful only in making it clear that the explanation of normative power is to be given by explaining what it is to exercise a power. We shall follow this method in the explanation of normative power given below. Often, however, the definition is regarded as a complete analysis of normative powers and normative acts are defined as acts which can be explained only by reference to norms, or rules. This view of powers is often connected with the view that power-conferring rules are constitutive rules. Constitutive rules will be discussed in the next chapter. But it is clear that on this interpretation of normative act the proposed definition of power is wrong. Paying income tax is on this view a normative act: it cannot be explained except by reference to the income tax law. Yet it is generally agreed that paying income tax is not the exercise of a power. If it were then by the same reasoning every act which is described as required by reasons or norms would be an exercise of a power.

Legal power is often explained as ability to bring about a legal change. A legal change is commonly interpreted as a change in the rights or duties of the power holder or of others. Generalizing, one may say that normative power is the power to effect a normative change. A normative change can be interpreted to comprise every change in the reasons for action that some person has. However, these characterizations as they stand cannot be the basis of the analysis of power. They too fail to distinguish between the exercise of a power and the performance of an act which is required by reasons. (If I had reason to take the medicine now and I did so, I have no longer reason to take it—my action has changed the reasons for action I have.) Moreover, they fail to distinguish between normative power and power as influence.[7] Influence is exercised by affecting people's reasons for action and their beliefs in them. One typical way in which influence is manifested is by manipulating the circumstances so as to make the realization of certain goals more difficult relative to others. This can be done by manipulation of money supply, by determining job or educational opportunities, etc. Such actions exercise an influence because they change the balance of reasons for or against certain actions, but they are not the exercise of normative powers.

It is worth noting that influence is exercised not only by control over the means by which people must realize their goals. Influence includes the power to affect the goals people have, their desires and aspirations. Beliefs in the desirability of pursuing certain styles of life are induced through educational institutions and the mass media. Desires for various patterns of consumption, for ways of spending one's leisure, for patterns of human relations in society, and so on, are greatly influenced by the operation of social institutions which are capable of being controlled and directed by people interested in securing or holding power or in promoting commercial interests or in affecting society for other reasons. These institutions are not always subject to such manipulation but they can be and often are so controlled. Influence, therefore, need not be power over auxiliary reasons only. It includes power over operative reasons. Normative power, also, includes both power over operative and over auxiliary reasons. Power to enact a mandatory norm is power to create a new operative reason. Power to sell property affects only auxiliary reasons. It applies an existing law to new people in a new way. The fact that a person has title in a property is not itself a complete reason for the performance of any action but in combination with the laws of property it is.

It might be thought that the distinctive mark of normative powers is that they are exercised not by manipulating 'objective' facts but by the performance of a speech act. The speech act itself is a reason for action or is taken as such. This suggestion points in the right direction but it cannot stand as it is. In the first place the exercise of a normative power may involve more than a speech act. In various legal systems, for example, sale required the weighing of metal on scales and its transfer from the buyer to the seller, or walking along the borders of the land bought or other acts. More important is the fact that influence is often exercised by the performance of speech acts. A person's influence may be manifested by the fact that all his requests are complied with. Consider, for example, an attractive young lady with a retinue of suitors or a charismatic leader who persuades his followers by fiery speeches.

This last point draws attention to the fact that one may have normative power to command or to order but not a (normative) power to request. A normative power to give an order is not the same as the ability to give it. One can give an order even if one lacks the normative power to do so: such an order is given with the intention that it be taken as both a first-order and an exclusionary reason and knowledge of this is important for the addressee in order to appraise his situation correctly. But if the person giving the order does not have the normative power to do so then the order is not binding. The gangster is as able as the parent to give an order but only the latter has the normative power to do so.

Having power to command is much the same as having the authority to do so. A command is valid only if the commander had authority, that is a normative power, to issue it. It is binding only if valid. The main practical significance of normative powers to issue orders is that they are necessary in order to settle whether orders are binding. The analysis offered above of the dimensions of norms can be applied to the case of orders: an order is binding if its addressee has reason to be guided by it, that is, to regard it both as a first-order reason to do as ordered and as an exclusionary reason to disregard some or all of the conflicting considerations.

Just as we distinguish between orders which are valid reasons and those which are not and which one may completely disregard, so we distinguish between requests which are valid reasons and those of which one need take no notice and which one may completely disregard.* But requests cannot be said to be binding. To say 'I am asking you to do A and this is binding' is to say that I am not making a request but giving an order. This seems to me to point to the explanation of why we can refer to a (normative) power to command but not to a (normative) power to request. The explanation of this difference between orders and requests cannot be that orders are either conclusive or very strong reasons whereas requests are not. This is simply not true. A request may be a conclusive or a very strong reason and an order may be a very weak reason. Nor are binding orders binding in the sense of being irrevocable. Barring special circumstances, an order, like a request, can be withdrawn. It seems to me that an order can be binding because if valid it requires that its addressee shall act on it disregarding other considerations. In other words it is binding because, unlike a request, it is also an exclusionary reason. It is binding by being exclusionary.

A normative power is an ability to affect exclusionary reasons which apply to one's own or to other people's action. This explains why the notion of a normative power does not apply to actions affecting only first-order reasons. One can ask whether a person was entitled to make a request, or whether the addressee of the request should regard it as a reason or as a conclusive reason. The same questions apply to the giving of orders. But with respect to orders and other acts intended to affect exclusionary reasons there is the further question of whether the person performing the act has power to make it, namely, whether the persons whose reasons he intends to affect are required to regard his action as affecting an exclusionary reason which applies to them.

Can we generalize from the case of a power to give orders and conclude that normative power generally is an ability to affect exclusionary reasons? It seems to me that we can, especially since the analysis of legal powers supports the same conclusion (see section 4.3 on the exclusionary force of the law). A normative power is tantamount to having an authority when it is a power over others. Thus we can equate power to command and instruct, which is exclusively power over other people, and power to make rules and regulations, which includes power over other people, with authority. Authority is one of the two main forms of normative power outside the law, the other being the power of undertaking commitments, namely, volun-

---

* It should be remembered that a request may be a valid reason even if it is not a conclusive reason. It may be overridden by stronger conflicting reasons.

tary obligations.* To complete my analysis of normative powers I will have to show that binding promises and voluntary obligations generally are exclusionary reasons. The examination of voluntary obligations will, however, take us too far afield and cannot be undertaken here.

We have considered so far only powers to affect exclusionary reasons. Similar reasoning would show that there are also powers to grant or revoke exclusionary permissions. The concept of normative power is particularly important for the analysis of norms, whether mandatory or permissive. We do not have much occasion nor great need to refer to normative powers which apply to exclusionary reasons which are not norms. Henceforth, I shall discuss only normative powers applying to norms.

A normative power is not just any power to affect a norm or its application. We have already noted that by this characterization every act in compliance with or in violation of a norm would be an exercise of a power. Nor can we overcome the problem by simply excluding all the acts which affect the application of norms just by complying with or contravening them. This would not explain the reason for the difference and it would not deal with other cases. By changing one's place of permanent residence from one town to another one changes the application of various tax laws and one's entitlement to various social services. Indeed one may choose to move to another town or country in order to be liable to lighter tax or entitled to more services. One's position changes in such cases in a way very similar to the changes produced by the sale of a car or a house or by joining the army. Yet the change of residence is not an exercise of power, whereas sale and joining the army are. The distinction does not depend on the normative change produced. It depends entirely on the justification for regarding such acts as effecting these normative changes.

An act is the exercise of a power only if the reason for recognizing it as affecting norms and their application is that it is desirable to enable people to affect norms and their application in such a way if they desire to do so for this purpose. Since the application of some norms depends on residence one can affect it by changing residence.

---

* In the law there are many different types of powers in addition to the power to legislate and make contracts. There are powers to sell, to appoint an agent, to get married, to establish a new corporation, etc. Many of these have analogues outside the law, especially in the context of voluntary associations. These are regulative powers and they will be explained below.

But the justification for making residence a condition for the application of the norms concerned was not to enable people to change their rights and duties by changing residence. Sale, on the other hand, is recognized as affecting the application of property laws precisely because it is, or is thought to be, desirable to enable people to change their rights and duties by sale if they so desire. An act is the exercise of a normative power if, and only if, it is recognized as effecting a normative change because, among other possible justifications, it is an act of a type such that it is reasonable to expect that, if recognized as effecting a normative change, acts of this type will be generally performed only if the persons concerned want to secure this normative change. A person has a normative power if and only if the performance of an act of his is an exercise of such a power.

A few comments on this definition would be in place here. A normative change is the creation or repeal of a norm (giving orders, legislating, etc.) or a change in the application of a norm (sale, marriage, joining the army, etc.). Thus we reject the wider definition of a normative change discussed on page 99 above. Powers to create or repeal norms are norm-creating powers. Powers to change the application of norms are regulative powers.

The exercise of normative power affects the existence or application of a norm normatively and not causally. I have a normative power to make my own will but only an influence over my wife with regard to her will. This distinction turns on the distinction between the result of an act and its consequences. 'The result of an act,' explains Dr Kenny, 'is the end state of the change by which the act is defined. When the world changes in a certain way there may follow certain other changes. . . . In that case we may say that the second transformation is a consequence of the first and of the act which brought the first about. The relation between an act and its result is an intrinsic relation, and that between an act and its consequences is a causal relation.'* An act affects a norm causally if its consequences effect a normative change. It affects a norm normatively if the act or its result affects the existence or application of the norm.†

* A. Kenny, 'Intention and Purpose in Law', in R. S. Summers (Ed.), *Essays in Legal Philosophy* (1968), p. 150. See also von Wright, *Norm and Action*, pp. 39–42, where this notion was first introduced.

† The act of successfully inducing a person to make a will produces a normative change in the right way, i.e. normatively and not causally, but it fails to qualify as an exercise of power under the test set above.

Normally only acts done with the intention of producing relevant normative change are recognized as producing it. But this is not always the case, and there are many exceptions particularly in the law or other institutionalized normative systems. One may make a binding contract without realizing that one did, for example. For this reason the definition turns, not on the intentions with which the act is performed, but rather on the reasons for regarding it as effecting a normative change.

Power-conferring norms

Normative powers, being powers to affect norms, are intimately connected to norms. But need we recognize a special type of norm which is a power-conferring norm?[8] If there are such norms they stipulate that the performance of the norm act by the norm subject has certain normative consequences. The norm need not, often it cannot, specify the precise nature of the consequences. The norm conferring the power to sell will specify only that certain people have the power, by certain actions, to effect a sale. The precise consequences of a sale will be spelt out in many other norms.

The reasons for recognizing power-conferring norms as a distinct type of norm differ with the type of power involved. The existence of a regulative power presupposes the existence of the norm(s) whose application it regulates. The only question is whether we can regard the power as conferred by the norm it affects or by a separate norm conferring this power. Are we to say that there is one norm forbidding all to handle the property without the consent of the owner, while other laws, some of them power-conferring, stipulate how ownership is acquired? Or are we to read all the ways of acquiring ownership into each law stipulating the consequences of ownership, such as that people are not allowed to handle the property without the owner's consent? There are several reasons for regarding regulative powers as conferred by norms other than the norms affected by the power, but only one need be mentioned here. The general purpose served by discourse about norms is to facilitate reference to considerations guiding human behaviour. We have seen that acts are the exercise of powers regulating the application of other norms because it is, or is thought to be, desirable that people will be motivated to engage in these actions if they wish to affect the regulated norm in the relevant way and refrain from them if they wish not to achieve these normative consequences. This means that the acts which are the exercise of a power are guided by a norm, be it the norm affected by the power or the one conferring it, if it is conferred by a separate norm. But the norm affected by the power guides another action as well. It guides the action required or permitted by it. Now, since it is the purpose of discourse concerning norms to clarify the way actions are guided by normative considerations, this purpose will be served best if every norm is conceived as guiding one act. This is the fundamental reason for recognizing a distinct type of norm, power-conferring norms, guiding those acts which are the exercise of power.

Norm-creating powers present different problems. The norms which can be created by their use do not yet exist and in many cases the norms which can be repealed by their use do not yet exist. Such powers cannot, therefore, be regarded as conferred by the norms whose creation or repeal they authorize. Regulative powers, since they regulate existing norms, are clearly conferred by norms. The only question is whether they are conferred by the norms they regulate or by a separate norm. The question with respect to norm-creating powers is whether they are conferred by a norm at all. The answer is dictated by the same considerations which determine whether there is a case for speaking of a mandatory norm. That is, if there are reasons capable of guiding the actions of the power-holder and to which we have occasion to refer without at the same time referring to the circumstances which justify those reasons, then we can and do regard the power as conferred by a norm. This is often the case when a power is invested in a person for a long period of time, or when it exists within an institutionalized normative system. Hence, we can and do refer to norms conferring norm-creating powers on parents with regard to their children and on committees, directors or other legislative bodies functioning in voluntary association or within the law.

These arguments do not purport to establish that all powers are conferred by norms. They indicate the type of considerations which determine which powers are so conferred. Powers to create mandatory norms can be regarded as conferred by mandatory norms of a special kind which I shall call obedience norms. These are norms requiring that their norm subjects obey the power-holder if and when he exercises his power. For example, 'children should obey their parents' could be regarded as the norm conferring authority on the parents. But if we have an option with regard to the logical form of norms conferring power to issue mandatory norms, we have no such option where the power includes power to issue permissive norms or power-conferring norms. In these cases the norm can only be represented as having the form specified above: the norm subject has power, by performing the norm act when the conditions of application apply, to effect a certain normative change. Since there are power-conferring norms, there are also powers to create, repeal and regulate the application of these norms, and norms conferring such powers.

In presenting the above arguments no distinction was drawn between powers affecting practised or prescribed norms from those affecting valid norms. The arguments apply to all these norms. If the norm affected is a practised norm then the reasons we look for in considering why an act is recognized as affecting it are reasons recognized and accepted by the persons or institutions practising it, and if the act affecting the norm is the exercise of a power and the power is conferred by a norm then this power-conferring norm is itself a practised norm. If, on the other hand, the norm affected is a valid one then the relevant reasons for which an act is recognized as affecting the norm are valid reasons and the power-conferring norm, if the power is conferred by one, is a valid norm.

Power-conferring norms resemble permissive norms and differ from mandatory norms in having a normative force without being themselves complete reasons for action. Their normative force is manifested by the fact that statements of such norms are premises of practical inferences which affect the conclusion of the inference. In considering whether to perform an action the fact that it has certain normative consequences is a relevant consideration. It is not itself a reason either to perform the act or to refrain from it. What one ought to do depends on whether one desires or has other reasons for or against bringing about the relevant normative change. But, like permissive norms, power-conferring norms are normative and can be said to guide behaviour because of their contribution to practical inferences, to the solution of practical problems.[9]

4 Normative systems

We often have occasion to refer to groups of rules. We talk of the rules of cricket or tennis or chess, of the rules of the university dramatic or debating society, of the regulations and rules of British Rail or Barclays Bank, of the rules of etiquette or the code of chivalry, or of the rules of morality, of the morality of the British working class during the nineteenth century. We refer to the highway code or to English land law, to the laws of Britain, France or Germany, and so on. It is evident that we group rules together by different criteria and for a variety of purposes. From the point of view of normative theory groups of rules are of interest only if the fact that the rules form a group is normatively relevant, if it has normative consequences.

Therefore we will not be concerned with groups of rules the common factor of which is, for example, that they apply to one group of norm subjects, or regulate one type of activity (for example, the highway code), or that they are followed by one group of people (for example, middle-class morality). Grouping rules in some such ways is important for many purposes, for example, for understanding a certain society or for knowing what to do when engaging in a certain activity. Such sets of rules are not, however, particularly significant from the point of view of normative theory. The fact that several rules apply to the same persons or that they are followed by the same people is not in itself indicative of any normative relations among the rules. They may be completely independent of each other in their force, and the existence of any one of them may have no impact on the operation of the others. In the present chapter we shall examine four types of normative systems which are of normative significance: systems of interlocking norms, systems of joint validity, autonomous systems and institutionalized systems. We shall later consider the special features of legal systems, which are the most important type of institutionalized systems in the modern world.

Constitutive rules

Several philosophers have suggested that there are two types of rules: constitutive and regulative. The difference is, we are told, a difference between rules of different logical types. Regulative rules stipulate that people ought to behave in a certain way. Constitutive rules are not normally formulated in this way. They resemble definitions. Their standard form is: 'Doing X counts as Y in context C'. Furthermore, regulative rules regulate, that is require or forbid, natural acts. Constitutive rules create new forms of behaviour, normative actions, which they regulate. Promising, legislating, getting married, playing cricket or chess and speaking a certain language are often given as examples of normative acts based on constitutive rules. Since Searle's treatment of the subject is best known I shall use it in order to show the various confusions on which the discussion of this topic is often based.[1]

The first mark of constitutive rules is, according to Searle, that they create new forms of behaviour. Not so regulative rules, which merely 'regulate antecedently or independently existing forms of behaviour'. The distinction is more subtle than might be thought. 'There is a trivial sense in which the creation of any rule creates the possibility of new forms of behaviour, namely, behaviour done as in accordance with the rule. That is not the sense in which my remark is intended. What I mean can perhaps be best put in the formal mode. Where the rule is purely regulative, behaviour which is in accordance with the rule *could* be given the same description or specification (the same answer to the question "What did he do?") whether or not the rule existed, provided the description or specification makes no explicit reference to the rule. But where the rule (or system of rules) is constitutive, behaviour which is in accordance with the rule *can* receive specifications or descriptions which it could not receive if the rule or rules did not exist.' (J. R. Searle, *Speech Acts*, 1969, p. 35 [italics added].)

In commenting on this passage I will disregard the (unjustified) assumption that all rules are 'created'. Let us compare the following two pairs of act descriptions:

1(a) 'Giving £50 to Mr Jones' (b) 'Paying income tax'
2(a) 'Saying "I promise" ' (b) 'Promising'

On a straightforward reading of Searle the availability of the two pairs of act descriptions demonstrates that both the law imposing income tax and the rule about promising are each of them both a regulative and a constitutive rule.* There is nothing in Searle's explanation to suggest that his classification is exclusive, that the same rule cannot be both regulative and constitutive. Searle assumes that the same act can be given different descriptions and that a rule is regulative if a description of a certain kind is available for acts in accordance with it, and that a rule is constitutive if a different description, which is of a kind logically independent of the first, is available to describe the same act. But it follows from his account that *all* rules are both regulative and constitutive.

Consider the two pairs of act descriptions given above. We assume that one can pay one's income tax by giving Mr Jones, who happens to be HM Inspector of Taxes, £50, and that one can promise (let us say, to pay £50 to Mr Jones) by saying 'I promise' (in reply to Mr Jones's request to promise to pay him £50). No doubt there are other ways of paying one's income tax, and other ways of promising, but this is irrelevant to our purpose. On our assumptions descriptions 1(a) and 2(a) specify acts which are in accordance with the rules in a way which could be given regardless of whether or not there is such a rule. Therefore, the rules are regulative. Descriptions 1(b) and 2(b) describe actions in accordance with the rules in a way which could not be given if there were no such rules. Therefore, the rules are constitutive, as well. Since for every rule one can formulate a similar pair of act descriptions, all rules are both constitutive and regulative.

One cannot refute this argument by replying that saying 'I promise' is not promising unless said with an intention of incurring an obligation thereby, and that the act description 'saying "I promise", with the intention of creating a voluntary obligation' presupposes the existence of the rule about promising. This refutation fails for two reasons. In the first place the revised act description does not presuppose the existence of the rule about promising, it merely presupposes the agent's belief that there is such a rule. Hence even the revised act description establishes that the rule of promising is a regulative rule. In the second place, and for precisely the same reasons, giving Mr Jones £50 is not a payment of one's income tax unless done with an intention of paying one's income tax. Otherwise

---

* I am overlooking the vagueness of 'behaviour in accordance with the rule'. Since it seems that constitutive rules, on Searle's account, do not require that an action be performed and cannot be infringed or violated, it is not clear in what sense one can talk of action in accordance with them.

it may be the fulfilment of the promise to pay Mr Jones personally £50.*

Searle's opening remark in the quoted passage and his comment that twenty-two people going through the movements of playing football are not playing football unless there are football rules, indicate a certain uneasiness with his distinction but they do nothing to counter my argument. Going through the motions of paying income tax, likewise, is not paying income tax unless there is an appropriate income tax law. There is a genuine and important distinction between normative and natural actions or act descriptions. Normative act descriptions are those of which a complete explanation must include reference to a rule. But this distinction between acts or their descriptions does not lead to a corresponding distinction between types of rules. Every rule regulates action which can be described without presupposing the *existence* of that rule (though sometimes it regulates only actions done with an *intention* of invoking the rule). Similarly every rule 'creates' actions which can be described only in ways which presuppose its existence.

Searle has an additional test for identifying constitutive rules. They can be and often are cast in the form 'X counts as Y in the context C'. He concedes, however, that every rule can be formulated in this way. In fact his test turns on the following remark: '. . . the phrase which is the Y term will not in general simply be a label. It will mark something that has consequences' (op. cit., p. 36). It is difficult to know how to interpret this test. Searle hedges by saying that consequences are 'generally' attached. But there is no indication how the test is applied when no consequences are attached to the act. Nor does Searle explain the nature of the consequences. Presumably he is interested only in normative consequences, and not in the natural consequences of actions. He does, however, mention penalties as one type of consequence which would turn any regulative rule whose violation is punishable into a constitutive rule.

Part of the difficulty in understanding Searle's analysis stems from the fact that he nowhere explains the normative force of constitutive rules. The little he says indicates that in his view all regulative rules are mandatory norms. He also says that constitutive rules regulate the behaviour they constitute. But he does not explain in what way they do so. Are they also mandatory norms? Or are they permissive

* Both tax laws and conventions concerning promising may establish 'objective tests' according to which one may pay one's debt to the income tax authorities or make a promise without intending to.

or power-conferring norms? Or are there constitutive rules of all these types? The plain truth is that Searle is very vague about the ways in which any rule guides behaviour. It may be that in proposing this second test Searle is groping towards the distinction between power-conferring and mandatory norms. It is at least quite natural to cast power-conferring rules in the form 'X counts as Y', 'ϕ-ing counts as making a contract or a will, or as promising, or selling, or legislating'. These are formulations often used in describing power-conferring rules.

If Searle is indeed struggling towards the idea of a power-conferring rule then we can understand why he regards promises, legislation, conducting a trial or a marriage ceremony as acts constituted by constitutive rules. But if that was his purpose then his analysis is very defective and incomplete. It has to be supplemented or replaced by the considerations advanced in the previous chapter. Moreover, if that was his purpose then his analysis is less relevant to the explanation of rules of games and of language than he thinks. Power-conferring rules may figure among the rules of games, but games include other rules as well, and there can be games with no power-conferring rules (see below on games and their rules). Furthermore, it may be doubted whether rules of language contain any power-conferring rules, but this is a subject which cannot be explored here.

Systems of interlocking norms

My feeling is that Searle failed to establish a viable distinction between two types of rules because he did not separate various ideas clearly. One distinction which he failed to draw is that between mandatory and power-conferring rules, but this is not the only one required. For the rest of this section I shall explore two other ideas which seem to underlie Searle's thinking, that of interlocking norms and that of systems of joint validity. We shall see that their analysis is very different from what he suggests.

Searle explored in vain the idea of rules regulating forms of behaviour which are created by them. Some of his remarks are, however, better suited to rules regulating forms of behaviour created by other rules. One norm can, for example, require that a certain person use a power given him by another norm in a certain way. Or it can prohibit or permit the exercise of such powers in certain circumstances. Immigration officers, for example, are given power to issue stay permits to aliens entitling them to reside in the country for a certain period. This power is conferred on them by law. Another law may require them to refuse applications from people who do not meet certain conditions. A third law may impose on them a duty to issue permits to a different category of people. They may have discretion (i.e. a weak permission) with regard to all other cases. In such a case the norm act of the mandatory norm requiring or forbidding the exercise of the power can only be described as a normative act presupposing the existence of the power-conferring norm. In our example the norm act is to issue or to refuse stay permits, and one cannot explain the nature of these acts except by reference to the norm giving the immigration officers power to issue stay permits. In such cases the mandatory norms are internally related to the power-conferring norm; they presuppose its existence and guide the use of the powers conferred by it.

Norms may be internally related in other ways as well. Compliance with or violation of one mandatory norm may be part of the conditions of application of other norms. For example, compliance with one norm may be specified in another as a condition in which a certain official is required to reward the person who complies with the first norm. A punitive mandatory norm may impose duties on any person who violates any norm. Another norm may give the police powers over persons if they violate certain norms, and so on.

In general a norm is internally related to another if the existence of the one is part of a sufficient condition for the existence of the other or if the content of the one can be fully explained only by reference to the other. There are many different types of internal relations between norms and there is no need to survey them all. Two further examples will suffice. A norm created by the exercise of a norm-creating power is internally related to the norm conferring that power. Every norm conferring regulative powers is internally related to the norms whose application is affected by the exercise of the powers.

Many normative terms serve primarily as bridge terms creating the link between two internally related norms. Terms such as 'sale', 'gift', 'will', 'contract', 'ownership', 'mortgage', 'trust' appear in the description of a variety of norms. Some of these norms confer powers to acquire ownership, others bestow powers on owners, still others require certain behaviour of owners or grant them exclusionary permissions, other norms require certain behaviour of other people with regard to the owners, and so on.

Many normative systems, such as the law, the rules of voluntary associations or of games, contain sets of interlocking, that is, internally related, norms. Sets of such norms need not be a part of a larger normative system. They can be, for example, some of the norms practised by a group of people. The fact that they are internally related endows them with a certain unity and interdependence which other practised norms lack. For this reason they can be regarded as one type of normative system. Systems of interlocking norms can be defined as any set of norms in which the relation of 'being internally related to' is connected.* Not all normative systems are, however, systems of this type. We may take the rules of games as examples of a different type of normative system.

Games as systems of joint validity

Philosophers interested in normative theory have often used the rules of games as a basis for their analysis of rules in general. Consequently, most of them have been at pains to emphasize the similarity between the rules of games and other rules. I shall also claim that rules of games are rules in the same sense as any other rules. My main purpose in discussing games is, however, to show in what way the rules of a game form a normative system and to contrast this with a different type of normative system to be discussed in the next section. This task will require the correction of various mistakes often made in analysing games. In particular I shall argue that games cannot be defined as sets of rules or norms.

Nowadays many games are highly institutionalized. There are organizations generally acknowledged as having authority to change the rules of games. They often organize competitions which are subject to many rules relating to qualification to participate, the behaviour of the participants, prizes, etc. In discussing games I shall disregard this institutional setting. I shall also disregard the role of the referee and the rules governing it. Our concern is only with the rules of the game itself.

The point to bear in mind throughout this discussion is that to explain the nature of games one must go beyond the rules of the game to their underlying reasons. One characteristic of games is that for each game there is one point underlying all their rules. Saying this is not saying much. Many norms depend on one common consideration for their justification. Respect for persons, for example, is

---

* I am regarding the relation of being internally related as a transitive relation. R is connected in $A \leftrightarrow (x)(y)(x \Sigma A \ \& \ y \Sigma A \ \& \ x \neq y \rightarrow xRyVyRx)$.

regarded by many as underlying numerous moral norms. In many such cases this fact does not affect one's reasons for complying with the rules. If one value justifies several rules then the reasons which should make a person practise one rule should also make him practise the others. Yet in most of these cases he should follow each of the rules even if he does not follow the others. Sometimes, however, different norms depend on a common justification in a way which makes conformity with one of them entirely pointless and worthless unless one conforms with all of them. This is true of games but not only of them. Even if several rules are based on the value of respect for persons there is reason to follow each of them regardless of whether one follows the others (though one should follow them as well). There is, however, no point in following just one rule of etiquette relating to conduct at formal parties, say. This will only make one look all the more ridiculous. If a person is to follow rules of etiquette at all he should follow a good number of them (though not necessarily all). Similarly there is no point, normally, in following one rule of a game unless one follows them all. This is one reason for regarding the rules of a game as forming a normative system.

Systems of this second type are normative systems of joint validity. They consist of norms each of which is valid for a person only if he follows all the others or certain designated norms from among the others. Normative systems of joint validity are analogous to norms which are valid only if practised (see the discussion of the dimensions of norms in section 2.3). A norm may be valid for each of its norm subjects only if he does or intends to practise it regularly, or only if it is regularly practised by all its norm subjects. Analogously a norm belongs to a normative system of joint validity if each of its norms is valid for each of its norm subjects if, and only if, he practises or intends to practise all or certain of the norms of the system.

Rules of games are normative systems of joint validity, but they have further peculiar features. Their most important feature is that the rules of a game are constitutive of the reason for their own validity, namely that the reasons for following the rules cannot be explained independently of the rules themselves. To explain this point we had better start by examining in greater detail the rules of games.

The rules of games

The rules of chess provide a simple example of one type of game. They contain rules of three types. The first are power-conferring rules.

They can be formulated as follows: 'A player who is to make the first move or whose opponent has made the last move, has power, unless he makes another move, to move his rook to any square lying horizontally or vertically on a straight line from its present position, provided that no other piece lies between its present position and that square and that the square to which it moves is not occupied by one of his own pieces.' I am assuming that a separate rule will confer power to castle and yet another will spell out the consequences of moving one of the pieces to a square on which there is a piece of the other player (excepting the King), namely that that piece is not used for any further purpose in the game. Similar power-conferring rules apply to all the other pieces in the game.

The precise formulation of the rules does not matter. In the rule formulated above the reference to the player who is to make the first move, for example, can be omitted since the rook can never be used in one's first move. It may be vacuously included if it is thought desirable to preserve a uniform pattern to all the power-conferring rules of the game. It is, however, important to see that these rules are power-conferring rules. Moving any piece to any square on the board is a normative act. It normatively regulates the application of the rules of chess. In the first place each move affects the powers of both players to make moves under the very same rule and under other power-conferring rules relating to the other pieces. In the second place it regulates the application of the continuity rule of chess, of which more below.

The rule as formulated above is incomplete. It does not specify the way in which the normative power to move the rook is to be exercised. It merely indicates the normative consequences of the use of the power—namely that the rook is moved to a new position. It is like a rule giving any adult the power to make a will without saying how a will is to be made. In fact there are various ways in which the power is commonly exercised: by physically moving a piece on a board, by pressing buttons which control an electrical machine which illuminates certain squares on a board, by saying aloud the new position of the piece when the game is played by memory and with no board, and so on. To be complete the rule should specify, for example, that the powers it confers can be exercised in any way agreed by the players.

Chess is governed by one mandatory norm. It can be formulated somewhat as follows: the opening player (determined in a certain way) and subsequently any player, within a reasonable (or a specified period of) time from the beginning of the game or from the time the other player made his last move, respectively, ought to use one of his powers as specified by rules of the first type. I am using this cumbersome formulation, rather than say 'ought to make a move', in order to make clear that this mandatory norm refers to and presupposes the power-conferring rules we have discussed. Therefore, every move by any player regulates the application of this mandatory norm. It determines the ways in which the players can comply with this mandatory norm.

The mandatory norm of chess is of a type which I shall call 'continuity norms'. Its purpose is to keep the game going, or more precisely, it partly determines what counts as playing the game. The penalty for persistently breaking the continuity norms is that the offender loses the game and is eliminated from it, though there might be lesser penalties for minor infringements of continuity rules. It is the fact that breach of a mandatory norm results in the game being lost which marks the norm as a continuity norm. For it is the fact that compliance with a mandatory norm is required to keep the game in progress that is the reason for calling it a continuity norm.

Every game must contain continuity norms. It may, of course, have other mandatory norms with other penalties for their infringement (like the rule against handling the ball in soccer or against intimidating bowling in cricket). When the game consists of a series of discrete moves its continuity rules are straightforward and easy to define. They are the injunction to make a move in chess or to bowl in cricket. In other games the continuity rules are more complex and less obvious. In soccer, for example, they include primarily the various rules for keeping the ball in the game, the duty to start at the initial position at the beginning of every half and after scoring a goal, the rules requiring a throw in if the ball goes over the sidelines, and the rest.

We have seen that the continuity rule of chess presupposes a set of power-conferring rules regulating its application. This is a characteristic feature of some games such as board and card games. In this they differ markedly from many other games, for example, from field games. The position of the players of the fielding side and the way the bowler throws the ball are designed to force the hand of the batsman just as a move in chess imposes a constraint on the moves of the other player. The difference is that the constraint in chess is entirely determined by the rules of the game and its goal. In cricket this is not so. The batsman's move is dictated largely by physical conditions, for example, by the speed and direction of the ball. Some games are completely normatively determined, others are not and leave scope for physical skills. The difference is determined by the rules of the various games.

Some rules of chess, and similar rules of other games, are neither mandatory norms nor power-conferring or permissive norms. I am referring to rules determining the number of players, the essential properties of the chess board and the number of pieces, etc. Such rules are not norms. They do not have any normative force because they do not in themselves guide behaviour; they do, however, guide behaviour indirectly. They have an indirect normative force because they are logically related to the other rules of the games which are norms. They partly determine the interpretation and application of these norms and for this reason they are regarded as rules of the game. They are explained by explaining their logical relations to rules which are norms. Their whole point and function is exhausted by their impact.

Games as autonomous normative systems

Our account of the rules of games was designed to show that such rules can be analysed on the model provided in the previous two chapters. The analysis did, however, disregard most of the features peculiar to games. This is a direct result of the fact that the notion of winning a game was not explained. The account of games given so far is consequently incomplete. No explanation of a game is complete unless it says that the game is played to win and to avoid losing and spells out what counts as winning and losing. But stating that games are played to win or avoid losing and specifying what counts as winning and what as losing is not stating yet another rule. It is to assert a value. Each game can only be defined as a normative system consisting of both rules and values.[2] Winning and not losing are values because they are operative first-order reasons for action. One plays the game in order to win and this goal guides one's moves in playing the game. There are no mandatory norms which require players to win; and if they fail to win, or if they lose, they do not thereby break any rule. They simply fail to achieve their goal. Nor is there any mandatory norm which requires the players to try to win. If they do not try to win or not to lose they do not break any rule. They simply fail to play the game. In this respect the values of winning and losing differ from the continuity rules. The latter apply to people who are playing the game, that is, trying to win and to avoid defeat. Continuity rules require certain behaviour of the players on pain of losing. But the fact that losing is 'a penalty' of sorts presupposes that not losing is a value for the players concerned.

It is important to see that the values of the game provide the test for determining whether the game is being played. It is only if the right number of people regard winning and avoiding defeat as values and guide their behaviour accordingly that the game is being played. As we shall see, what counts as winning and as losing can only be stated by reference to the rules of the game. Following the rules is in general a necessary condition of winning the game. Hence those playing the game necessarily play it by and large by the rules. But acting in accordance with the rules is not a sufficient condition for playing the game. To play one must follow the rules in order to win or to avoid defeat. Consider two people playing chess in the following way: each move both of the white and of the black is decided by consultation. Each time they decide on a move they do so with the intention of making the best move available from the point of view of the white or the black, depending on whose move it is. They follow all the rules, but they are not playing chess. They merely solve a series of chess problems.

The foregoing remarks illustrate the two ways in which the values of a game serve as a reason for action for the players. They are for them a reason for following the continuity rules of the game, because by definition this is necessary to avoid defeat. They are also reasons for following the other mandatory rules of the game because, as will be seen below, violating them makes one liable to a penalty which reduces one's chances of winning. But the values of the game are not only reasons for following the rules. They are also reasons for selecting between various strategies of playing the game. They are a reason for preferring the strategy which is most likely to avoid defeat and to lead to winning the game. (Needless to say the fact that every game has at least two values, winning and not losing, may lead to conflicts in the choice of strategies. Games with more than two sides in which the result is a complete ordering of the parties to the game often create even greater complications.)

Cannot one play a game in order to lose? Do not parents, for example, sometimes play with their children intending that their children shall win? One may pursue other values than winning and one may pursue contradictory values—like winning and losing— during the same time. But in the imagined situation the two values are not pursued in the same way. The parent really wants to lose and does not want to win at all. But he pretends that he plays in order to win and not at all to lose. So we may say that to play a game one must at the very least pretend to be playing to win rather than actually do so. It is worth noting, however, that pretending to play in order to win entails choosing 'moves' because the player thinks that they are or will be thought to be useful as part of a strategy designed to win. Hence even when merely pretending that one holds winning as a value directing all one's actions in the game one is actually holding it as a value at least on occasion and directs some of one's moves in the game by it. (One should bear in mind that in any case it is not a *desire* to win which is postulated but merely the holding of winning as a value guiding one's behaviour.)

This analysis fits most categories of games very well and is valuable in distinguishing between cases of playing a game and those cases of playing which are not the playing of a game. The two cases shade into each other and some games come very close to the borderline. These might be called fragmented games. Many children's games are of this type which could be regarded as a primitive kind of game. I shall use 'hide and seek' as an example of a fragmented game.

The distinctive feature of fragmented games is that the game is broken up into stages or phases. Each phase is structurally identical with the other—for example, in each phase all the players hide except one who has to find at least one of the others. Fragmented games do not have a 'natural' end. The game can be continued, one phase following the other indefinitely. This open-endedness reflects the fact that there is no overall winner or loser in such games. Instead there is something like a winner and a loser at every phase. The players are assigned distinctive roles. Their roles in any given phase are determined by the outcome of the preceding phase. Indeed, unlike the game itself, the phases have a natural end; they come to an end the moment the roles of the players in the next phase are determined. In hide and seek, the first person to be discovered by the seeker has to look for the others in the next phase. The others have to hide. Success is defined for every role. The players in hiding 'lose' if they are discovered. (There is no winning for them. They can only avoid losing.) The seeker succeeds if he discovers somebody and the sooner the better. As in all games the players play only if they adopt the values of the game—trying to hide or to discover the others according to their role. Here we see again that the values are different from the rules and dictate not merely the reasons for following the rules but also the strategy adopted in playing—the choice between the various options permitted by the rules.

As we have seen, fragmented games too are structured by a combination of rules and values and their values share many features of winning and losing. Such values differ, however, from ordinary winning and losing first in being merely the result of a phase and by leading to another phase, and secondly in being more loosely defined and perceived: the quicker the seeker is in discovering one of the hiding players the more successful he is. But there is no precise definition of success or failure. It is all a matter of degree.

Games of mere chance also present some peculiar features. These are games where either the players have no choice—each move being dictated by the rules (which often introduce some random decision procedure such as throwing a dice) or where the outcome of the game is merely randomly related to the players' choice of moves. Such games are in fact elaborate lottery systems in which one's luck is determined by a combination of draws, and the dominating value, the winning, is an autonomous value in the sense explained below.

Because these are games of mere chance there is no question of choosing moves in order to win. Yet, unlike some other lottery systems, such games require the players to act and participate in drawing the lots and they would not be considered as playing the game if they were merely to do so mechanically. They have to do so in order to win or at least to pretend to hold winning as a value.

Winning and avoiding defeat are not, for most players, ultimate values. Most players do not just want to win for winning's sake. For most of them winning is an instrumental value. It could be a means of winning a money prize, or a bet, of being selected for some competition, of keeping fit, of acquiring a certain social status or winning the approval of friends, or to annoy somebody. People may regard winning as a value for any reason under the sun. One common reason is that they enjoy playing the game. Therefore, they regard winning as a value which makes it possible for them to play the game. They play in order to win, but they try to win in order to play.

To play the game it is necessary to regard (or to pretend to regard) winning and avoiding defeat as values. But they need not be regarded as ultimate values, nor need they be regarded by the players as the only values relevant to their behaviour in playing the game. Not only do general moral values apply to these as to any other situations but there are various values which are particularly relevant to games. Playing beautifully and in a sportsmanlike way are values often regarded as even more important than winning. Again they may be considered as reasons for following the rules of the game, and more importantly, they carry considerable weight in determining the strategies a player will follow in his game.

It is interesting to examine the relation between the specific values of the game and its rules. What counts as winning or as losing a game can only be defined by reference to the rules of the game. One can checkmate one's opponent only if one reaches a checkmate position by a series of moves in accordance with the rules. But the value of the game need not be entirely determined by the rules. A loser's chess, in which being checkmated is winning, has the same rules as ordinary chess. Yet it is a different game, which shows once again that the game is defined by reference to its values and rules, and not by its rules only. On the one hand the rules contribute to the identification of the values. On the other hand the values establish the validity of the rules. The rules are binding and one ought to follow them because this is necessary or useful for the realization of the value. Here we must distinguish between the various justificatory questions concerning rules. The values of the game do not explain why we should have such rules in the first place. Since the values depend on the rules for their identification they presuppose that we already have them. The reasons for having these rules rather than others depend on considerations such as whether the rules contribute to the making of an enjoyable and exciting game. The question of validity has nothing to do with these considerations. It assumes that we have the rules and is exclusively concerned with their binding force; it asks if people should follow these rules. The answer to this is yes, because this is necessary or useful for realizing the value. This answer presupposes that the persons concerned do indeed regard the values of the game as values. It applies, in other words, only to people who play the game, for only they regard winning as their value and guide their behaviour accordingly.

We must distinguish between the continuity rules of the game and those rules which are internally related to them and the other rules of the game. Observance of the continuity rules is necessary to playing the game. Persistent disregard of such rules results in the loss of the game. Therefore their validity is directly established by the value of the game. Through them the values indirectly establish the validity of the rules which are internally related to the continuity rules. Other rules, like the rules concerning handling the ball or off-side in soccer, are not so intimately connected with the values of the game, but they nevertheless depend on them through the penalties for their violations. The penalties are normative results which are generally disadvantageous from the point of view of realizing the values of the game. In this way the values provide reasons for observing these rules as well.[3]

We have noted that other values can also guide the behaviour of the players. They need not. To play the game it is necessary for the players to be guided by the values of the game. They may but need not be guided by other values. Since the game is logically governed by its values, all its rules depend on them for their validity—this is really a definition of what counts as a rule of the game. The players may observe many rules while playing the game, not all of which need be rules of the game. Only those whose validity can be established by the values of the game are rules of the game. Hence the rules of the game are its continuity rules, its other mandatory rules with penalties relevant to the realization of the values, and rules internally related to them.

Mandatory rules of games are exclusionary reasons. Disregarding them may be right on the balance of reasons and may make the game more interesting; yet it is not justified for the rules require excluding all such considerations. Rules of games are norms in the same sense as any other norm. The uniqueness of games as normative systems depends on the special nature of their values. They are artificial values because they are not inherently connected to wider human concerns. We cannot ask of the values of games whether they are justified in the abstract. They may be justified or binding on one person at one time and not binding on another person or the same person at another time. We can determine whether at any given time a person guides his behaviour by them or whether he should do so, that is whether he should play the game in a given concrete situation, but there is little sense normally in asking when precisely any person should be guided by the values of chess or football. Sometimes this question does make good sense. 'A professional chess player should play chess four hours a day' may be a true statement. But it depends on knowledge of the special interests of the man concerned. Because the values of a game are not inherently related to wider human concerns there is little point in inquiries about their general justification. Such inquiries make sense only once we have more information concerning the situation in question and the desires and interests of the persons involved. This is the reason that games are merely games.

We began our examination of games by saying that they are normative systems of joint validity. There is no point in following one of their rules unless one follows all the continuity rules of the game. We have also seen that games may consist of or contain sets of interlocking rules. But neither of these features explain the distinctive nature of games. Games are unique in being autonomous normative systems. I call them autonomous for two reasons. First, as normative systems they consist of interdependent rules and values: the values can be identified only in terms of the rules, and the rules depend for their validity on the values. Secondly, their values are artificial values in that they are not systematically related to wider human concerns.

4.2 INSTITUTIONALIZED SYSTEMS: PRELIMINARY REMARKS

A preliminary analysis

Using 'institutions' in the widest possible sense it is clear that many institutions are set up and governed by norms. One can regard the norms regulating the institutions of marriage and family relations, or property or contract as normative systems of joint validity. However, when discussing institutionalized systems we will be concerned not with any institution created by norms but with a special type of institutions, those which are not only established by norms but whose function is to create and apply norms.

Many normative systems contain either norm-creating or norm-applying institutions or both. Sports associations, social clubs, educational institutions, trade unions and many other organizations have one or the other, or both, of these institutions. Legal systems are the most important type of institutionalized system today and I shall use them throughout to illustrate the analysis. But the features of legal systems discussed in this section are not peculiar to legal systems. They are typical of many institutionalized systems. There are, of course, normative systems based on institutions to which my analysis does not apply. Systems of common origin and systems of absolute discretion (both to be discussed below) are examples of such systems. My claim is merely that the analysis provided in this section and the one below applies to one type of system of which legal systems are the most notable example. In the next chapter we shall examine the features which mark out legal systems as a special kind of institutionalized system.

The purpose of the present section is to examine the conditions under which the presence of norm-creating or of norm-applying institutions turns a set of norms into a normative system, and to review their normative impact on the relations between the norms of the system and between them and other norms. These remarks presuppose that the existence of norm-creating or of norm-applying institutions is crucial to the understanding of at least some normative systems such as legal systems. Is this assumption justified? I shall argue that it is justified with respect to normative systems with an independent criterion for being practised.

It is a feature common to legal systems and the rules of a college or a political association or a golf club, etc., that we can talk of 'the law of the community C' or 'the rules of C' implying that we are referring to the normative system practised in C. Similarly we use expressions such as 'the legal system which is in force in C' or 'which exists in C' and these, again, refer to the system practised in C. We contrast such expressions with others which do not presuppose that the system is practised: we may refer to the system which was once in force in the Roman Republic, or to that which a revolutionary group is trying to establish in a certain community or which a group of scholars has recommended to the parliament of a certain country.

Is there any significance in the fact that on such occasions we refer to the normative system which is in force and not to the norms which are practised, to the law of C, not to the laws of C? Consider legal systems: no doubt if all or almost all the norm subjects of mandatory or permissive legal norms accept these norms as binding and guide their behaviour accordingly we will have no doubt that the system is being practised. Indeed this state of affairs can be regarded as an ideal for any legal system or any other institutionalized system.

It is, however, an ideal which is rarely realized. Wherever we turn we find legal systems in force in countries in which some or many of the norm subjects are either unaware of the content of many laws applying to them or reject many laws as unjust or oppressive or because they are imposed by a foreign ruler or by tyrannical government or for other reasons. In short many of the norm subjects of almost every legal system do not regard some or all of its norms as binding on them and do not guide their behaviour by the norm as a norm. This sometimes leads to law-breaking behaviour, but it need not always do so. Many conform to the law without being guided by it. They conform because they have other reasons for doing what the law requires, reasons which have nothing to do with the fact that these actions are required by law. They may think that there are moral reasons or self-interested reasons for them to do what is in fact required by the law, regardless of whether it is in fact required by law.

People may conform with the law on many occasions for the reason, among others, that it is the law, without accepting its norms as guides to their behaviour. They may do so because they realize that others regard the law as binding and would react in certain ways to their own violations of the law: the police will arrest and prosecute them, their neighbours will resent them, etc. As we have seen, such considerations may lead individuals to accept the norm and guide their behaviour accordingly. This would be the case whenever a person resolves that, because if he disregards a norm which is generally followed and believed in he may suffer unpleasant consequences, he had better adopt it himself and guide his own behaviour accordingly. The cases we are envisaging here are different. They are cases in which a person who does not guide his behaviour by a norm decides to conform to it on a particular occasion because he is aware of a policeman around the corner or a neighbour in the window upstairs, and knows that since they accept the norm their reaction to his violation of it on this occasion would be such that he had better conform to it.

I have elaborated this point for it is important not to take the mere fact that the population by and large conforms to the law as evidence that it accepts it and guides its behaviour by it. There is no denying that some level of general conformity with the law is a necessary condition for a legal system to be the law of a community. We would not say of a legal system that it is in force if the community to which it applies respects it only in the breach, that is, if the community generally disobeys it. The problem is that general conformity, though a necessary condition, is not a sufficient condition for judging that a legal system is in force. It should be remembered that the degree of conformity required is not very high. A legal system may be in force in a country suffering from a crime wave, many of the laws can be generally disregarded, some of the regions may have a particularly bad record in law observance, etc. Given that the standard of conformity required is not very high, and given that conformity to law presupposes neither knowledge of the law nor behaviour for the reason that this is what is required by law, it is possible for a community to conform to legal systems which are not in force in it. We can imagine a model legal system proposed by a group of legal scholars which, because it partly overlaps with existing laws or with various social practices, is in fact generally conformed with by the population of the United Kingdom today. This does not establish that the proposed legal system is the law of the UK.

The criteria for judging that a legal system is the law of a community must, therefore, include the condition that it is generally conformed to and some additional condition or conditions which must fall short of requiring that all the norms of the system are actually practised.[4] H. L. A. Hart (in *The Concept of Law*, pp. 109–14) has suggested that the additional condition is that at least the officials of the system accept the norms of the system and guide their behaviour accordingly. This test will explain why the model legal system in our example is not the law of the United Kingdom— it is not regarded as binding by the officials of the system. Hart's test does in fact conform with our intuitions and explains the grounds on which we judge whether a legal system is the law of a community. A legal system is the law of a community if, and only if, it is generally conformed to by the norm subjects of the laws and the officials set up by the laws of the system endorse them and follow them. The same test applies to other institutionalized normative systems. Some features of the test will be further examined below. For the time being let us draw attention to some of its consequences.

The first major trait of institutionalized systems is that they have a criterion for being practised or in force which is not identical with all their norms being practised, and which assigns considerable weight to the activities of officials and institutions. This is closely connected to their second major trait.

All the norms of legal and similar institutionalized systems have internal relations with those norms which set up either the norm-creating or the norm-applying institutions. For every kind of normative system we require a criterion for determining which norms belong to the system. The rules of a game are, as we have seen, identified by their relation to the values of the game. The rules of institutionalized systems are identified by their relation to the institutions which characterize those systems. This is a simple result of the importance of these institutions in the system. We have seen that the working of such institutions plays a large part in determining whether the system as a whole is practised. It is true that the fact that the system is practised is not a simple function of its norms being practised but it is reasonable to assume that every norm is somehow relevant to the facts which determine whether the system of which it is part is practised. If this were not so the criteria for determining that a system is practised would be arbitrary; they would lack any relevance to the norms of the system, or to some of them. Hence the conclusion that normative systems with this kind of criteria of being practised consist of norms which have internal relations to the norms setting up and regulating the institutions the working of which determines whether the system is practised.

The nature of the unifying relation between the institutions and the norms of the system will be examined below, but even a superficial survey of such normative institutions presents two types of relationship as candidates for the role. To the extent that the relation is to norm-creating institutions it is bound to be that they enacted the norms under some conditions. To the extent that the relation is to norm-applying institutions it is bound to be that they apply the norms under some conditions.

The first two features of institutionalized systems together yield a third important feature: the systemic validity of norms belonging to such systems is conditioned by the system being practised. A norm is valid if its norm subjects ought to endorse and follow it. A normative system is valid if its norms are valid. There could be many different grounds on which a norm may be judged valid. Norms which belong to normative systems may be valid on grounds which are completely independent of the fact that they belong to such systems. Legal systems contain norms prohibiting murder and requiring that certain agreements be respected. These rules are usually considered as valid rules independently of their belonging to any legal system, though many will maintain that the fact that they are legally binding rules is an alternative ground for their validity. Let us say that a norm has systemic validity if it is valid on grounds which depend on its belonging to a certain normative system. A normative system is systemically valid if, and only if, all its norms are systemically valid relative to that system, i.e. if they are valid because, among other things, they belong to that system. In discussing the validity of normative systems we are normally concerned with their systemic validity, i.e. with whether the fact that their norms belong to that system is a reason for judging them to be valid.

It must be clear by now that I am using 'valid' in a different sense from that of 'legally valid'. A norm is legally valid if and only if it belongs to some legal system. A norm may be legally valid without being valid and without being systemically valid: it may belong to a legal system but its norm subjects may not be justified in following it. For a legal norm to be systemically valid it is of course necessary that it is legally valid, but this is not a sufficient condition. Sentences of the form 'x is a (legally) valid norm' and similar sentences are standardly used either to assert that x belongs to a legal system or that it is valid (i.e. a justified norm which ought to be followed), or that it is valid on the supposition that the law ought to be obeyed (on the nature of such statements, cf. section 5.4).

The third main feature of legal and similar systems is that they are systemically valid only if they are practised systems. A norm belonging to the Roman legal system or to a proposed legal system sponsored by an institute for law reform may be a valid moral norm or valid on any other grounds. But the fact that it belongs to a proposed or an extinct system is no reason for regarding it as valid. The fact that a norm belongs to a legal system is relevant to its validity only if that legal system is in force, i.e. actually practised. As indicated, this conclusion is based on the aforementioned features of institutionalized systems. A norm is systemically valid if and only if the fact that it belongs to a system is (part of) a reason for its validity. Roughly speaking a norm belongs to a certain institutionalized system only if it was enacted by the organs of that system or is applied by them. It follows that the systemic validity of the norms must depend on the fact that they were created or are applied by the relevant institutions. In other words the systemic validity of institutionalized norms depends on the authority of the norm-creating or the norm-applying institutions to regulate behaviour and settle disputes. The authority in question is social authority—authority over a community. And the question is not whether it would be good for the society to be governed by these institutions, nor whether they should have authority in the community but whether things being what they are they do have authority and should be obeyed. Since the social authority of the institutions must depend on their ability to regulate adequately social relations in the society, it is necessary in order for them to have authority that their rule be effective, that the normative system they create or administer be actually practised. That it is practised is not sufficient to establish that it regulates adequately social relations. But if it is not practised it does not regulate them at all and the institutions lack authority, however much they may deserve to have it. Hence the conclusion that the systemic validity of institutionalized systems depends on their being practised.

We have mentioned three main features of legal and similar normative systems. Firstly, they have criteria for being practised which depend in part on the operation of their norm-creating or norm-applying institutions. Secondly, the test for belonging to such systems depends on having certain internal relations to the norms setting up the relevant institutions. Thirdly, the systemic validity of such systems depends on their being practised. In enumerating these features I have relied on our general knowledge of the law and similar systems. These features make clear the importance of institutions to some normative systems. What has not been established is that whenever we have such institutions we also have normative systems of this kind. To clarify this point we must have a closer look at the nature of normative systems based on these institutions.

Systems of a common origin

So far we have not distinguished between the role played by the norm-creating and the norm-applying institutions. But are both kinds of institutions of equal importance to the understanding of legal systems and other similar systems? Legal philosophers have long been divided between those who emphasize the role of the law-creating institutions and those who think that the key to the systematic nature of law lies with the functioning of the law-applying institutions. I have argued at length for the latter view elsewhere. Let me explain briefly the nature of the shortcomings of the other view. The preliminary analysis suggested that normative institutions are crucial to our conception of some normative systems in two respects: first, in determining whether the system is in force, whether it is practised; secondly, in determining via their role in the criterion of identity of the system which norms belong to the system. I shall suggest that from both points of view norm-applying and not norm-creating organs are of primary importance.

The view I am concerned to criticize regards legal systems and similar normative systems as systems of a common origin. There are two main variants of this type of theory.[5] One, represented most notably by Hobbes and Austin, defines a legal system as the set of all the norms issued, directly or indirectly, by one legislator. The second variant, of which Kelsen's work is the best example, regards a legal system as a set of all the norms deriving their legal validity, directly or indirectly, from one norm. A norm is made directly by a legislator if made by an act of his. He is said to have issued it indirectly if it was enacted by the exercise of a power conferred by a norm which he enacted, directly or indirectly. A norm derives its legal validity directly from another norm if it is enacted by the exercise of powers conferred by that other norm. It derives its legal validity indirectly from a norm if enacted by the exercise of powers which are conferred by a third norm which itself derives its legal validity directly or indirectly from the relevant norm.

According to both views every legal system has a common origin. Austin maintains that there is one legislator called 'the sovereign' who is ultimately the source of all the laws of the system. He either enacts them himself or delegates power to subordinate legislators to enact them. According to Kelsen there is one norm called the basic norm which is the source of all the laws of the system. It confers power to enact them or to enact laws which confer powers to enact them. There are many important differences between these two types of theories, and there are many objections which apply to the one but not to the other. There are, however, at least two major objections which apply to both. These objections show that only the simplest forms of institutionalized systems are systems of a common origin. Such systems are usually those governing the activities of a small group of people for a relatively short period of time. Complex systems such as legal systems and similar systems of the kind mentioned in the beginning of the section are not systems of a common origin. The models of systems of a common origin cannot account for two major features of complex institutionalized systems; they fail to explain the unity and the existence of these complex systems.

The first objection (from unity) argues that some legal systems include more than one ultimate legislative authority.[6] They include several legislators such that the authority of each is not derived either from a norm made by the other or from a norm which confers power on the other. In Britain, for example, the authority of Parliament is not derived from the Common Law, nor the authority of the Common Law from Parliament. Yet the Common Law confers in effect norm-making powers on the courts and these are not derived from parliamentary legislation. Nor is there any other norm conferring powers on both the courts and Parliament. No *one* norm can do this. The powers of the courts and of Parliament differ very much both in their scope and in the manner of their exercise. Consequently if they are conferred by law at all they are conferred by at least two different norms. Hence there is no origin common to all the norms of the legal system of the United Kingdom. Moreover, some legal systems are based on customary laws. Many of their laws are binding laws because they are based on certain practices without there being any legislated law which instructs people to obey those customs. In such systems there is, of course, no single legislator of all the laws, nor a norm conferring powers to enact all the laws for the simple reason that many of the laws are not enacted at all.

The second objection concerns the existence of complex institutionalized systems. Having seen that a common origin is not a necessary condition for belonging to a legal system, it is worth pointing out that having a common origin is not sufficient to explain the nature of most institutionalized systems. We have seen that these systems can be in force even if not all their norms are practised. In some way yet to be explained the fact that they are practised by some institutions is crucial to establishing that the system is practised. This test cannot turn on the practice of the norm-creating institutions. These can at best practise those norms addressed to them and there is no reason to regard a system as in force simply because it is acceptable to those who lay down its rules. That it is in force must depend somehow on what happens to those who are the norm subjects of the norms of the system. Since we have seen that if on the one hand it is not necessary that they shall practise the norms and on the other hand it is not sufficient that they conform with them we are forced to rely on the practice of the norm-applying institutions. If they regularly enforce the norms on those of their norm subjects who have not conformed with them then we can regard the system as practised even if the bulk of the population does not practise its norms. The reason why this is a plausible step is that even if not practised by the norm subjects the norms are applied to them by the norm-applying organs. We are relying on facts which are relevant to the behaviour of the norm subjects with respect to the norms. If they do not follow the norms of their own accord they are forced to do so by the police and the courts, etc. This is, of course, a very crude and imprecise statement of the situation but it brings out the reasons for regarding the practices of the law-applying institutions as an essential part of the test for determining whether the system is in force. As explained above this conclusion in itself requires that the test for the unity of the system, the test for determining which norms belong to the system, will also relate to the norm-applying rather than to the norm-creating institutions.

4.3 INSTITUTIONALIZED SYSTEMS: AN ANALYSIS

Norm-applying institutions

Norm-applying institutions and not norm-creating institutions provide the key to our notion of an institutionalized system. Institutionalized systems are sets of norms which either set up certain norm-applying institutions or which are internally related in a certain way to these. To understand the nature of institutionalized systems we have to explain first what are norm-applying institutions, and, secondly, what are the relations between the norms creating these institutions and the other norms of the system.

What are the distinguishing marks of norm-applying organs? This is a notoriously difficult question. We have only to look at the debate concerning the nature of courts to become aware of the difficulties. Lawyers and sociologists have offered various incompatible explanations and the controversy is still raging. Given this history of disagreement the first thing to note is that the various theorists studying this question are really tackling a variety of problems. Lawyers studying the defining features of a court or a tribunal may be concerned with solving any one of a variety of legal problems arising under a specific legal system: a certain court in that system may have supervisory powers over all judicial determinations by judicial bodies; the law of evidence or some of its rules may apply to proceedings before every judicial body, etc. When a lawyer faces the question 'What is a court?' he is usually concerned with one or more of the many problems to which such laws give rise. Is body A a judicial body subject to the supervisory jurisdiction of the relevant court? Do the general principles of the law of evidence apply to proceedings before A? And so on. Social scientists have their own problems which are quite different, though usually indirectly related to those of the lawyer. They may be interested in the classification of different social methods of settling disputes, or of the different channels for the articulation of demands, etc. Our purpose in looking for the identifying traits of norm-applying institutions is primarily to establish the nature of the institutions whose presence is a defining feature of legal and similar systems. An adequate answer to our question need not be a satisfactory solution of the problems of the lawyer or the sociologist, nor is it intended as an answer to their questions.

Some have attempted to define judicial and other norm-applying organs by the social functions they fulfil. Others have looked to the norms which establish these institutions for an answer. I shall follow the latter approach. Norm-applying institutions are first and foremost normative institutions established by norms and it is to these that we must turn for a clue to their identity. It may be true that they are established to serve some social functions, but it is likely that the same functions can be and are served by other means as well. Norm-applying institutions should, therefore, be identified by the way they fulfil their functions rather than by their functions themselves. This does not detract from the importance of studying the functions which the institutions serve. It merely means that the institutions have to be identified by other means.

Of legal systems it can be said that every act by a public official which is the performance of a duty or the exercise of a power is generally regarded as a law-applying act. A policeman arresting a suspect, an official granting a trader's licence, a court rendering judgment in which Doe is ordered to pay a sum of money to Roe— all these are commonly regarded as instances of the application of law by public officials. These cases differ from similar acts of private individuals who pay taxes, sell property, give orders to their employees, etc., only in being the acts of public officials. Therefore, on the most general interpretation of 'norm-applying institutions' these are identical with public institutions (in one sense of the word 'public').

What are the identifying features of public officials? This is a problem which is both important and difficult. It is, however, a problem which it would be best to avoid here, for, though we will find public officials in all institutionalized systems, not all of them must exist in the system if it is to count as an institutionalized system. Instead we should try to identify a subclass of norm-applying institutions, namely those the presence of which is necessary in all institutionalized normative systems.

The terminological contrast between 'norm-creating' and 'norm-applying' draws attention to one important class of norm-applying institutions—those which apply norms not by making other norms but by physically implementing them. The courts apply the law by rendering judgments which are themselves norms. The prison service or public officials instructed to pull down a house against which a demolition order has been issued physically enforce the law. I shall call norm-applying institutions of this kind 'norm-enforcing' institutions. There is no doubt that norm-enforcing institutions play an important role in all modern legal systems. Yet for two reasons they cannot be regarded as the key to the identification of legal and similar systems. First, though all legal systems regulate the use of force and ultimately rely on force to ensure compliance with the law (see section 5.2), not all of them need have law-enforcing institutions. There may be normative systems which share all the characteristics of legal systems and do not have any law-enforcing machinery. Once a judgment is given its execution is left to the parties to the dispute. In such a system an individual is not allowed to use force to secure his rights whenever he likes. He is obliged to go to a court and obtain an authoritative declaration of his rights. But once he is in possession of a decision he is entitled to implement it using reasonable force and he may be entitled to authorize others to use force in his name for this purpose. Such a system is clearly a legal system. It does not have law-enforcing institutions but it has other norm-applying institutions which warrant regarding it as an institutionalized system. Secondly, we must remember that there are institutionalized systems other than legal ones. Normative systems governing voluntary associations, for example, may not regulate the use of force at all or at any rate may not provide for the use of force as a means of norm-enforcement and consequently may not have any norm-enforcing institutions.

We must, therefore, look elsewhere for the kind of norm-applying institutions which are crucial to our understanding of institutionalized systems. I shall suggest that the type of institutions we are looking for are those which combine norm-making and norm-applying in a special way. Let us call these institutions primary (norm-applying) organs, to indicate their importance. Primary institutions are just one kind of norm-applying institutions. Norm-enforcing organs are another kind of such institution and there are others as well. Norm-enforcing organs are concerned with the physical implementation of norms and this determines their character as norm-applying. Primary organs are concerned with the authoritative determination of normative situations in accordance with pre-existing norms. Consider judicial bodies. Courts and tribunals have power to determine the rights and duties of individuals. But cannot any person do the same? Cannot John determine whether he owes £100 to Alan or whether Paul owes money to Jack? He may be ignorant of the facts but like a court he may investigate them. He may be ignorant of the law but like a court he may study it. The difference between a court and a private individual is not merely that courts are provided with better facilities to determine the facts of the case and the law applying to them. Courts have power to make an *authoritative* determination of people's legal situation. Private individuals may express their opinions on the subject but their views are not binding.

The fact that a court can make a binding decision does not mean that it cannot err. It means that its decision is binding even if it is mistaken. My specification of the legal situation is not binding at all because it is not binding if it is mistaken. To be a binding application of a norm means to be binding even if wrong, even if it is in fact a misapplication of the norm. This seemingly paradoxical formulation illuminates the nature and function of primary norm-applying organs.

The paradox is generated by the problem of how we can say of a determination (decision or declaration) both that it applies a pre-existing norm and that it is binding. We may feel that we regard a determination as norm-applying if it merely determines which rights and duties individuals have in virtue of pre-existing norms, whereas we regard a determination as binding only if it changes the rights and duties of individuals. Only with regard to a new norm imposing duty on individuals or releasing them from their duties, investing them with rights or divesting them of their rights, can we ask whether it is valid or not. If the determination purports merely to ascertain what rights and duties they already have and not to change them then the only question arising is whether the determination is correct or incorrect. The question of the binding force arises only with respect to creative determinations—those which change the normative situation. Creative determinations can be binding or not but cannot be either correct or incorrect. The reverse is true of applicative determinations.

On this view a determination cannot be both binding and norm-applying. This is, however, an over-restrictive view of the sense of 'binding'. A determination can be binding even if it does not change the normative situation, provided it would have been binding had it changed it. Consider a new piece of legislation which, though its authors may be unaware of the fact, merely repeats the contents of an old but valid law. The new legislation can be judged to be either valid or invalid, even though it is clear that it does not change anybody's rights or duties. The point is that if valid it would have changed the legal situation had the old law no longer been in force. Put it another way: if valid it creates another basis for the rights and duties imposed by the old law. In the same sense a court's determination that Doe owes money to Roe is binding even though the debt existed by a pre-existing norm, provided that it is binding even if there would have been no debt but for the decision of the court—hence my original formulation that a norm-applying determination is binding only if binding even if mistaken.

Now we are in a position to describe the defining features of a primary norm-applying organ. They are institutions with power to determine the normative situation of specified individuals, which are required to exercise these powers by applying existing norms, but whose decisions are binding even when wrong. A few comments on this characterization are in place here.

(1) The definition attempts to identify one kind of institution. The nature of institutions in general is presupposed and is not explained in it. It is important to stress that we are concerned with primary *institutions*. Institutionalized systems are not identified merely by the fact that they contain norms conferring powers to make binding applicative determinations. They must contain norms conferring such powers on institutions, i.e. on centralized bodies concentrating in their hands the authority to make binding applicative determinations.

(2) Courts, tribunals and other judicial bodies are the most important example of primary organs. But other officials, such as police officers, may also be primary organs. There are obvious reasons to impose on primary organs a duty to follow judicial procedures, but this need not be always done. It does seem reasonable to suppose, however, that the notion of a primary institution provides a necessary step in any attempt to analyse the nature of judicial institutions.

(3) The definition of a primary organ has to be further refined. As it stands it applies only to final and absolutely binding determinations. It has to be modified to allow for the possibility of appeal, re-trial, etc., and also for the possibility that the determination is binding for one purpose but not for others. In many legal systems there are applicative determinations which are binding only in respect of the cause of action whose litigation resulted in the determinations.

(4) The definition identifies organs by their power to make binding applicative determinations. This is compatible with the fact that the same institutions have other powers and functions. In particular, courts often have power to create precedent and lay down general rules, to issue orders to individuals to perform certain actions and to determine authoritatively the facts of the case (the *res judicata* doctrine). All these are either entirely different or, at best, overlap with the power to make binding applicative determinations. Applica-

tive determinations are determinations of the rights or duties of individuals in concrete situations and are entirely different from the power to create precedent or to issue orders instructing individuals to pay damages or fines or be jailed, etc., because they disregarded their duties or the rights of others. Applicative determinations are most closely related to declaratory judgements. In fact the definition suggests that a declaratory judgement is an ingredient in many courts' decisions. This is part of the effect of the *res judicata* doctrine. But this doctrine is wider and applies also to purely factual findings, and not only to determinations of rights and duties in particular situations.

The claim that the presence of a primary organ is a defining feature of institutionalized systems is based not only on our common knowledge of typical cases of legal and similar systems but also on the crucial role such institutions, when present, play in regulating social relations. The presence of primary institutions indicates that the normative system concerned provides for an institutionalized and authoritative way of settling disputes. Every normative system which recognizes voluntary obligations implicitly allows for authoritative settlement of disputes through agreed arbitration and similar methods. But the difference between normative systems which provide systematic and institutionalized methods of settling disputes and those which do not is of momentous importance to their utility and function in regulating social behaviour. Hence the claim that the presence of primary institutions is a defining characteristic of an important class of normative systems.[7]

Institutionalized systems and systems of absolute discretion

One reason for the importance of primary institutions is that they provide an authoritative institutionalized method of settling disputes. The other important aspect of primary institutions is, of course, that their duty is to apply existing norms. The significance of this fact can be gauged by comparing normative systems which have primary organs with a hypothetical system based on dispute-settling methods of a completely different nature. I shall call this system a system of absolute discretion. Its norms set up tribunals with powers to solve certain categories of disputes. It may also contain other norms: some norms specify the qualifications for service and the method of appointment to the tribunals; other norms specify the conditions of service, the procedure of adjudication and the precise powers of the various tribunals (some may have power to deal with cases of personal injury, others with purely financial disputes, etc.). A system of this nature may or may not make it obligatory for individuals to refer disputes to the tribunals. I shall assume that it does not and that it does not provide machinery for the enforcement of the decisions of the tribunals. But it does follow from the norms of the system that once a tribunal declares the rights and duties of an individual its decision settles the matter conclusively.

The tribunals of a system of complete discretion are not primary institutions for they are not required to decide on the basis of any specified norms. Indeed it is the defining characteristic of a system of complete discretion that its tribunals are subject to one instruction only concerning the reasons on which their decisions are to be based: they are always to make that decision which they think to be best on the basis of all the valid reasons. There are no legislated, customary or any other standards which they have to apply. Nor do they have to follow their own precedents. The tribunals of this peculiar system are not entitled to decide in an arbitrary way. They are to act on reasons but the selection of the reasons which determine the cases is within their own absolute discretion. They must act on their own sincere and unfettered judgement.

Systems of absolute discretion differ from legal and similar systems primarily in one respect. Since their tribunals are not obliged to follow any common standards and can decide whatever they think best, such a system does not provide any guidance to individuals on the behaviour which would entitle them to a decision in their favour, should a dispute arise. Different tribunals may believe in the validity of different reasons. The same tribunal may change its mind at any time. There is no requirement of consistency over time imposed on the tribunals, and litigation before them always involves, at least potentially, questions of ultimate values. Legal and similar systems, on the other hand, do provide guidance to individuals. They contain norms determining the rights and duties of individuals. These are the very same norms that the primary institutions are bound to apply and that is the reason that they also provide guidance to individuals as to their rights and duties in litigation before the primary organs.

Institutionalized systems based on primary institutions contain norms guiding the behaviour of individuals, and not only norms instituting tribunals. Since primary institutions are norm-applying there must be norms for them to apply. This truism, which forms the basis of the distinction between systems of absolute discretion and institutionalized systems, has two important implications. In the first place it reveals that institutionalized systems are co-ordinated guidance and evaluation systems. They contain norms guiding behaviour and institutions for evaluating and judging behaviour. The evaluation is based on the very same norms which guide behaviour. Indeed the test by which we determine whether a norm belongs to the system is, roughly speaking, that it is a norm which the primary organs ought to apply when judging and evaluating behaviour. (This test will be discussed and somewhat modified in section 5.1.) Thus legal and other institutionalized systems can be said to possess their own internal system of evaluation. We can assess behaviour from the legal point of view, for example, and the legal point of view consists of the norms by which courts are bound to evaluate behaviour which are the very same norms which are legally binding on the individual whose behaviour is evaluated.

The second important consequence of the difference between institutionalized systems and systems of absolute discretion is that the former contain, indeed consist of, norms which the courts are bound to apply regardless of their view of their merit. A more accurate formulation would be that institutionalized systems consist of norms which the primary organs are bound to apply and are not at liberty to disregard whenever they find their application undesirable, all things considered. It does not follow that primary organs are computing machines always applying pre-existing rules regardless of their own views of which rule or which decision is the right one. But it is a consequence that they are to follow a certain body of norms regardless of their views of their merits and are allowed to act on their own views only to the extent that this is allowed by those norms. The law, for example, sometimes instructs judges to decide cases by whichever principle they find just or appropriate.* In many other cases the law requires the courts to render judgment in cases for which the body of laws they are bound to follow does not provide one correct answer. Because of the vagueness, open texture and incompleteness of all legal systems there are many disputes for which the system does not provide a correct answer. Even if it rules out certain solutions as wrong, it may have others which are neither wrong nor right in law. If the system requires with respect to some such cases, as all legal

---

* Such instructions are usually subject to various restrictions designed to preserve the coherence of purpose of the body of laws which governs cases similar to the one before the courts.

systems in fact do, that the courts should not refuse to settle the dispute but should render judgment in it, then they are thereby required to determine the case in accordance with their own conception of what is right. Needless to say, even in such cases their discretion can be limited by general legal principles, but these will not eliminate the element of personal judgement of the merits.

One objection to this view might be considered overwhelming. In many legal systems, for example in all Common Law jurisdictions, there are courts with power not only to settle at their discretion unsettled cases but also to overrule established precedent. They are entitled, in fact, to repeal laws and replace them with rules which they judge to be better than the old ones. That might be claimed to provide a counter-example to my claim that the law consists only of rules which the courts are bound to follow. It is, of course, possible to argue (indeed, I wish to argue) that such courts derive their power to repeal or overrule settled law from laws of the very same system. But this is no answer to our problem. For even so how can it be that the courts are bound to follow laws which they are at liberty to disregard? The answer is that this is quite impossible and yet the supposed counter-example fails for it misdescribes the situation.

A rule which the courts have complete liberty to disregard or change is not binding on them and is not part of the legal system. But the courts in Common Law jurisdictions do not have this power with respect to the binding Common Law rules. They cannot change them whenever they consider that on the balance of reasons it would be better to do so. They may change them only for certain kinds of reasons. They may change them, for example, for being unjust, for iniquitous discrimination, for being out of step with the court's conception of the body of laws to which they belong. But even if the court finds that they are not the best rules for some other reason not included in the permissible list, it is nevertheless bound to follow the rules.

The situation is paralleled in other areas of practical reasoning. People have an obligation to keep their promises. This entails that they are not at liberty to break their promises whenever they find that all things considered it would be best to do so. But this does not mean that they ought to keep their promises come what may. The presence of reasons of a certain kind will justify breaking a promise. It follows that the fact that one is under an obligation is consistent with being at liberty to disregard it in certain circumstances, provided that one is not at liberty to disregard it whenever one finds that on the balance of reasons it would be best to do so. For this reason the purported counter-example fails. All it shows is that in Common Law jurisdictions there are courts which are sometimes at liberty to repeal some valid laws. Since they are entitled to do so only for certain specific types of reasons* (and not whenever this is desirable, all things considered) their liberty to use their power to repeal those laws is consistent with the fact that they are under an obligation to follow them.

Institutionalized systems and exclusionary reasons

It is time to retrace our steps and draw conclusions. There are normative systems consisting of norms guiding individuals but providing no institutionalized methods for settling disputes, not even those arising from the application of the norms of the system. There can also be normative systems (our systems of absolute discretion) which do not include any norms for guiding the behaviour of ordinary individuals but which do provide institutions for settling disputes. It is characteristic of legal systems as well as of many other institutionalized systems that they combine both features: they include both norms for guiding individuals and norms setting up institutions for settling at least some categories of disputes (these include, but are not always confined to, disputes concerning the proper application of the norms of the system). It follows that such institutionalized systems are characterized by the fact that they contain norms setting up primary norm-applying institutions.

Institutionalized systems may include other kinds of norm-applying institutions and their primary organs may have powers beyond that of making authoritative applicative determinations. These additional institutions and powers may vary from one institutionalized system to another. But all such systems have norms instituting primary organs since they contain both norms guiding individuals and institutionalized ways of settling disputes arising from the application of such norms. In this they differ from systems of absolute discretion since primary organs are sometimes bound to act on certain standards regardless of their view as to whether it is

* The fact that their liberty is to act on reasons of types specified by the law does not negate the personal discretion of the court. They have discretion, not only to establish whether the facts justify the conclusion that reasons of that type are present in the situation, but also a discretion to act on their personal view of what counts as a valid reason of that type—for example, what is an unjust law.

best that they should so act. But institutionalized systems also differ in a radical way from normative systems which provide no institutions for settling disputes.

The introduction of primary organs is not a simple addition to a normative system. Their introduction radically transforms the system adding to it a whole new dimension, that of authoritative evaluations of behaviour. Of course, people do evaluate behaviour on the basis of the norms of other types of normative systems as well, but only institutionalized systems provide for primary organs the function of which is to evaluate behaviour authoritatively on the basis of the norms of the system. We can thus talk of evaluation from the point of view of the system (from a legal point of view, etc.), meaning by this evaluation on the basis of those standards which the primary organs of the system are bound to apply. The official evaluation of behaviour by the primary organs must of course coincide with the guidance given by the system to ordinary individuals. If the system judges an individual to be doing what he ought not to do this entails that its norms guide him not to do that act, and *vice versa*. Hence if the primary organs do not regard themselves as bound to apply a certain norm it does not belong to the system. Thus the introduction of primary organs affects the criterion for membership in the system: if the system's guidance and evaluation are to coincide it must be regarded as containing only those norms which its primary organs are bound to apply. Some legal theorists concluded that the law consists of all the standards which the courts do in fact apply. This, however, makes it impossible to say that the courts are wrong on a point of law and confuses institutionalized systems with systems of absolute discretion.

So far I have freely referred to institutionalized systems as consisting of *norms* without justifying this usage. Norms are exclusionary reasons or permissions or are logically related to such reasons or permissions. Are laws or the rules of other institutionalized systems exclusionary reasons or permissions? Are the power-conferring rules of institutionalized systems logically related in the right way to exclusionary reasons? Where is the exclusionary element in institutionalized systems to be found? The answer is implied by the analysis of primary organs. We saw that they are institutions which are bound to act on certain reasons even if they do not think that on the balance of reasons they ought to do so. That means that primary organs are institutions which ought to act on certain reasons to the exclusion of all others, namely institutions which are subject to an exclusionary reason not to act on certain reasons. Moreover we also saw that the standards on which primary organs ought to act even when they are overridden are the rules of the system under which they operate and that they ought to exclude standards which are not part of the system. The conclusion which emerges from these deliberations is that an institutionalized system consists of a set of rules some of which institute primary organs and all of which the primary organs are bound to act on to the exclusion of all other conflicting reasons.[8]

Let us again use the law as our paradigmatic case. If a man is legally required to do A in C then the courts are bound to hold that he failed to do what he ought to have done if he fails to do A in C. They will refuse to listen to arguments to the effect that failing to do A in C is really what he ought to have done since there were extra-legal reasons which override the reason that the legal requirement provides. Many may feel inclined to modify this statement to the effect that the courts hold the man to have done what *in law* he should have done. They judge him from the legal point of view only and pass no judgement on what he ought to have done all things considered. This is one way of making the same point but it may mislead because of the looseness of 'a point of view'.

When we say of John that he always judges moral questions from the Christian point of view we imply that he does not believe in the validity of other reasons. The Christian point of view includes all the reasons relevant to the judgement of moral issues in the validity of which he believes, and that is why he judges moral questions from this point of view. Here we refer to his point of view as a way of identifying the nature of the reasons in whose validity he believes. But the judges who judge a man from the legal point of view do not necessarily deny the validity of other reasons which bear on his action. They may well believe that there are other reasons which, all things considered, justify his action. Yet they may condemn it because theirs is a judgment from the legal point of view only. In a way this use of 'point of view' is indicative of a partial, incomplete judgement. It is somewhat like a Minister of Transport saying, 'From the economic point of view we should close down many rural railway lines but since they serve an important social function the government ought to provide subsidies to keep them open.' Here when judging what ought to be done from a certain point of view one does not deny the existence of other valid reasons. In this usage a judgement from a point of view is merely a partial judgement of what ought to be done. Judges rendering judgment from a legal point of view do not deny that there are other valid reasons applicable to the situation and, therefore, can be regarded as issuing a partial judgment of what ought to be done. However, there is a big difference between the Minister of Transport in our example and the judge. The Minister has formed a partial judgement from the economic point of view but his action is based on his total assessment of the situation. He cannot admit that his judgement is incomplete, that it disregards other valid reasons, and at the same time act on this partial judgement. The judge, on the other hand, both regards his judgment as based on a partial assessment of the valid reasons and as justifying action. This means that he regards himself as justified in acting on some reasons to the exclusion of others. Hence, though it is true that judgment from the legal point of view is a partial and incomplete judgement it serves as a basis for action because this point of view includes an exclusionary reason requiring one not to act on reasons which do not belong to it.

The courts, as we saw, judge individuals on the basis of legal rules excluding all other conflicting reasons.* They therefore must judge individuals as if they should take the legal requirements as exclusionary reasons. The courts are in effect bound to regard individuals as acting in accordance with legal standards to the exclusion of all other reasons. Since, as was argued above, the rules of the system which apply to ordinary individuals are identical with the rules by which the primary organs ought to judge individuals it follows that all the legal rules are both first-order and exclusionary reasons.

The last point requires a more precise formulation. We ought to distinguish between the different kinds of legal rules as follows:

(1)   Every legal rule requiring the performance of an action (or its omission) is a reason for the performance (or omission) of that act and also an exclusionary reason for not acting on conflicting reasons which are not themselves either legal norms or legally recognized reasons.

(2)   Every permissive legal rule is also an exclusionary permission, that is, it is a permission to perform the norm act and a second-order permission not to act on reasons for not performing the norm act which are not themselves legal norms or legally recognized reasons.

(3)   Every legal power-conferring rule is related to legal mandatory or permissive norms in the way described in section 3.2.

An analogous analysis applies to the rules of other institutionalized

---

* Though one should always remember that the exclusion is not total in scope. Sometimes judges have discretion to overrule.

systems. This argument is designed to show that a normative system which includes both norms guiding ordinary individuals and norms setting up institutions for solving disputes arising from the application of such norms, that is a system based on primary organs, is necessarily an exclusionary system. Its norms exclude the application of reasons, standards and norms which do not belong to the system or are not recognized by it. The legal point of view and the point of view of any other institutionalized system is an exclusionary point of view. Legal norms may conflict and in deciding what, according to law, ought to be done one may have to balance different conflicting legal considerations, but law is an exclusionary system and it excludes the application of extra-legal reasons.

Exclusionary reasons are involved in the analysis of institutionalized systems in yet another way. We saw that applicative determinations of primary organs are binding even if wrong. This means that an authoritative determination of a primary organ to the effect that x has a duty to perform a certain action is an exclusionary reason for x to perform that action. That a primary organ has so decreed is a reason on which x should act regardless of what conflicting reasons apply to the case. The special feature of the applicative determinations of primary organs is that they exclude not only all reasons from outside the system but exclude also the conflicting rules of the system itself—that much is implied by saying that authoritative applicative determinations are binding even if wrong. Suppose that by the laws of England x ought to forbear from doing A. Suppose further that an English court mistakenly determines that x ought to do A. Here we have two conflicting legal evaluations of what x ought to do. Of course, the decisive evaluation is that based on the court's decision— but that means that the court's decision is an exclusionary reason for x to disregard all conflicting laws. The court's decision has not changed those laws, they are still there unchanged. A mistaken decision by a court should not be confused with an exception created by legislation. They may both have the same practical consequences (for example, that a man shall be liable to be jailed) but these consequences are achieved through different normative routes since a legislated exception cancels the original reason x had by modifying the law which was that reason. A mistaken judicial decision does not modify the law. To suppose that it does is to claim that it rectifies itself automatically, as it were, so that if the decision fails to conform to the law the law is made to conform to the decision. A mistaken judicial decision can achieve the same practical consequences as a legislated exception because it is an exclusionary reason excluding action on conflicting laws.

Institutionalized systems consist of norms surrounded by a parameter of exclusionary reasons excluding the application of all reasons other than norms of the system and at their core are authoritative applicative determinations excluding all other reasons including other norms of the system.

Rules of recognition

In one of the most important contributions to our understanding of institutionalized systems H. L. A. Hart has advanced his doctrine of the rule of recognition as a solution to many of the problems which have long bedevilled all attempts to explain such normative systems. His doctrine has been extensively discussed in a number of articles and books and it is not my intention to undertake a thorough examination of it.[9] It may, however, be of interest to compare the arguments presented above with the doctrine of the rule of recognition. In discussing Hart's doctrine I shall consider its applicability to institutionalized systems in general. Hart himself applies it only to the law and regards it as one of the distinctive features of law. But his arguments when valid apply to other institutionalized systems as well and when they fail they fail with respect to all such systems.

According to Hart:

(1) A rule of recognition is a rule requiring officials to apply rules identified by criteria of validity included in it.
(2) Every legal system has at least one rule of recognition.
(3) No legal system has more than one rule of recognition.
(4) Every rule of recognition is accepted and practised by the officials of the system to which it belongs.
(5) But the officials need not approve of it as a morally good or justified rule.
(6) A legal system consists of its rule of recognition and all the rules identified by it.

The considerations advanced in this section support all these theses except for (3) and (6) which have to be modified or abandoned. The first proposition is acceptable as a definition of a rule of recognition. There is just one comment which need be made: one should not confuse rules of recognition with second-order reasons to act on a reason. The rules which rules of recognition require officials to apply are not confined to rules addressed to those very same officials. They apply to such rules but also to many other rules addressed to ordinary individuals (directing them to pay their taxes, not to assault other individuals, to keep their contracts, etc.) as well as rules granting powers and permissions to individuals. A rule of recognition is not a second-order reason requiring the officials to regard some other rules as their norm subjects should. It requires the officials to treat these rules as valid when using their powers to issue authoritative applicative determinations, for example, not to pay taxes as if the tax law applies to them but to declare that x, who is subject to the law, ought to pay the tax or that he has failed to pay the tax owed, etc.

The second proposition is clearly true. It is a direct consequence of the fact that institutionalized systems have primary organs with power to settle disputes concerning the application of their norms. This entails that such systems contain norms addressed to the primary organs requiring them to apply certain norms—and these are rules of recognition. There is no reason, on the other hand, to assume that a legal system can contain only one rule of recognition. The unity of the system does not depend on its containing only one rule of recognition. The unity of the system depends on the fact that it contains only rules which certain primary organs are bound to apply. The primary organs which are to be regarded as belonging to one system are those which mutually recognize the authoritativeness of their determinations. Some remarks in *The Concept of Law* suggest that Hart regards it as essential that the different criteria of validity will be ranked to prevent the possibility of conflicts between equally valid rules. But there is no reason to believe that valid norms belonging to one system cannot conflict (cf. p. 145).[10] We should, therefore, conclude that, though every legal system must contain at least one rule of recognition, it may contain more than one.

Must rules of recognition be customary rules practised by the officials of the system? The answer is obviously yes if the system under consideration is in force, for it is part of the test for a system's being in force that primary organs apply its rules, which entails that if it is in force then its primary organs practise and follow its rules of recognition.

That the primary organs follow and apply the rules of recognition does not entail that they hold them to be morally justified. This thesis of Hart's has been so often overlooked or misinterpreted that one cannot repeat it often enough. It is normal to find that some at least of the subjects of an institutionalized system hold it to be morally

justified. It is even more common to find that many of its officials
share this view. But it is of great importance to remember that these
facts though common and widespread are not logically necessary.
Moreover, it is not only logically possible but also not uncommon for
an official of the system to follow its rules of recognition without
regarding them as morally justified. In the first place, that a rule is
followed by a person requires only that he holds it to be valid, i.e.,
believes that the norm subjects are justified in following it—justified,
perhaps, only because it already exists and is practised and despite
the fact that it should not have been made and that it should even
now be changed. Moreover, the official may follow the rule either
without having any beliefs about why he is justified in doing so, or
for prudential reasons (his best way of securing a comfortable life or
of avoiding social embarrassment, etc.), or even for moral reasons
which are based on his moral rejection of the system. An anarchist,
for example, may become a judge on the ground that if he follows
the law most of the time he will be able to disobey it on the few but
important occasions when to do so will tend most to undermine it.
Another may become a judge because he holds that he is justified in
applying the law of which he disapproves when he is bound to do so
if he makes good use of the powers judges have to make new laws
and change existing laws on occasion.

Finally, though it is true that legal systems contain all the rules of
recognition which apply to their primary organs and all the rules
which these require the primary organs to apply, they may contain
other rules as well. Basically (and subject to the modification introduced in the next section) an institutionalized system consists of the
norms its primary organs are bound to apply. These include, first, all
the norms addressed to them and, secondly, all the rules addressed
to ordinary individuals which the primary organs are required to
apply by norms addressed to them. The second class of norms consists of the norms identified by the rules of recognition of the system.
The first class includes rules of recognition but may include other
norms as well. There is no reason why an institutionalized system
should not include rules addressed to its officials even though they
are neither rules of recognition nor rules identified by the rules of
recognition. The only limitation is that if the system in question is in
force then those rules must not only be addressed to the primary
organs, they must also be followed by them.

5 Legal systems

Legal philosophy is nothing but practical philosophy applied to one social institution. Most of the discussion in the preceding chapters applies equally to the law and to other norms and normative systems; this made it possible to use legal examples to illustrate aspects of norms and normative systems which are not specifically legal. In examining legal systems as such we will still often be dealing with problems of wider application. The aim of the present section is to point to the unique features of law. But the other parts of this chapter, dealing as they do with the normativity of law and with normative statements, raise problems which are by no means confined to legal philosophy.

In the preceding discussion we treated legal systems as typical examples of institutionalized systems. Consequently, the discussion has done a lot to explain the nature of legal systems. However, all the features which have so far been mentioned are not unique to legal systems but are shared by other institutionalized systems. The present section will show in what respects legal systems differ from other institutionalized systems. These features also account for the fact that legal systems are the most important of all institutionalized systems and this is so as a matter of logic. It is a direct result of the defining features of law.

Institutionalized systems in general are characterized primarily by their structural properties. They consist of norms setting up primary organs and all the norms which these institutions are bound, by norms they practise, to apply. Legal systems differ from other institutionalized systems primarily by their relations to other institutionalized systems in force in the same society. These relations can be best illuminated by attending to the spheres of human activity which all legal systems regulate or claim authority to regulate.

What does it mean for a normative system to regulate a certain sphere of behaviour? Every norm regulates that behaviour which is its norm action, that is the behaviour which the norm either requires or permits or which it turns into the exercise of a power. A normative system regulates all the acts regulated by its norms. This means that a normative system regulates all the acts permitted by norms of the system which grant exclusionary permissions. But a system does not regulate acts which are merely weakly permitted by it, that is acts permitted merely because of the absence of a norm requiring their omission. A normative system claims authority to regulate all those acts which it regulates and which can be regulated by norms which can be enacted directly or indirectly by the exercise of powers recognized by norms of the system.

The attempt to characterize legal systems by the spheres of activity which they regulate or claim authority to regulate cannot be a very precise one. The general traits which mark a system as a legal one are several and each of them admits, in principle, of various degrees. In typical instances of legal systems all these traits are manifested to a very high degree. But it is possible to find systems in which all or some are present only to a lesser degree or in which one or two are absent altogether. It would be arbitrary and pointless to try and fix a precise borderline between normative systems which are legal systems and those which are not. When faced with borderline cases it is best to admit their problematic credentials, to enumerate their similarities and dissimilarities to the typical cases, and leave it at that.*

Three features characterize legal systems.

Legal systems are comprehensive

By this I mean that they claim authority to regulate any type of behaviour. In this they differ from most other institutionalized systems. These normally institute and govern the activities of organizations which are tied to some purpose or other. Sport associations, commercial companies, cultural organizations or political parties are all established in order to achieve certain limited goals and each claims authority over behaviour relevant to that goal only. Not so legal systems. They do not acknowledge any limitation of the spheres of behaviour which they claim authority to regulate. If legal systems

---

* International law is a borderline case of a different sort. It meets the conditions laid down in this section but there are doubts whether it can be regarded as an institutionalized system.

are established for a definite purpose it is a purpose which does not entail a limitation over their claimed scope of competence.

We should be careful to see precisely the nature of this feature of comprehensiveness. It does not entail that legal systems *have* and other systems do not have authority to regulate every kind of behaviour. All it says is that legal systems *claim* such an authority whereas other systems do not claim it. Furthermore, legal systems do not necessarily *regulate* all forms of behaviour. All that this test means is that they *claim authority* to regulate all forms of behaviour, that is, that they either contain norms which regulate it or norms conferring powers to enact norms which if enacted would regulate it.

The authority which all legal systems claim is authority to regulate any form of behaviour of a certain community. They need not claim authority to regulate the behaviour of everybody. It should also be remembered that an action is regulated by a norm even if it is merely permitted by it. Furthermore, the test requires that every legal system claims authority to regulate behaviour in some way but not necessarily in every way. Therefore, the test is satisfied by those legal systems which contain, for example, liberties granted by constitutional provisions which cannot be changed by any legal means. Such systems may not claim authority to regulate the permitted behaviour in any other way but they regulate it in one way by permitting it.

Finally, it should be remembered that this test sets at most a necessary condition and not a sufficient condition for a system to be a legal system. We should not be surprised, therefore, to find that some systems which are not legal systems meet this condition, though there are probably few such cases. The laws of various churches qualify by this test, but then many of these meet the other conditions as well and are ordinary legal systems. If there are religious normative systems which meet this test but not the others, they would be borderline cases.

Legal systems claim to be supreme

This condition is entailed by the previous one and is merely an elaboration of one aspect of it. The condition means that every legal system claims authority to regulate the setting up and application of other institutionalized systems by its subject-community. In other words it claims authority to prohibit, permit or impose conditions on the institution and operation of all the normative organizations to which members of its subject-community belong.

Once again this condition is a weak one in allowing for the possibility that a system claims only authority to permit the functioning of some such organizations. It seems to me, however, that this does not deprive this condition of its importance since claimed authority to grant exclusionary permission by a norm is a most significant feature of a normative system and is not to be compared with the mere existence of a weak permission because the system does not regulate the behaviour concerned and does not claim authority to regulate it.

Are legal systems necessarily incompatible? It is evident that two legal systems can co-exist, can both be practised by one community. If they do not contain too many conflicting norms it is possible for the population to observe both systems and the institutions set by them could all function. This would in most cases be an undesirable and an unstable situation but it can exist and it need not always be undesirable or unstable. But in asking whether two legal systems can be compatible I am not asking whether they can co-exist as a matter of fact but rather whether they can co-exist as a matter of law. Can one legal system acknowledge that another legal system applies by right to the same community or must one legal system deny the right of others to apply to the same population? Of course, almost every legal system permits some normative systems to apply to its subject-community, but perhaps it does not permit this if the other system is also a legal system?

There is no doubt that many legal systems are incompatible with each other, but there is no reason for assuming that this is necessarily true of all legal systems. Most legal systems are at least partly compatible; they recognize, for example, the extra-territorial validity of some norms of other systems. Cases of relatively stable and mutually recognized co-existence of secular and religious laws in various countries provide examples of different degrees of compatibility. All legal systems, however, are potentially incompatible at least to a certain extent. Since all legal systems claim to be supreme with respect to their subject-community, none can acknowledge any claim to supremacy over the same community which may be made by another legal system.

Legal systems are open systems

A normative system is an open system to the extent that it contains norms the purpose of which is to give binding force within the system to norms which do not belong to it. The more 'alien' norms are 'adopted' by the system the more open it is. It is characteristic of legal systems that they maintain and support other forms of social grouping. Legal systems achieve this by upholding and enforcing contracts, agreements, rules and customs of individuals and associations, and by enforcing through their rules of conflict of laws the laws of other countries, and so on.

Norms which are recognized for such reasons are not normally regarded as part of the legal system which gives them its sanction. They are, however, recognized and made binding in such systems by norms which require the courts to act on and enforce these norms. Therefore, the criterion of membership in an institutionalized system must be modified to exclude these norms. A test is needed which will identify as belonging to a system all the norms which its norm-applying institutions are bound to apply (by norms which they practise) except for those norms which are merely 'adopted'. But how are we to characterize the adopted norms? How are we to define with greater precision the character of an open system?

Many have tried to find the distinguishing mark in the manner or technique of the adoption. It seems to me that this is a blind alley. These distinctions inevitably turn on formal and technical differences irrelevant to the basis of the distinction, and lead to counter-intuitive results. We must rely on the reasons for recognizing these norms as binding, for our purpose is to distinguish between norms which are recognized because they are part of the law and those which are recognized because of the law's function to support other social arrangements and groups.

Norms are 'adopted' by a system because it is an open system if, and only if, they fulfil one of two tests. The first test requires that they belong to another normative system which is practised by its norm subjects and be recognized as long as they remain in force in such a system as applying to the same norm subjects. In this case they must be recognized because the system intends to respect the way that the community regulates its activities, regardless of whether the same regulation would have been otherwise adopted. The alternative test requires that they be norms which were made by or with the consent of their norm subjects by the use of powers conferred by the system in order to enable individuals to arrange their own affairs as they desire. The first half of the test applies to norms recognized by the rules of conflict of laws, etc. The second part of the test applies to contracts, the regulations of commerical companies, and the like.

Norms which meet these requirements are recognized by a system but are not part of it. If a system recognizes such norms it is an open system and, as I said, all legal systems are open systems.* It is part of their function to sustain and encourage various other norms and organizations.

The importance of law

I have relied on our general knowledge of the law and human society in claiming that legal systems are institutionalized systems characterized by the combination of these three conditions. If my claim is right it is easy to see that they provide the beginning of an explanation of the importance of law. There can be human societies which are not governed by law at all. But if a society is subjected to a legal system then that system is the most important institutionalized system to which it is subjected. The law provides the general framework within which social life takes place. It is a system for guiding behaviour and for settling disputes which claims supreme authority to interfere with any kind of activity. It also regularly either supports or restricts the creation and practice of other norms in the society. By making these claims the law claims to provide the general framework for the conduct of all aspects of social life and sets itself as the supreme guardian of society.

5.2 LAW AND FORCE

The problem of the normativity of law

So far we have freely referred to laws as norms. This entails that they are reasons for action. Does that assumption require justification? Not necessarily. The use of so many normative terms such as 'rules', 'duties', 'obligations', 'rights' or 'powers' to describe both laws and legal situations is ample justification for regarding legal rules as norms. The only possible doubt might be that legal rules may not be exclusionary reasons. The arguments provided in section 4.3 were meant to establish that they are. But if the use of normative language in describing the law is justification enough for the assumption that legal rules (like other rules) are norms, it does little to explain how it is that they are norms and what precisely is meant by saying so. The fact that normative language is used to describe the law helped to

---

* Saying that all legal systems are open systems is not to commend them. They may 'adopt' the wrong norms and refuse to adopt those that should be 'adopted'.

perpetuate two of the great fallacies of the philosophy of law. One is the fallacious belief that laws are of necessity moral reasons* (or that they are morally justified or that there are always moral reasons to obey each one of them) and the other is the equally ill-founded belief that a legal system can exist only if the bulk of its subject community believe in its moral validity. The second fallacy was discussed in the previous chapter. The first will be examined below. Thus it is the main purpose of the rest of this chapter to explain what precisely is meant by saying that legal rules are norms (i.e. reasons for action), and what justifies the use of normative terms to describe the law. Let us preface the inquiry by mentioning two or three possible solutions which cannot be regarded as adequate to our probem.

It is obviously often the case that people have reason to perform actions which are in fact required by law. This in itself does not explain how *all* laws can be said to be reasons. But suppose it can be shown that one always has reason to perform every action which is in fact required by law. That would still fall short of solving our problem. We will also want to know whether it is the fact that those actions are required by law which is held to be the reason for performing them. Similarly we will not be content to learn that individuals ought to follow rules which are also legal rules. We would like to know whether they ought to follow them because they are legal rules. It is not merely the validity of the norms which has to be established but their systemic validity. We want to know what difference the fact that a norm belongs to a legal system in force in a certain country makes to our practical reasoning. We cannot be satisfied with an answer which shows that laws coincide with systems of valid norms.

A sanction-based solution

Consider the case of Julie. She is required by law to pay a certain sum in income tax. Moreover, her employer will sack her if she does not do so, and her ailing father will be greatly distressed to learn that she indulges in tax dodging. The fact that there is a law which requires her to pay is a reason for her to pay. To be more precise, the fact that there is such a law is part of at least two complete reasons. Her employer's reaction to law-breaking behaviour and her desire to keep her job, together with the existence of the income tax law, are one

* To simplify the argument I shall refer directly only to mandatory norms. The same arguments apply, *mutatis mutandis*, to other norms.

complete reason for obeying; this might be called a prudential reason. The distress which she causes to her ailing father, together with some suitable value concerning the prevention of suffering and the existence of the law, are another complete reason for Julie to pay her tax; this could be called a moral reason.

In Julie's case the law is a real (part of the) reason. But for the law she would not have a reason to pay the money to the tax authority. Yet we rightly feel that these facts and others like them are not enough to explain the use of normative language in describing the law. One reason why such facts cannot provide the solution to our problem is that there is no guarantee that they are always present. Since we are ready to refer to a legal rule as a norm we must explain that by pointing to features present in all the situations to which that rule applies. The explanation cannot depend on the fact that one norm subject happens to have an ailing father with certain views.

Many legal theorists, following some such line of reasoning, concluded that the answer to the problem of the normativity of the law must lie in the fact that the law stipulates that sanctions be applied against those who violate the law. Others were moved by similar considerations to endorse the view that it is the sanctioning of the systematic use of force against law-breakers which lies at the core of the normativity of law. What can be said of these explanations? They certainly do not lack plausibility. By definition sanctions and the use of force against one are things which people normally prefer to avoid. Hence if sanctions or force are to be applied against law-breakers then for normal people in normal circumstances this would be a reason for obeying the law. But are law-breakers always subjected to sanctions or to the use of force? Or (for only this is to our point) are law-breakers always subjected to sanctions or force because they are law-breakers?

It is obviously not the case that all violations of law are met by sanctions or by the use of force. But it is true that some weaker generalization applies. I shall call it the motivational generalization. It goes something like this: it is normally, or usually or frequently, the case that violations of law are the occasion for the imposition of sanctions or the use of force against their perpetrators. The precise force of the generalization is not important but it is important to see why such generalizations are true. It is based on two assumptions. First, the law provides for sanctions or the use of force against all violations of law. Secondly, the law is by and large efficacious and its sanctions are generally applied when deserved.

Taken together these assumptions, if true, justify the motivational generalization. They establish that the mere fact that a violation of law has occurred is a reason for believing that a sanction is likely to be applied or force used against the offender. Of course, further information may falsify the conclusion. When the precise circumstances of a crime are established it may emerge that the criminal is likely to die before the police will reach him, or that his crime will never be detected, or that by the time it will be he will have left the country for good, or that his security has been bought by bribing the police, and so on and so forth. Like all probabilistic generalizations the strength of this one depends on its evidential basis. The motivational generalization has a very narrow evidential basis; it depends only on knowledge that an act is a violation of law.

Are the assumptions in fact true? We may, perhaps, accept the second on the ground that the whole argument is meant to apply to legal systems which are in force in a certain community and legal systems are in force only if they are by and large efficacious. The more interesting assumption is the first. Is it true that a sanction is stipulated for every violation of a legal duty? Is it true that the law directs that force be used against all law-breakers? Here we must distinguish between the use of force and sanctions. It is sometimes assumed that the two are identical but they clearly are not. Some sanctions, like capital punishment or whipping, consist in the use of force against a person. But most sanctions consist in the withdrawal of rights or the imposition of duties (for example, duty to pay fines and compensation or duty not to leave a certain area or building). Nor is the use of force according to law confined to its use as a sanction. In fact it is rarely used as a sanction. Most often the use of force is provided for as an enforcement measure to ensure compliance with ordinary law (for example, compliance with building regulations or public health requirements which involve the destruction of property and the forcible confinement of animals and humans) as well as compliance with sanction-imposing orders (for example, seizing property when a fine is not paid or using force to prevent an escape from prison).

A sanctionless legal system

Is every law supported by another providing for sanctions or the use of force against law-breakers?[1] Is it necessary that this be so? It cannot be denied that all known legal systems are based on widespread

resort to sanctions and that all of them rely ultimately on the use
of force. The question is whether something more precise can be said
about the extent to which legal systems resort to sanctions and the
use of force. It is dangerous to generalize over all known legal
systems but it seems to me that it can be safely said that all regulate
the use of force, i.e. prohibit it in certain cases and permit or require
it in others. Furthermore, though they differ very much in the way
they regulate the use of force they have at least two features in
common. First, all known legal systems prohibit the use of force
against the officials of the system when those are engaged in their
official duties. Secondly, they all authorize the use of force to enforce
compliance with sanctions.

These generalizations, modest as they are, may suggest that if the
law is based on sanctions then at one remove it is based on the use of
force, for the enforcement of sanctions is guaranteed by officials who
are authorized to use force to enforce these sanctions and who may
not be resisted by the use of force. Can one make a similar generalization about the law's use of sanctions? Perhaps there is a third feature: all known legal systems provide for sanctions for intentional
violation of all legal rules *addressed to ordinary individuals*. This
formulation is designed to be compatible with the fact that sometimes the application of a sanction against an individual may be
blocked by his personal immunity (as a foreign diplomat or a member of the legislature, for example) or by a statute of limitation, or
the like. These 'exceptions' do not affect the validity of the explanations of normativity we are considering.

Do these three generalizations establish the truth of the assumption
they were invoked to prove? It seems to me that they do not. The
assumption was that the law provides for sanctions or the use of
force against all violations of law. This is meant to be a necessary
truth. Our three generalizations allow for the existence of mandatory
norms addressed to *officials* which are not backed by sanctions, but
more important still they are empirical generalizations true of known
legal systems. They do not represent a logical feature of our concept
of law. The first of these points hardly needs elaboration. We all know
that courts, presidents and other high-ranking officials are subject to
duties which, so far as the law goes, they can break with impunity.

The second point is more difficult. Is it possible for there to be a
legal system in force which does not provide for sanctions or which
does not authorize their enforcement by force? The answer seems to
be that it is humanly impossible but logically possible. It is humanly

impossible because for human beings as they are the support of sanctions, to be enforced by force if necessary, is required to assure a reasonable degree of conformity to law and prevent its complete breakdown. And yet we can imagine other rational beings who may be subject to law, who have, and who would acknowledge that they have, more than enough reasons to obey the law regardless of sanctions. Perhaps even human beings may be transformed to become such creatures. It is reasonable to suppose that in such a society the legislator would not bother to enact sanctions since they would be unnecessary and superfluous. If such a normative system has all the features of a legal system described above then it would be recognized as one by all despite its lack of sanctions.

It is doubtless controversial to claim that resort to sanctions, though universal and likely to remain so (so long as human nature is not transformed), is not a feature which forms part of our concept of law. The controversy is both old and complex. Let me add only three comments in defence of my view.

(1) Even a society of angels may have a need for legislative authorities to ensure co-ordination. Angels may be in agreement about both their values and the best policies for implementing them. But the sort of society described above does not presuppose such a measure of agreement. Its members may pursue many different and conflicting goals and they may share our difficulties in settling disputes and resolving conflicts of interests by mutual agreement. They differ from us only in having universal and deep-rooted respect towards their legal institutions and in lacking all desire to disobey their rulings. They have, therefore, all the reasons that we have for having legislative authorities and an executive.

(2) It might be thought that our imaginary society would have no use for courts and therefore no legal system. But this is a mistake. It would require courts for at least two reasons. In the first place there would be many factual disagreements and disputes about the interpretation of legal transactions and their legal effects. In the second place there would be many at least partly unregulated disputes, i.e. those whose solution is not uniquely determined by existing law but requires the exercise of discretion by the courts. When a dispute is entirely unregulated then its solution does not require a primary organ. But most such disputes are only partly unregulated. The law rules out certain solutions but does not decide between some other possible solutions. To settle such disputes one needs a court which is

a primary organ and also has discretion. For these reasons the imagined community would have more than enough reasons for having a proper legal system with primary organs. We should not think of the imagined society as a community of self-denying saints. Its members pursue their self-interest when they think they are right to do so, and they may be wrong.

(3)   Since accidental damage might occur in our community and since damage may result from people acting wrongly because they misapprehend the facts or misinterpret the law, our society would have laws providing for remedial rights and duties. People would have to pay compensation and damages, for example. Does not that establish that the law provides for sanctions? Even if these are sanctions it would still be true that our society would not have criminal sanctions (though it would have criminal laws), nor authorize the use of force to enforce sanctions; there would be no need for such measures. But are the civil remedies provided for in our imaginary legal system sanctions? They are not designed to deter people from breaking the law (which is one purpose of civil remedies in all existing legal systems) and they are made with the knowledge that they will be applied only to people who fail to perform their duty through accident or ignorance, and who will be ready to comply with their remedial duties once they are convinced that these apply to them. Is a provision in a rent agreement by which the tenant undertakes to make good damage caused by him a sanction-stipulating provision? Should we not deny that the remedial duties in our imaginary legal system are sanctions?

This is a complex and difficult problem which we need not resolve here. For it may well be argued that to explain the normativity of law it does not matter whether a sanctionless legal system is possible. It is true that there will have to be some other explanation of the normativity of the laws of a sanctionless legal system. Sanction- or force-oriented explanations will not apply to such a system but this does not mean that they are not true of all known legal systems of which the three generalizations are true. One may be reluctant to believe that the explanation of the normativity of law varies from one legal system to another. But the three generalizations can be said to be true not only of all known legal systems but of all which are possible in human society, given that human nature is what it is. One may accept an explanation of the normativity of law which applies to all humanly possible legal systems and admit the necessity for a different explanation of the normativity of law in radically different circumstances.

So the possibility of a sanctionless law does not prevent the three generalizations providing the basis for a sanction- or force-oriented explanation of the normativity of human law. True there is still the problem of the many sanctionless norms addressed to officials. Perhaps a solution can be found which could be regarded as no more than a minor modification of a sanction-oriented explanation. Nevertheless, the sanction-oriented explanations must ultimately fail, for a completely different reason.

Sanctions as auxiliary reasons

The fact that a law of a system in force provides for a sanction is no doubt a reason for action, but it is a reason of the wrong kind.* A sanction-backed norm is at best only an auxiliary partial reason. The complete reason must include the agent's desire to avoid the sanction or the fact that it is against his interests for it to be applied to him. This is the operative reason: it is because the agent wants to avoid the sanction that he has reason to take notice of the law. The law itself identifies the action which will result in the infliction of the sanction and establishes the sanction, thus determining for which action the operative reason is a reason.

The fact that so far as sanctions go the law is merely an auxiliary reason is not intended to belittle the importance of legal sanctions. They are a most important way of securing social co-ordination and of providing people with reasons for conforming to law. But the fact that laws are auxiliary reasons cannot explain how it is that some laws are mandatory norms. For mandatory norms are complete operative reasons as was established in section 2.3 above. Moreover if some laws are mandatory norms then they are exclusionary reasons as well as first-order reasons. But the fact that a law is backed by a sanction is never an exclusionary reason. It is a simple (auxiliary) first-order reason. The inevitable conclusion is that, despite the undoubted importance of sanctions and the use of force to enforce

* Some may want to deny that it is a reason for action at all. They may say that it is merely a reason to believe that if the law should be broken a sanction would be applied. Only this fact is a reason for action. But this temptation ought to be resisted. When a fact A is evidence for the occurrence of fact B because it is the cause or the reason for the occurrence of B, and if B is a reason for an action, then we often rightly regard A as a reason for the same action.

them in all human legal systems, the sanction-directed attempt to explain the normativity of the law leads to a dead end. It explains one way in which laws are reasons. But it fails to explain in what way they are norms.

5.3 LAW AND MORALITY

The claim

The explanation of the uniqueness of law (in section 5.1) was also an explanation of its importance. Law is not necessary for the existence of human society. We know of various forms of social organization which are not based on the existence of a legal system. But in those societies which have law it is the most important institutionalized system in the society. The law provides the general normative framework within which organized social activity takes place. Given the importance of law there is little surprise that the problem of the relation of law and morals has always been regarded as one of the central concerns of legal theory. Many aspects of this problem have been considered by legal theorists. Many of them turn not on the relation of law and morality as such but on the relation of law and the moral views which are accepted and practised by the society in which the law is in force. Thus people have wondered about the impact of popular morality on the development of law and the impact of law on the development of popular morality. They have asked whether it is right that the law should enforce accepted moral beliefs as such. They have speculated on whether it is a necessary truth that a legal system can be in force in a certain society only if the bulk of the members of that society believe in its moral validity.

Much attention has also been focused on the relation between law and morality proper. At the centre of these deliberations stands one major problem: is there a necessary relation between law and morality? Is it a necessary truth that law, every law, has moral worth? Those philosophers who think it a criterion of adequacy for theories of law that they answer these questions in the affirmative are usually called 'natural law theorists'.[2] There are many radically different natural law theories and our examination of them will be neither detailed nor comprehensive. We are interested in them only to the extent that they suggest a solution to the problem of the normativity of law. According to some natural law theories laws are norms because they are morally valid. They can be regarded as valid moral norms. They are, to be sure, derivative moral norms, deriving their validity from ultimate moral norms and values. Nevertheless they can be regarded as morally valid norms and it is this fact which explains why we are entitled to regard laws as norms and to apply normative language to their description.

Natural law theories can be classified by the strength of the claim they stake. In a descending order of strength we can distinguish between the following claims:

(1)   Every single law is on balance morally good and therefore morally valid and ought, morally, to be followed.

(2)   A single law considered on its merits may be morally neutral or even bad and yet there are, always and of necessity, general reasons to obey any law which outweigh or exclude all possible considerations of the wrongness of an individual law or indeed of the wrongness of any number of laws. Such considerations (such as that breaking one law will lead to the breakdown of society or that all law is laid down by legitimate authority) are enough to establish that all laws regardless of their content are morally valid and ought, morally, to be followed.

(3)   Every legal system necessarily contains at least some laws which are morally valid and ought, morally, to be followed.

One can no doubt draw further and subtler distinctions but these will suffice for our present purpose. Only one further comment is called for here. It is not assumed that the moral reasons one has to follow the law (or some laws) are absolute reasons. They may be overridden on occasion by, for example, the need to bring an injured man to hospital, or to prevent the oppression of a minority group. Considerations such as these may justify breaking the law despite the reasons one has for respecting it; the reasons are outweighed by the circumstances. Some natural lawyers thought that the moral validity of law is absolute and nothing could justify breaking it. I will not, however, refer to arguments necessary to establish this view. The criticism to be levelled below against the weaker versions of natural law theories apply, *eo ipso*, to the stronger versions.

The definitional argument

Many people, and not only natural lawyers, believe that the laws of their community are morally valid. But for most the moral validity of the law is contingent on its content or on the nature of the regime which created it. A given Education Act is good and therefore morally valid but there could have been a different Act which would have been bad and morally invalid. The laws of a given government are morally binding because it is a genuinely democratic government, but if the army were to stage a *coup d'état* then its laws would not be morally binding. The natural lawyer on the other hand is committed to the view that the moral validity of law does not depend on contingent fact. He is committed to the view that it is the nature of law as law which is sufficient to establish its moral validity.

It is tempting to think that the best way to explain such a conceptual link between law and morality is to show that it is reflected in one's account of the identifying features of law. One may indeed regard it as an essential part of this approach that law is defined by explicit reference to morality in a way which guarantees its moral worth. This could be called the 'definitional method'. It consists in defining law by a set of properties one or more of which are openly moral properties, for example, that every law is morally valid, or conforms to the precepts of justice or is laid down by a morally legitimate authority. This is not the only possible way of establishing the required conceptual connection, as will be seen below. But first I should like to advance three arguments against the definitional method.

(1)   The definitional approach has to explain away many counter examples. We are all sadly familiar with laws which are racially discriminating, which suppress basic individual liberties such as freedom of speech or of worship. We also know of tyrannical governments pursuing evil goals through the machinery of law. Supporters of the definitional method would argue that though such cases are unfortunately all too frequent they fail to rebut their claim since by definition a bad law is not a law, or at any rate a law of a government without moral authority is not law. This answer is, however, misconceived. All it shows is that the theory is consistent on this issue, not that it is correct. It is precisely because such obvious laws are ruled out as non-laws by the theory that it is incorrect. It fails to explain correctly our ordinary concept of law which does allow for the possibility of laws of this objectionable kind.

(2)   The first objection merely states a fact about our ordinary notion of law. The second objection can be taken as an explanation of this fact. I shall call it the objection to the heterogeneity of law. If all the characteristics a thing may possess are divided into evaluative and non-evaluative then the definitional method differs from other methods of defining law by insisting that law can only be identified as possessing both evaluative and non-evaluative charac-

teristics. All other theorists, including other natural lawyers, identify law on the basis of non-evaluative characteristics only.

There is of course little agreement on what precisely the non-evaluative identifying criteria are, but there is a general understanding what they should be: they should single out those phenomena which form a special sort of social institution, an institution to be found as an important component of many social systems and which differs significantly from other social institutions. It is precisely here that the weakness of the definitional method is to be found. It implies that to be a law it is not enough that the norm belongs to the social institution, it must also meet some moral test. Now, it is clear that the study of social institutions is an important task, regardless of their moral value. Not that we should be oblivious to moral values, but we should recognize that it may be, and indeed it is, the case that the same social institution may sometimes be used for the right ends and sometimes for the wrong ends. The fact that it is sometimes good and sometimes bad need not depend on its character as a social institution. It may depend on other circumstances. If a certain norm functions in precisely the same way as other norms, if its effects on economic or social activities are just as significant as the effects of the other norms, if the attitude to it of the police or the courts is the same, then it should not be denied the status of law simply because it is unjust. To do so would be to misclassify norms in a way which distorts one's view of the social institutions to which they belong.

(3) It is common ground that in principle one can know what the law is. What the law in force is can on occasion be a controversial question, but it is in principle soluble. This entails that the natural lawyer who follows the definitional approach is committed at least to a qualified moral objectivism. He is bound to claim that what is morally right or wrong, good or bad, is capable of being known at least in principle and at least in those areas of morality which may be relevant to the identification of law. All those who reject moral objectivism or who wish to support a more restricted objectivist doctrine (i.e. that only the solution to some moral issues can, in principle, be known, but that other moral issues may also be relevant to the moral validity of law) are bound to reject the definitional approach.

The derivative approach

The objections to the definitional approach are objections in principle: it is based on a misconception of the nature of morality and it distorts the most fundamental feature of legal systems, i.e. that they are normative systems identified by features which indicate their role as a social institution, as a certain mode of social organization. Most of the hostile criticism of natural law theories in recent times has concentrated on these defects. Consequently the impression was formed that all natural law theories are based on the definitional approach. This is a mistake. There can be natural law theories which admit that the law is to be identified as a kind of social institution and which do not presuppose moral objectivism. Such theories do nevertheless insist on a necessary link between law and morality in virtue of which all law, as law, has moral value. Without entering into a detailed inquiry I should like, briefly, first to explain why there is no objection in principle to this kind of approach; secondly, to indicate the nature of the arguments which may be used and the difficulties to be overcome by natural lawyers of this persuasion; thirdly, to argue that even if successful this type of natural law theory cannot explain the normativity of law.

I shall call this approach the derivative approach because it accepts the need for a socially oriented identification of law. Law is primarily a form of social organization and has to be identified as such. Natural lawyers of this persuasion can accept in principle Bentham's or Kelsen's or Hart's characterizations of law. To the extent that they disagree with all or some of these their criticism will not reveal their support of natural law. It will be the sort of criticism which could also be supported by non-natural lawyers. Once the law has been correctly identified as a social institution, contends the supporter of the derivative approach, it can be successfully argued that a normative system of this kind, if it is in force in a human society, has, of necessity, moral worth. In other words the moral properties that all legal systems possess depend on their non-moral properties.

The following seems perfectly sound. If every legal system in force in some society has, in virtue of its identifying features, or in virtue of the conditions which must obtain if it is to be in force, certain moral attributes, then the derivative approach is successful in establishing a necessary link between law and morality. The question is whether the identifying features of legal systems or the conditions necessary for them to be in force entail that such systems always possess some moral worth. One does not have to be a moral objectivist to accept the possibility that they do, since nothing is implied about the 'epistemological status' of moral views. So, for all I know, this approach to natural law may be successful though its success has yet to be demonstrated.

Consider the possible arguments for such a version of natural law. One may argue that the very existence of a legal system, even the worst legal system imaginable, is good (the argument from mere existence) or one may argue that all legal systems must contain some good laws (the argument from content). Let us take arguments from mere existence first. Can one argue, for example, that, since by definition law provides the framework for social life in those societies in which it exists, it must have some moral merit? The argument does not presuppose that but for law there would be no society. There can be societies which are not subject to law. Nor does it presuppose that the choice is between law and anarchy. On most occasions the choice is between one legal system and another, and the other may well be the better of the two. All the argument claims is that in those societies which have a legal system it contributes to the maintenance of the social organization existing in those societies and as such has some moral merit. This is compatible with saying that, since one could at little cost (by a bloodless *coup d'état*, for example) replace the existing legal system with a better one, one should not, on the balance of reasons, obey the law. All that the argument is designed to establish is that one always has a *prima facie* reason to obey the law because where it exists it contributes to the maintenance of the existing social order.

There could be other arguments from mere existence. One can argue that by definition a legal system provides a method for settling disputes through its primary organs and that it provides for general rules guiding the behaviour of individuals—these can be regarded as enshrining certain values. However bad the laws may be, the subjection of human behaviour to the government of rules on the basis of which certain disputes are to be settled is of itself of moral value or ensures the realization of some moral values: a certain conception of justice according to law, for example, can be regarded as a moral value which is inseparable from law.

All such arguments are based on moral assumptions which can be disputed. Is it true that there is some moral value in the existence of every human society, however wicked? Is there a coherent notion of justice according to law which is inseparable from law and the manifestation of which is always of moral value? I do not wish to express any view on these difficult moral problems, for it is clear that even if the arguments are sound they do not solve the problem of the normativity of law. To explain legal norms as morally valid norms it is not enough to show that there is some moral merit in them. It is true that one does not have to show that there are morally conclusive reasons for following the law. But one has to show that the moral merits of the law are greater than its moral shortcomings. If one has overriding reasons not to follow the law these must be extraneous reasons like the occurrence of an emergency (for example, an earthquake or war). They cannot be reasons which will show that the law is not morally valid. All they can show is that it is morally right to disregard it in certain circumstances. Since the aim is to explain that every legal rule is a norm, the arguments have to show that every legal rule is morally valid. The arguments from existence aim to point to pervasive moral attributes. They do not single out one law or one group of laws which all legal systems have and which are of moral value. They prove that the system as a whole is of value. But what are the implications of this to the moral validity of individual legal rules? These will vary with the circumstances and the type of argument involved.

Arguments based on the maintenance of society may establish the moral validity of those basic constitutional laws necessary for the perpetuation of the legal system or other laws the undermining of which will undermine the existence of law or its ability to play its role in maintaining the fabric of society. But there will obviously be many laws (for example, obscure regulations of commercial law or planning law or public health or traffic law) which will be affected little, if at all, by such arguments. Their moral validity cannot be guaranteed in this way. Similarly if law inevitably embodies some values of justice these will be more relevant to some laws than to others. It may be a consideration sufficient to ensure the moral validity of some legal rules, but there will be many others of which this will not be true. It may be that the value of justice embodied in all law confers some value on each law and provides a reason for its validity. But, though the point cannot be definitely established without detailed examination of specific arguments, it seems unlikely that such an argument will suffice to override all the reasons telling against the validity of a law which is, in its content, a very bad law.

Similar difficulties beset arguments from content. Legal systems are identified by their institutionalized character and may have any rules with any content whatsoever. Nevertheless it could be argued that if a legal system is to be in force in any human society for any length of time then it must have certain laws with a certain content. In the previous section I suggested three generalizations concerning the minimum regulation of force and sanctions. It can be argued that legal systems must also include laws regulating property, voluntary obligations and sexual behaviour at least to a degree. The necessity referred to is factual not logical necessity. These are not part of the identifying features of law. They are features which a legal system must have if it is to enjoy enduring existence in human society.

H. L. A. Hart, who did more than anyone to clarify the nature and status of the claim that there are common elements to the content of all legal systems, regards these arguments as explaining whatever truth there is in the natural law approach. This may be true. But if it is, more will have to be established than that there must be in every legal system some laws regulating the use of force, property, voluntary obligations or sex. One would have to show that these areas of conduct have to be regulated in a morally good way. Cannot the use of force or the institution of property be regulated in a morally obnoxious way? Can it not be regulated to support oppressive slavery, for example? But, again, we can suspend judgement on this issue. It is clear that whatever else can be said of arguments from content they cannot explain the normativity of law. The reason is very simple: these arguments are designed to show that all legal systems must contain some just laws. They may be sufficient to establish the validity of these laws. But what of others? Those laws whose violation undermines the very existence of the legal system may derive some force from such arguments. But is it always sufficient to ensure their validity? And what of the many laws violation of which in no way endangers the existence of the system?

Finally, there is another argument which is both simple and decisive and which applies to all versions of natural law theories, definitional and derivative. It is not designed to refute them. It is designed to show that they are incapable of explaining the normativity of law.* We all use normative language in describing the law. We all (a few philosophers excluded) regard it as consisting of rules, i.e. norms, as explained above. Many people who do not accept the natural law view of the necessary morality of law, indeed many who reject it, are happy to apply normative language to the law. This must mean that the explanation of the use of normative terms to describe the law and legal situations cannot depend on the truth of the controversial natural law theories—and it is the explanation of the use of normative language which lies at the heart of the problem of the normativity of law.

* It should be remembered that much of the motivation to endorse natural law theories derives from the belief that they provide the best explanation of the normativity of law.

My point is not that an explanatory theory of the use of normative language in legal contexts must already be accepted by all and sundry. This is obviously false. My argument is that if natural law theories are to explain the use of normative language in such contexts they must show not only that all law is morally valid but also that this is generally known and thus accounts for the application of normative value to the law. Since this assumption is false, natural law cannot explain the normativity of law.

5.4 THE NORMATIVITY OF LAW

The legal point of view

The use of force and sanctions on the one hand and moral considerations on the other may be reasons for people to follow the law, but neither can explain why legal rules are norms. Both natural law theories and sanction-oriented doctrines have one thing in common. Both attempt to explain the normativity of law by showing that laws are valid reasons for action. A third approach to the problem also has a long jurisprudential tradition behind it. According to this approach the key to the problem of the normativity of law is not that laws *are* valid reasons but that people *believe* that they are.

The problem of the normativity of law is the problem of explaining the use of normative language in describing the law or legal situations. One may well argue that the mere fact that legal rules are valid norms can never count as an explanation. The explanation of the common use of normative language must be found in the beliefs (justified or unjustified) of those who use that language. Legal rules may be valid reasons for action or they may not. But this is irrelevant to the explanation of the use of normative language in a legal context.

As will appear below, I believe that belief-based explanations come nearer the truth than validity-based explanations. Yet belief-based explanations are not without their difficulties. One major difficulty had better be mentioned right away, though its examination will have to be postponed to the second half of the section. Belief-based explanations have traditionally been concerned to establish that no legal system can be in force unless some people believe in the validity of its laws. But this line of inquiry seems inadequate in principle. What has to be established, it can be argued, is that those who use normative language to describe the law believe that laws are valid reasons. But everyone can use normative language to describe a legal system. People who live on the other side of the world or who live thousands of years after the period during which the legal system was in force can use normative language to describe the law. It cannot be that the beliefs of all the people who may refer normatively to law are a necessary condition of the law being in force. This, it is argued, shows that even if it is true that a legal system can be in force only if some people believe that its laws are valid reasons, it is irrelevant to the problem of normativity. I shall deal with this objection below. I shall first examine the view that some people must believe that laws are valid reasons for the law to exist and only later examine the way this fact helps explain the normativity of law.

The discussion of the conditions necessary for a legal system to be in force (see section 4.2) showed that it is not necessary that the population at large will follow the law nor, for the reasons advanced there, that they should believe that laws are valid reasons. But, as was argued there, it is necessary that the courts should follow the law. Judges, acting as judges, act on the belief that laws are valid reasons for action. Furthermore, as was argued in section 4.3, they hold laws to be exclusionary reasons in that they disregard all nonlegal reasons except where allowed by law to act on non-legal reasons.

The legal point of view (of system S), we could say, consists of the norms of S and any other reasons on which the norm subjects of S are required by the norms of S to act. The ideal law-abiding citizen is the man who acts from the legal point of view. He does not merely conform to law. He follows legal norms and legally recognized norms as norms and accepts them also as exclusionary reasons for disregarding those conflicting reasons which they exclude.

It is not necessary for a legal system to be in force that its norm subjects are ideal law-abiding citizens or that they should be so (i.e. that legal norms are morally valid). But it is necessary that its judges, when acting as judges, should on the whole be acting according to the legal point of view. This entails also that the courts must regard ordinary citizens as required to be ideal law-abiding citizens and judge them accordingly.

Normative statements

Belief-based explanations usually divide normative statements about the law into two groups. Some are made by people who believe in the validity of the legal point of view; they make such normative statements to assert what valid reasons for action there are. The second group consists of statements about people's beliefs and attitudes to norms.

There is no doubt that statements of both types are often made. It even seems reasonable to regard them as having some logical priority in the following sense: the full richness and variety of normative discourse is reflected in discourse about the law and legal situations. All kinds and manner of normative statements are used and can be used in legal contexts. The employment of all other types of statement presupposes the availability of one or other of two basic types: first, statements of what (valid) reasons or norms there are, and, secondly, statements of the fact that norms are followed or practised or that people act on certain reasons or believe in their validity. Statements of these two types could have been made even if none of the other forms of normative statements were available.

The fact that these types of statements are primary indicates that belief-based explanations are the right kind of explanation. But the assumption that they are the only kind of normative statement possible leads to gross distortion. Without aiming at completeness either of classification or of explanation of normative statements I should like to draw attention to one further kind of statement which is of great importance to our understanding of discourse about the law as well as normative discourse in other contexts.[3]

'A ought to pay £80 income tax', 'One is not allowed to park for more than two hours within the zone'—such sentences in their primary use are uttered to state what reasons for action people have. They make it clear that the reasons are 'legal': income tax and zones are the creatures of law. But to say that such reasons are legal is like saying that economic reasons forced one to cancel the trip to Bermuda: such qualifying phrases qualify and define the nature of the facts which are reasons. They do not entail anything concerning their force as reasons. 'The legal system in the Ottoman Empire allowed males to marry more than one wife.' Such sentences are standardly used not to state reasons but to assert what legal systems are or were in force or what laws systems which are or were in force contain.

The difficulty is that sentences like 'A ought to pay £80 income tax' are often used not to state what action A has reason to perform but simply to state what his legal situation is. To make clear that that is what is stated one often uses sentences such as 'A is required by law to . . .', 'According to law he ought to . . .', 'Legally speaking you ought to . . .', and the like. But it should be noted that sentences of both kinds can be used to make statements of the kind we are concerned with, i.e. those stating what the legal situation is. How can such statements be analysed? A detailed analysis is impossible here. But some attempts at an explanation should be rejected and the general direction of an analysis can be suggested.

The analyses to be rejected assimilate the statements under consideration into one or the other of the basic types of statement. One such explanation claims that to say:

(1) According to law A ought to ϕ

is an elliptical form of saying:

(2) If A wants to be law-abiding he ought to ϕ.

This explanation must be rejected even by those who favour this line of analysis. The explanation attempts to reduce statements 'according to law' and the like to statements of what (valid) reasons there are. It interprets the qualification 'according to law' and similar qualifications as indicating that the sentence is used elliptically to assert a conditional. Just as a conditional whose consequent is an ought-sentence is not an assertion of a reason so, and in the same way, a statement of what ought to be done according to law is not a statement of what there is reason to do. It is a disguised conditional assertion of what one has reason to do. But on this type of analysis the antecedent of the conditional must state in perfect generality what conditions would be sufficient to make what ought legally to be done into what ought to be done. That one wants to be law-abiding is just one such sufficient condition. There could be others. So the analysis must be modified into:

(3) If there are reasons to follow the law then A ought to ϕ.

But the very same objection which led us to reject (2) as an analysis of (1) shows that (3) ought also to be rejected. For even (3) does not state in full generality all the sufficient conditions for accepting what in (1) is said to be required by law as what ought to be done. There may be grave faults in the legal system sufficient to justify disobedience to large parts of it and yet there may be reason to do what is required by law according to (1) for the reason that it is required by law. There may be reason to respect parts of the legal system—perhaps most of it—because of the importance of having some legal system or even because the one in force is fundamentally sound, and yet the ideal of the law-abiding citizen may be unjustified since many laws should be disobeyed. In a situation such as this one ought to ϕ because it is legally required but the antecedent of (3) is false. Hence (3) does not meet the conditions which could justify regarding it as an analysis of (1).

Let us assume that (1) is true in virtue of the law L. Can one regard the following as an analysis of (1):

(4) If L is systemically valid then A ought to ϕ.

Considerations of the same kind show that (4) also fails. L is systemically valid only if it is systemically valid for all its norm subjects. But it is enough that A will have reason to follow L for the 'ought' in (1) to become unconditional. What then of the following:

(5) If L is systemically valid as applied to A then A ought to ϕ.

This also fails as an analysis of (1) for L may require some action of which ϕ-ing is an instance and L may not be valid as applied to A and yet the fact that L also requires ϕ-ing may be a reason for A to ϕ. So it seems that the conditional analysis results in the assertion that:

(6) If because according to law A ought to ϕ A ought to ϕ then A ought to ϕ

is an analysis of

(1) According to law A ought to ϕ.

And this is clearly absurd.

No more successful is the alternative of explaining (1) as a statement about people's attitudes to norms. Is the following an analysis of (1)?

(7) The population of C largely conforms to and the courts generally follow the norms of a legal system according to which A ought to ϕ.

There are two comments to make on this suggestion. (1) states what the situation is according to some legal system. In so far as (7) is merely intended to identify which legal system is referred to it is unobjectionable but should be recast as:

(8) According to the legal system conformed to by the population of C and followed by the courts, A ought to ϕ.

The legal system according to which the situation is as stated by such statements may be in force in a certain society or it may be a system which was once in force. It could also be a system which has never been in force at all, a system proposed by a reformer or by a movement, for example. Reformulation along the lines suggested by (8) will not necessarily refer to the practice of individuals or communities. When such a reference is made it serves merely to identify according to which system A ought to ϕ. It does not explain the sense of 'legally ought' or 'ought according to law'.

If (7) is to count as an analysis of (1) then the reference to the practices of the community cannot be taken as merely identifying the legal system according to which A ought to ϕ. It must somehow explain what it means to say that one legally ought to ϕ. Presumably the intention in (7) was to explain what one legally ought to do in terms of what people believe one ought to do or what certain people order one to do, etc. If so then (7) is quite inadequate since nothing follows from it as to people's beliefs or attitudes to the proposition that A ought to ϕ. If the intention is to reduce (1) to a statement about people's beliefs, etc., then (7) must be replaced with a much more detailed statement of the beliefs, attitudes or actions of parliaments, courts, etc. The problem is that it is not the case that for every legal statement there is a statement about the beliefs, attitudes or actions of people which is even logically equivalent to it, let alone synonymous.

What, then, is the way to explain statements of what ought to be done according to law? The beginning of wisdom is to allow that such statements are not reducible to one or the other of the basic types. Such statements simply state what one has reason to do from the legal point of view, namely, what ought to be done if legal norms are valid norms. But they do not state this conditional. They do not state that if the law is valid that is what ought to be done. Nor do they state what ought to be done. They do not presuppose that the law is valid. They are like statements made on the assumption that something is the case, for example, that a certain scientific theory is valid, which are not conditionals of which the assumption is the antecedent, nor do they presuppose that the theory is true. We could say that they state what is the case from the point of view of the theory or on the assumption of the theory.

The use of this type of normative statement is more frequent than might be thought and is not confined to law. If I go with a vegetarian friend to a dinner party I may say to him, 'You should not eat this dish. It contains meat.' Not being a vegetarian I do not believe that the fact that the dish contains meat is a reason against eating it. I do not, therefore, believe that my friend has a reason to refrain from eating it, nor am I stating that he has. I am merely informing him what ought to be done from the point of view of a vegetarian. Of course the very same sentence can be used by a fellow vegetarian to state what ought to be done. But this is not what I am saying, as my friend who understands the situation will know.

Some may object to this interpretation. It is true, they will say, that as I am not a vegetarian I do not regard the fact that there is meat in the dish as by itself a reason for not eating it. But I do regard this and the fact that my friend is a vegetarian as a reason. This, however, seems to be a very strange reason. I do believe that if my friend believes that the dish contains meat and eats it this shows inconsistency or weakness of character. But since my friend does not know of the fact he has no reason to refrain from eating the dish, and what other reason do I see? Naturally I have, or believe I have, a reason to tell my friend about the meat. I may want to spare him the embarrassment or regret he is bound to feel when he learns about the meat or I may want to help him to live according to his ideals. But these are *my* reasons for telling him something which I know he will regard as a valid reason. I do not believe that *he* has a reason nor do I state that he has. I state what reasons there are from a certain point of view because I know that that is his point of view.

Consider next a textbook on chess. It contains many statements as to what White or Black ought to do under various conditions. Again, these state what ought to be done from the point of view of someone who plays the game and wants to win. The author of the book does not state what ought to be done, *tout court*. He does not make conditional statements about what ought to be done if one wants to win. Nor does he state that this is what is believed by experts, etc. He makes a normative statement from a point of view.

When giving legal advice a solicitor or any other person is stating what is the case from the legal point of view. He may do so because he believes that the man he is advising endorses this point of view completely or in part. But sometimes he makes no such assumption. He may know that the man he is advising is not law-abiding, that his interest is merely to find what view the police or the courts are bound to take of his behaviour. A law lecturer or a legal writer normally does the same. He states what is the case from the legal point of view without normally making any specific assumptions about the reasons which may make his audience interested in his lecture or book—they may just be interested in the information (in order to pass an examination or for any one of a variety of reasons).

A barrister arguing a case before a court may do no more. He may simply state what is the case according to law in the knowledge that the judges hold themselves bound to act according to law. Naturally a barrister, a solicitor, a lecturer or any other person talking about the law may, as we noted above, state what reasons there are on account of the law. But it is important to see that they may not do this. They may merely state what ought to be done according to law.

The foregoing remarks do not amount to an analysis of statements made from the legal point of view. They are designed primarily to establish that this type of statement is not reducible to the two primary types and to show that it is widely used outside the law. They also indicate two features of such statements which point the way to their analysis: first, they are true or false according to whether there is, in the legal system referred to, a norm which requires the action which is stated to be one which ought to be done; secondly, if the statement is true and the norm in virtue of which it is true is valid, then one ought to perform the action which according to the statement ought legally to be performed.

Such statements are widespread in legal contexts. It should be emphasized again that statements from a point of view or according to a set of values are used in all spheres of practical reason, including morality. Their use is particularly widespread when discussing reasons and norms which are widely believed in and followed by a community, and perhaps especially in the case of an institutionalized system which is in force in the community. There are always people who accept the point of view and want to know what ought to be done according to it in order to know what they ought to do. In the case of practised norms, especially those enforced by norm-applying organs, there are also many who have a derivative practical interest in what ought to be done according to such systems or norms. The fact that other people follow such norms and that institutions enforce them may itself become a reason for people who do not believe in the validity of the norms or systems concerned. In section 5.2 we saw several examples of the way the fact that the law requires an action can become a reason for doing it—through its stipulation of sanctions or the impact of law-breaking on one's reputation, etc. All these cases depend on the fact that some people believe in the validity of the norms and follow them. That is the background for the widespread use of statements according to law—the fact that even people who do not endorse them have a practical interest in what is required by law. This leads them to make normative statements from a point of view which they do not necessarily accept as valid.

Postscript to the Second Edition: Rethinking exclusionary reasons

Not long after the original publication of this book in 1975, and somewhat to my regret, my work changed direction and drifted away from
consideration of practical reasoning. Coming back to these issues I have
to contend with the wish to expand, modify and improve many parts of
the book. Most of this can only be done in new, independent writings.
This postscript is an opportunity to reassess the credentials of the book's
central new idea concerning practical reason.[1] That idea is of the importance of exclusionary reasons for the understanding of some rules and
related normative concepts. The very claim that there are reasons of the
kind I called exclusionary was met with skepticism on the part of many
readers. I shall first discuss the notion of an exclusionary reason and then
argue that not only do many people believe that there are exclusionary
reasons, but they are sometimes right to think so because some exclusionary reasons exist. Only then shall I turn to the connection between
exclusionary reasons and rules, promises, decisions, authoritative directives, and others.

REASONS TO ACT FOR A REASON

Let us start with a familiar distinction and introduce a couple of terms to
mark it. If the need to give Jane moral support while she struggles with
her homework is a reason for Derek to stay at home, then he conforms
with that reason if he does stay at home. Generally people conform with
a reason for a certain act if they perform that act in the circumstance in
which that reason is a reason for its performance. If Derek not only stays
at home but does so because he realises Jane's need and that it is a reason
for him to so act, then we would say that he complies with the reason.

Is there anything wrong with mere conformity? Obviously people
who conform with a reason do not act against it. Other things being
equal, they are not irrational. Other things need not be equal. Their reasons for action may have been misguided or irrational. But they need

not be. Derek may have decided to stay at home because he was expecting an important telephone call, or to watch a good TV program. In staying at home he did in fact give Jane moral support. But this was not the reason for his staying at home. Has he failed in any way?

Clearly Derek fails to have a proper sensitivity to Jane's need, or at least he fails to display it on this occasion. But this is a failure in having a proper attitude, not a failure to give Jane moral support. Does it not follow that, so far as the reason to give her moral support is concerned, he has done all that can be expected? Things are not that simple. Had he been sensitive to Jane's needs—I mean, had he been so sensitive on that occasion as he should have been—he would have been motivated by her need for moral support. Does it not follow that he had reason not only to give Jane moral support but also to do so because of her need for it? I think that he had such reason. He had reason not only to conform with the reason there was to give Jane moral support, but also to comply with it. Jane's need, in other words, is a reason not only for conforming behaviour, but for complying behaviour as well. It is a reason to give her moral support, and a reason to do so for the reason that she needs it. Her need is, if you like, a self-reflexive reason. It combines, in the terminology I used in the book, a first-order reason to give Jane moral support with a second-order positive reason to do so for the reason that she needs it.

This terminology may be a bit of a mouthful. The important issue is: are reasons for action reasons for conformity or for compliance? That is, does one do all that one has reason to if one conforms with the reasons which apply to one, or need one comply with them, so that one is at fault if one does not?[2] The issue goes deep into our understanding of reasons for action. Do they aim at action, so that if the action occurs all is as well as it should be? Or do they aim at one's reasoning as well, so that they demand, as it were, to figure in one's reasoning and/or in one's motivation? The view that reasons for action are always reasons for compliance fits well with the idea that practical reasons are guides to action. If one is not guided by them, then one is failing to behave as one should. If reasons for action are understood as reasons for conformity,[3] then one may still talk of reasons for action as guides for behaviour, but only in the sense that, other things being equal, it is legitimate, i.e. alright, for them to figure in one's reasoning or motivation.[4] They are guides in the sense that the Michelin guide to Paris is a guide. I may use it, but I do not have to. I do not even have to be aware of its existence. There is absolutely nothing wrong in using another guide, if it is as good. The important thing is that I get to see the things which are worth seeing in Paris. Similarly, on this understanding of reasons the important thing is that the act for which the reason is a reason gets done (unless the reason is defeated). It does not necessarily matter if it is done for this or some other (good) reason.

Which understanding of reasons is correct? The main justification for thinking that reasons for action are always reasons for compliance is that, as our example of Derek may be thought to show, failure to comply always shows failure of appropriate sensitivity. Depending on the nature of the reason, this may be failure of moral sensitivity, or of appropriate concern for one's own well-being, or of loyalty to the state; or it may be an inadequate response to beauty, etc. However, there need be no failure in sensitivity in cases where the reasons neither figure in our reasoning nor motivate us. For example, there is no such necessary failure where we are not motivated by a reason because we are unaware of the circumstances which make it relevant to the case at hand. Suppose that I go to visit a friend because I am bored and think that he will not mind my dropping in for a brief visit. In fact, unbeknown to me, he had bad news earlier that day and is in need of being distracted from his resulting gloom. My conversation distracts him. I conform to the reason I have to help my friend, though, being unaware of his news, I do not comply with it. Still, given that I am generally sensitive to his needs, happy to help when needed, and that there was no fault in not knowing of his situation on this occasion, there seems to be no failure in my sensitivity as a result of the fact that I merely conformed and did not comply with the reason I had to distract him.

Three general considerations suggest that reasons for action are, barring special circumstances, merely reasons to conform. First, there is no fault in not basing our beliefs on some reasons for belief that we have. If our beliefs are at odds with our reasons for belief, then we are irrational, or at any rate guilty of some epistemic fault. So long as our beliefs (to the extent that they should be reason-based) are well-founded on reasons we have, we are rational. There is nothing wrong with us just because our reasons for holding certain beliefs do not exhaust the reasons for that belief which are available to us. Reasons for action may be different. But there is some reason to think that they resemble reasons for belief rather closely.[5]

Secondly, there is nothing wrong in not being aware of, and not being motivated to act for, reasons which are overridden or otherwise defeated. If I stay at home I will be able to weed the garden. I leave home to meet my mother who requires help with her shopping, or to renew my car insurance which expires tomorrow. I am completely oblivious of the state of the garden.[6] Surely there is nothing wrong in that. The view that reasons must guide might suggest that on such occasions I should consider the defeated reason and become aware of its existence. If that is, as I think it is, too intellectualized a view of the way reasons guide people, at least it would suggest that one is torn between conflicting motivations. On the one hand one should be moved to stay at home to weed the garden; on the other, winning, hand one is motivated to go out to renew the insurance or to meet one's mother. This seems to me to be clearly false.

Thirdly, there is the case of omissions. Again they may be a special case, but a unified account of practical reasons is preferable. It is not a fault in me that the reason I never killed anyone is simply that I never felt the slightest bit inclined to kill anyone, that the thought simply never crossed my mind. My failure to become a murderer was not motivated by the fact that it is wrong to kill. I do not mean that I do not know that it is wrong to kill. Such ignorance would be wrong. All I mean is that whenever I am with people such that an opportunity to kill them arises (i.e. whenever I can kill someone), the thought of doing so has never crossed my mind. I never had any reason for my continuous omission to kill. And that is, I believe, the best mental background for this, as for many other omissions to commit wrongful acts. That is, I feel that the moment we are morally motivated in such cases we are behaving in a less admirable way than those to whom the thought of the wrongful act simply does not occur.[7]

These observations do not prove that reasons are reasons for conforming behaviour, but they seem to support this view. The position I took concerning moral omissions runs counter to the Kantian view that acts lack moral worth if not undertaken out of respect for the moral law. The appeal of the Kantian view is often enhanced by a confusion of thought. Some people equate it with the view that an act lacks moral worth if it is not undertaken for a moral motive. This last view is very plausible given that the moral worth of an act is related to the way it contributes to, manifests, or is evidence of, a moral character trait or a moral virtue. Moral virtues, it is plausible to believe, are manifested only by actions which do not merely coincide with moral requirements but are undertaken for the right (moral) motives. Kant, however, went one step further. The often controverted aspect of his view is that only respect for the moral law is an appropriate moral motive. Many people believe that various motives (regarded by Kant as mere inclinations) are appropriate moral motives for various actions. For example, love of one's children is an appropriate motive for performing parental duties towards them.

Those who conform with those duties, but for reasons other than love for their children, are at fault: they do not manifest the required moral attitudes which parents ought to possess and to be motivated by.[8]

Consider such a view a little further. Assume that the un-Kantian view I am describing accepts that respect for the moral law is a reason for action.[9] One has a reason (the moral law) to look after one's children out of love for them. The love is a love for them, not a love for the moral law. One has to love them for their own sake, not to love them because this is good for business or because this is necessary for the salvation of one's soul or in order to meet the moral law. Indeed, one may well say that love is a genuine love only if it is not undertaken instrumentally, for an extraneous purpose. The moral law, therefore, is a reason to come to love one's children. But it is a reason to come to love them for their own sake, not for the sake of one's conformity with the moral law. If this is so, then there are reasons for having reasons which necessarily have to stay in the background. They cannot, without defeating their point, be one's motivational reasons at the time of action.[10] In pointing to an example of one, admittedly rather special, kind of reasons (the moral reason to act out of love for one's children) which are reasons for conformity rather than for compliance, this consideration somewhat reinforces the view that reasons for action are, barring special circumstances, reasons for conformity only.

But there is one last twist to the story (and it is necessary to complete the analysis of Jane and Derek's case). One has reason to do whatever will facilitate conformity with reason. More narrowly, one has reason to do whatever is a sufficient condition for the realisation of some good, including the good of conformity with reason. Complying with a reason will, trivially, lead to, or rather constitute, conformity with it. Hence one always has reason to comply. But such instrumental reasons disappear if their end is achieved some other way. If my only reason for opening the door is to be able to get into the room, there is nothing wrong, no loss whatsoever, in the door's being accidentally opened by the wind or by someone else. Similarly, there is no loss, no defect, blemish, or any other shortcoming, in conformity with reason achieved not through compliance with it, but for other reasons.

EXCLUSIONARY REASONS

The arguments of the previous section, like most of the arguments to follow, are merely tentative. They attempt to analyse reasons and considerations which are somewhat unusual and escape the rough-and-ready analyses of practical rationality which populate the writings on the subject. There may well be better ways of understanding the phenomena I am concerned with. All that can be claimed for the proposed analyses in this book is that they draw attention to features which are sometimes neglected and provide (or rather begin to sketch) an account which shows how they fit in a general understanding of practical reasons.

The type of reason I was particularly concerned with is exclusionary reasons: reasons not to act for certain reasons. This gives them the appearance of paradox. Some readers regarded it as a necessary truth that there cannot be valid exclusionary reasons. Such reactions are understandable. After all, reasons are there to guide action. Surely there cannot be reasons for not being guided by reasons whose very nature is that they should guide. The argument of the preceding section helps dispel the air of paradox. It shows that reasons are merely legitimate guides. One does not have to be guided by them. Other things being equal, so long as one conforms with them there is nothing wrong with one.

In one respect exclusionary reasons are less paradoxical than ordinary conflicting reasons. A reason which is overridden by conflicting reasons may not be conformed to. One may not follow an overridden reason.[11] An overriding reason therefore requires us to act against what we have positive reason to do. An exclusionary reason merely requires us to avoid something which other reasons make legitimate, but do not require.

In another respect exclusionary reasons are more paradoxical than most conflicting reasons. When I have reasons both to enroll in a university and to abandon my studies and get a job right away (in order to support my young family, for example), the reasons are independent of each other. The benefits of education and the need to support my young family are independently intelligible. They conflict accidentally, because of the circumstances of my life. In other circumstances they would have been mutually satisfiable, and there would have been no conflict. Exclusionary and excluded reasons conflict necessarily. The very point of an exclusionary reason is to exclude acting for another consideration which is a valid reason for action. Can there ever be a reason to deny a valid reason for action its guiding role?[12] The answer is that here again some ordinary conflicting reasons do precisely that. Ascetic or self-denying reasons are an important case in point. Self-denying reasons are reasons to avoid doing, or having, things one has reason to do or have. Their entire point will be lost if what is denied one are actions or possessions one has no reason to take or to cherish. The point of a (self-denying[13]) fast is that we forgo what we value and have reason to pursue.

It is possible that there are no valid ascetic reasons. But if so this seems to be due to contingent factors. There seems to be no logical incoherence in the idea of ascetic or self-denying reasons.

The preceding discussion was meant to dispel the air of paradox which appears to surround the idea of exclusionary reasons. Some readers may feel that it only reinforces their doubts about the possibility of conflicting reasons at all. Before I comment briefly on that issue, let me pursue the notion of exclusionary reasons. It is easily confused with several similar but distinct ideas. First, it can be confused with a reason to avoid thinking, considering, or attending to certain matters. I contributed to that confusion myself by giving some examples in which it appeared that the need to avoid anxiety or mistakes likely to occur if one were to consider certain matters, is the reason for an exclusionary reason.[14] But in all these cases my assumption was that the anxiety and so forth are caused not by attending to or thinking about certain matters, but by the fact that one does so because certain reasons should guide one's behaviour, and that is why one has to establish what they are. If one ought not to act for these reasons, one would be relieved of the pressure which brings the undesirable side effects in its wake. So that while the good to be achieved has to do with one's thinking, the reason it provides is a reason not to act for certain reasons. So long as that reason is complied with, there is little objection to actually engaging in thought about the matter. So long as one knows that one's reflections will not affect one's action, the ill effects of such thoughts are avoided.

I raise this point here not to justify the claim that there are valid exclusionary reasons, but merely to clarify the nature of the notion and the way it was discussed in the book. In the same spirit I would draw attention to another possible confusion. Exclusionary reasons are reasons for not acting for certain valid reasons. They do not nullify or cancel those reasons (in the way that the death of a person to whom I made a promise often cancels whatever reasons arise out of my promise[15]), nor are they reasons for not acting on my belief in certain reasons. They are reasons for not acting for those reasons as they are, rather than as I think that they are. Later, when we come to consider whether there are valid exclusionary reasons, this last point will require careful attention.

Exclusionary reasons, I said in the book, are second-order reasons because they are reasons about how to relate to other reasons. But reasons can be second-order in various ways. For example, there can be a reason to bring about a situation in which other reasons do or do not exist. For example, those in a Prisoner's Dilemma-type situation have reason to change the structure of their reasons. Besides, people have reasons to avoid situations in which the best one can do is the lesser of two evils.[16] Exclusionary reasons are not second-order in this sense. They are simply reasons for acting in ways the full specification of which essentially refers to other reasons. They are reasons for not being motivated in one's action by certain (valid) considerations. They are not reasons for not conforming with the reasons. They exclude reasons from being one's motivation for action, but the excluded reasons may be conformed to, if they are conformed to through compliance with other non-excluded reasons (or even through a false belief in some reasons). In fact it is better that the excluded reasons be conformed to. They are reasons for performing certain actions, and, other things being equal, the fact that they are excluded by an exclusionary reason merely means that they should not be complied with, not that they should not be conformed to. The best course is if they are indirectly obeyed, i.e. if the action they indicate is performed for some other, independent, reason.

Think of it this way:[17] Think of John, who is subject to an (undefeated) exclusionary reason. Let us assume that it affects the outcome of his deliberations, i.e. that the action indicated by the balance of all first-order reasons is different from the action required by the balance of the unexcluded reasons only. John, I have argued, is acting correctly only if he disregards the excluded reasons in his deliberations. I do not mean that he must not think of them, only that he must not base his action on them. He must not act *for* those reasons. From his perspective before he acts, the right action to take is the one which is indicated by the unexcluded reasons. How is he to judge his own conduct after he acts? Assume that he acted correctly from the point of view of the *ex ante* considerations. His action may be out of step with the balance of first-order reasons, but on the other hand it is in accord with the exclusionary reason, and this explains and justifies the deviation from first-order reasons. He could not conform both to them and to the exclusionary reason, and the exclusionary one prevails. Well, this is almost right. He could not conform to both the balance of first-order reasons and the exclusionary reason if he reasons correctly.

Assume, however, that he made a mistake. While completely disregarding the excluded reasons and letting them play no part in his motivation, John nevertheless performed the action which is in fact indicated by the balance of all the first-order reasons. He simply miscalculated. Paradoxically his mistake seems to be rather fortunate. Because of it he managed to conform both to the exclusionary reason (he did not act for any excluded reason) and to the balance of first-order reasons. Up to a point this is a familiar puzzle. It is a general feature of the difference between judging actions *ex ante* and judging them *ex post*. Sometimes when trying to act on the evidence before us we make a mistake which turns out to be a lucky one: we perform an action which the partial evidence available at the time, correctly evaluated, did not justify, but which is in fact justified in light of all the facts of the case.

This is the case with exclusionary reasons, as is evidenced by the stories of Ann, Jeremy, and Colin (pp. 37–9 above). Many exclusionary reasons are, as the case of Ann exemplifies, 'evidential' in character. That is, their justification is that conformity to them will lead to improved conformity with the excluded reasons. This is the case, for example, when a person refrains from acting on new information because he is too tired or intoxicated to trust his judgement of its significance. Clearly if by luck his action conforms to the reasons furnished by the information he dismissed, no one can complain. The same is true if the exclusion is justified on rational grounds of saving labour, time, or anxiety. Certain reasons are justifiably excluded. One does not act for them. Supposing that the exclusion would have led to a sub-optimal action, but that a miscalculation led the agent to the optimal action, we simply count him lucky. There is no mystery or paradox in this.

At other times the exclusion is justified directly by motivational considerations. If Colin promised to disregard his own interest in deciding on the education of his son, then he has discharged his duty if he did indeed disregard his interest. If fortuitously his misunderstanding of the merits of various schools led him to choose one which suits his interests, then all we can say is that he is lucky. Perhaps we should also say that his son is unlucky, for had this mistake not been made a school better for the son would have been chosen. But this is no ground for condemning the decision. After all, the parent's interests matter as well, and we are assuming that they outweigh, in this case and within these bounds, those of the son.

CONFLICTS OF REASONS

In trying, in the preceding section, to explain the notion of an exclusionary reason, and to dispel some of its paradoxical air, I have been assuming that reasons can conflict. One way of avoiding some of my conclusions is to deny that premise. Some philosophers think that there are independent grounds for denying the possibility of conflicting reasons. Such views reflect a misunderstanding of the nature of reasons.

The reasons for an action are considerations which count in favour of that action. Other things being equal, they are sufficient grounds for taking the action, and, barring reasonable ignorance or other excuses, grounds for finding fault with the actor's conduct, if he fails to take the action. We can think of them as the facts statements of which form the premises of a sound inference to the conclusion that, other things being equal, the agent ought to perform the action.[18] Considerations which establish that the action also has disadvantages do not in the least show that the reasons do not exist, nor do they show that they are subject to an 'exception'. The original reasons are still there. The inference from them to the conclusion that, other things being equal, the act ought to be done is still sound. The conflicting considerations merely show that there are conflicting reasons, i.e. that there is also a sound inference to the conclusion that, other things being equal, the act ought not to be done.

Conflicting reasons, while they may defeat the reasons they conflict with, do not create exceptions to them. Rules, not reasons, have exceptions. Rules belong to the lower level of any two-level way of understanding practical reasoning. Usually each rule is based on a number of reasons, and they reflect a judgement that those reasons defeat, within the scope of the rule, various, though not necessarily all, conflicting reasons. Rules are, metaphorically speaking, expressions of compromises, of judgements about the outcome of conflicts. Here talk of exceptions comes into its own. Characteristically, cases are 'simply' outside the scope of the rule if the main reasons which support the rule do not apply to such cases. Cases fall under an exception to the rule when some of the main reasons for the rule apply to them, but the 'compromise reflected in the rule' deems other, conflicting reasons to prevail. It is in this sense that 'You may deceive to save life', if right, is an exception to the rule, 'Never deceive', if there is such a rule. Since exceptions belong to the logic of rules and do not apply to reasons, they cannot be used to show that reasons do not conflict. In fact exceptions to rules exist precisely when reasons do conflict.[19]

The 'other things being equal' premise necessary to sustain a conclusion regarding what ought be done excludes defeating considerations of any kind. These need not be conflicting reasons. They may be, for example, facts which cancel the reasons stated by the other premises supporting the 'ought'-conclusion.[20] Once a reason for an action is cancelled it stops being a ground for the action, or for faulting or regretting its non-performance. But the cancelling circumstance is not itself (i.e. not under the same description) a reason for any other action. The cancelling facts show how the act will no longer achieve its desired result (the rain is accompanied by such high winds that an umbrella is useless, or the person for whom the medicine is intended has died), or that the result is no longer desirable[21] (my terminally ill friend's deterioration means that prolonging his life is no longer desirable). Cancelling facts relate to the reasons that they cancel. Conflicting reasons are essentially independent considerations which point to the desirability of the non-performance of that action.

Conflicts of reasons, as we know, occur when the agent has reason both to perform and not to perform a certain act (e.g., that its non-performance is necessary for him to be able to perform some other act he has reason to perform). Sometimes if a reason is overridden it is completely frustrated: that is, the good that conforming with it would have secured will not be achieved. But often this is not the case. Often the good that conformity with the reason would achieve can be secured, completely or partly, in some other way, which may be open to the agent or to some other people. Assume, for example, that I have reason to give each of two patients a certain medicine, but I have only one dose of it. I may be able to find an alternative medicine, or some other course of treatment which will be effective for one but not the other of the patients. This alternative may be slower to work, or may have unpleasant side effects. It may be a second best, but if I cannot give him the best medicine at least I should give him the second best one.

Whenever at least one of two conflicting reasons need not be completely frustrated, the conflicts are partial conflicts. Let us take the case of two conflicting reasons, one of which, if overridden, would be completely frustrated, whereas the other need not be frustrated at all (i.e. there is an equally effective alternative way of realising the good that conformity with it will have achieved). In such a case the reason which would be frustrated overrides the one that will not be. The overridden reason will then serve as a reason for an alternative action which will achieve the good that conformity with it would have secured. This principle of conflict resolution may have to be modified when it is unlikely that the alternative action will be taken. For example, it might be that only someone else can take it, and that person is unlikely to be appropriately motivated to do so (only another doctor can offer the alternative treatment but that doctor has an unjustified conscientious objection to that form of treatment). Or it might be that even though I can take the alternative action, I am less likely through some weakness of mine to do so. Furthermore, the principle has to be refined to take account of the fact that the reason for the alternative action itself may conflict with yet another reason.

Things become even more complicated when the reason which is not completely frustrated is partially frustrated. In such cases depending on its importance and on the degree that it will be frustrated, it may override. We need not explore such complexities here. I mention them to make the point that judgement that one reason overrides another has often little to do with judgement, rightly considered by many to be mysterious in many cases, that one reason is more important than another. At least as common are cases in which judgements that one reason overrides another rest on assessment of possible alternatives in partial conflicts.[22]

In the book I suggested that exclusionary reasons do not compete in weight with the reasons they exclude; rather, they always win in such conflicts. It is possible to account for this result by regarding the relations between exclusionary reasons and the excluded reasons as governed by general considerations affecting partial conflicts. Exclusionary reasons partially conflict with the reasons they exclude. Colin's promise not to act out of concern for his own interest (that his son go to a state school, enabling him to resign his job and write a book) conflicts with that interest of his. They conflict in that there is a way of conforming with the excluded reason (i.e. sending his son to a state school in order to be able to resign his job) which the exclusionary reason, i.e. his promise, is a reason against. Colin may, however, decide to send his son to a state school (and this suits his interests), while not acting out of regard for his interest. Since it is possible to satisfy both the excluded reason and the reason which excludes it, the conflict between them is merely partial. Given that the conflict is only partial, and that complying with the excluded reason (Colin's sending his son to a state school in part because it is in his—Colin's—interest to do so) will completely frustrate the exclusionary reason (the promise) whereas not complying with the excluded reason will conform to the exclusionary reason while leaving a possibility that the agent will conform with the excluded reason, it follows that exclusionary reasons defeat the excluded reasons to the extent that one may conform with the excluded reason only in ways which conform with the exclusionary reason as well.

Wherever there is a reason not merely to conform to a reason but specifically to comply with it (i.e. what I called a positive second-order reason in this book), it conflicts with any reason to exclude that reason in an ordinary way, and considerations of their relative importance, or of the relative damage to the goods which conformity to them will serve, determine which overrides the other.

This way of explaining the status of exclusionary reasons is not free from difficulty. While clearly they only partially conflict with the excluded reasons, such conflicts are special in several ways. At the very least we should observe that as they remove the legitimacy of being guided by the excluded reasons, they can be expected to reduce the chance that one will conform to them. Nevertheless, I think that the considerations above are sound, and that they account or come close to accounting for the priority of exclusionary over the excluded reasons. Not every conceivable exclusionary reason is valid. If they make conformity less likely, that may count against their validity (though not necessarily conclusively).[23] But, as will be argued below, this is not always the case. If there are circumstances in which an exclusionary reason makes conformity with the excluded reason more likely, then that exclusionary reason is valid just for that reason alone. As was argued above, what matters is conformity with reason. Compliance is important in itself only in certain special cases. Normally compliance matters only because attempting to comply is the only reliable route to conformity. But this is not always the case, and where the attempt to comply makes conformity less likely there is a case for an exclusionary reason against acting for that reason.

So the conflict rule giving the upper hand to the exclusionary reason regardless of considerations of relative weight (of the exclusionary and the excluded reasons) is justified. The very point of exclusionary reasons is to bypass issues of weight by excluding consideration of the excluded reasons regardless of weight. If they have to compete in weight with the excluded reasons, they will only exclude reasons which they outweigh, and thus lose distinctiveness. Their function is to escape the linear comparison of reasons and create a separate stratification alongside the ordinary one. This is achieved only if they do succeed in their aim of excluding other reasons regardless of weight.[24]

EXCLUSIONARY REASONS AND RULES: THE CONCEPTUAL ARGUMENT

Nothing in the discussion so far directly shows that there are valid exclusionary reasons. But inasmuch as it clarifies the concept and removes the a priori objection to the possible validity of exclusionary reasons, it does all that need be done to establish their validity. The rest is a matter of fact. Has anyone ever made a promise such as Colin's? If so then such a promise was binding, being in all other respects an ordinary promise. Hence that person had a valid exclusionary reason. The aim of the book was, however, more ambitious. It set out to show that exclusionary reasons are more than occasional features of this or that person's situation. They are systematically related to central structures of practical reasoning, in that rules and commitments are by their nature exclusionary reasons. The issues are complicated and space does not permit their full examination here. I will rehearse some of the arguments as I now see them, though what I can say here can only be a preliminary to a full inquiry.[25]

Rules and commitments are what I call protected reasons, i.e. a systematic combination of a reason to perform the act one has undertaken to perform, or the one required by the rule, and an exclusionary reason not to act for certain reasons (for or against that act). This statement is too sweeping. 'Rules' is used in a variety of ways, and not all rules conform to the analysis proposed here. The analysis is designed to apply to rules of one easily recognisable, important type, which I call 'mandatory rules'. Here, and throughout when I refer to rules, I will have only mandatory rules in mind. Directives issued by authority are one subspecies of mandatory rules, and it is convenient to use them to illustrate the general case. In discussing authoritative directives and other rules and commitments, there is no need to distinguish between justified and unjustified directives and rules. The basic structure of reasoning involved in relying on either is the same. Since those who rely on them believe that they are justified, their basic structure is determined by that of justified, or valid, rules.

Authoritative directives are issued for reasons, which are deemed to justify them. Typically, these are reasons which show that the prescribed act is one which those subject to the authority have good reason to perform, reasons which defeat other countervailing reasons. The building committee, for example, considers how much residents should contribute towards the cost of communal services and imposes a duty to pay a sum proportionate to the size of one's flat, or to the number of people in one's household, or to some other factor or combination of factors deemed to reflect the right rate of contribution.[26] The common view, crudely described, is that in deciding whether to pay the prescribed sum, residents should consider the reasons for each of them to pay that amount—i.e. the independent reasons which would have applied even if the house committee had not reached the conclusion it did—adding to them the reasons which arise out of the fact that the committee has decided as it did, and balance them against whatever reasons there are against paying that sum.

The reasons which arise out of the fact that the money has been authoritatively demanded include whatever damage to the effectiveness and credibility of a legitimate authority may be caused by disobedience.

This consideration is covered by the duty to support just institutions.[27] But there must be more to it than that or else there will be no harm in undermining the effectiveness of just institutions. The further considerations must point to the fact that the authoritative intervention makes it the case, or makes it more likely, that the act required by the authority is the act which best realises whatever value one can realise in one's action on that occasion. Such considerations point to the greater expertise of the authority, which makes it likely that the action its directive requires is better than whatever alternative action may appear to me, the non-expert, as best. Or they may point to the fact that the authority's directive gives the prescribed act salience which makes it the best course to achieve some desirable coordination, which would not be achieved in any other way.

There are two problems with this approach. First, it fails to represent the way authoritative directives actually figure in practical reasoning. Secondly, it cannot explain fully the advantages of having, where appropriate, legitimate authorities. Both problems are solved by the account here offered, according to which authoritative directives are protected reasons. On this view each legitimate authority has the right to issue directives within the sphere of its jurisdiction. Jurisdiction is determined by the range of actions the authority can command: the house committee can require paying to a common fund, but not attending church services. It is also determined by the type of reasons the authority may rely upon: in determining contributions it can rely on use of common services, and the like, but not on whether one individual deserves them more than another (one neighbour may be doing a lot of voluntary work in the community while the others do not, and therefore arguably he deserves priority in access to some services during the little free time that he has), nor on need or ability to pay (charity can only be decided upon by each individual separately and cannot be required of one by the committee). In deciding whether one ought to obey the authority's directive, one ought to exclude all the reasons both for and against paying the required sum which were within the jurisdiction of the authority. One ought to weigh the directive in the balance with whatever reasons for or against the act it requires are outside the authority's jurisdiction, adding to them whatever reasons arise out of the duty to support just institutions in the situation at hand.

How can one show that the protected reason account captures the logic of reasoning with reference to authoritatively promulgated rules better than the common account? We will assume that the two accounts can be made to yield equivalent verdicts on when one should or should not obey the rules. The only issue is whether those verdicts are reached by one process of reasoning or the other. Since this dispute is conceptual, and not moral, its outcome depends on which account provides the more accurate representation of the structure of reasoning which is necessarily involved when reflecting on authoritative rules. Here the common account is at fault for failing to take notice of the fundamental point about authority, i.e. that it removes the decision from one person to another.

The common account concentrates on the way, once a legitimate authority has ruled on a certain issue, its ruling affects one's reasons. The protected reason account pays equal attention to the reasons for having an authority in the first place. These may be that it is desirable to change the reasons for action one has, but they need not be. They always are, they must always be, reasons to have the matter decided by someone else. This is, typically, either because there is reason to change the reasons confronting the agent (e.g., for him to escape from a Prisoner's Dilemma-type situation) or because he is more likely to conform to reason if he does not attempt to work out what it requires, but follows someone else's more expert judgement. In both cases there is reason to believe that the agent will better conform with reasons which apply to him if he does not attempt to comply with those reasons (directly) but submits his action (in the sense explained by the protected reasons account) to the judgement of an authority.[28]

Necessarily the attitude of those who accept the legitimacy of an authority is one of reasoned trust. We have reasons to take the authority's ruling as evidence that there are adequate reasons to do as we are told. The authority's directives become our reasons. While the acceptance of the authority is based on belief that its directives are well-founded in reason, they are understood to yield the benefits they are meant to bring only if we do rely on them rather than on our own independent judgement of the merits of each case to which they apply. That is the whole point of admitting that the decision-making power should be with the authority.

In sum, the case for authoritative rules depends on the advantages of the indirect approach, the attempt to maximise conformity with certain reasons (which I will call 'the underlying reasons') not through compliance with them but through compliance with an alternative set of reasons, i.e. the rules, which are tailor-made so that compliance with them maximises conformity with the underlying reasons. This has long been recognised in discussions of rules, especially in discussions of various forms of rule-utilitarianism.

The puzzle has always been, how can one avoid the following dilemma? If a rule is justified by certain reasons, then either the action it requires is invariably the action required by the underlying reasons,[29] in which case one might just as well rely on the reason rather than the rule, or else the action the rule requires deviates from that justified by the underlying reasons, in which case following the rule is unjustified. Hence rules are either redundant or unjustified. One escapes from the dilemma in those cases where conformity with the underlying reasons is improved if one does not attempt to comply with them. In such cases conformity with the underlying reasons is secured by complying with the rule, or rather a better degree of conformity than can otherwise be achieved is so obtained. This can justify complying with the rule even when it requires action which the underlying reasons do not. Such compliance may still be the best strategy to maximise conformity with the underlying reasons. The reason not to comply with another reason is an exclusionary reason. Since rules can only function as rules if one takes them as reasons for action and avoids trying to comply with the underlying reasons, all rules are exclusionary reasons.

Similar arguments apply to other rules. In the book I have equated such rules with generalised prior decisions. The reason is simple. Rules laid down by authority are like decisions about what to do taken by somebody else. Other rules which people have are like decisions about what to do which are taken by the agents for themselves but in advance of the circumstances in which the action is called for.[30] Just as the advantages of handing over decision-making powers to another depend on following an indirect strategy in attempting to secure conformity (i.e. on securing conformity not through compliance), so the advantages, whenever there are any, of deciding in advance of the action depend on adopting a similar indirect strategy, i.e. in securing conformity with the reasons which justify the rule by attempting to comply not with them but with the rule itself. Space restrictions preclude my explaining the details of the argument here, but they are readily extrapolated from the case of authority-generated rules.

RULES AND COMMITMENT: JUSTIFICATORY ARGUMENTS

The preceding section showed that reasoning with rules is reasoning with protected reasons. It did not establish that it is ever justified to reason with rules. It did not establish that any authority is ever legitimate. Nor is it the function of this book to argue for such conclusions.

But it is its function to show that rules can be valid, that there could be circumstances in which protected reasons are valid. This requires a demonstration that, where there are advantages in having authorities (for again I will take the case of authoritative rules first) one needs the protected reason account to show what they are. Such advantages, I will argue, are always a result of the indirect strategy for conformity with reasons, i.e. maximising conformity with reasons not by trying to comply with them, but by following someone else's judgement about what one should do. Having argued for this in detail elsewhere, I will not repeat the argument here beyond mentioning its core idea.[31] The two basic arguments for authority depend on its ability, through concentrating expertise on various issues, to overcome common ignorance and on its ability to help solve common difficulties in securing coordination. Overcoming both problems requires adopting an indirect approach to conformity to reason, that is, it requires securing conformity not through an attempt to comply. In the case of failure to conform due to ignorance (or to anxiety about decision taking, etc.), the cure is in deferring to the judgement of the expert rather than trying to rely on one's own judgement of the balance of reasons.[32]

A similar indirect strategy can be useful in securing coordination. One common difficulty in achieving coordination is the need for each to have assurance that other people's cooperative behaviour is likely. This often depends on their having come to the conclusion that coordination is needed in a certain type of case.[33] In some cases one can rely on the fact that people accept an authority: if the authority tells them that a coordination problem exists, and that a certain course of action should be followed to solve it, then they will take that course. In such cases the problem of assurance is solved. Therefore, since everyone has reason to secure coordination when needed, where one can trust an authority's identification of such problems and their solutions, everyone has reason to follow that authority's directives rather than judge for himself whether a coordination problem exists in the matter covered by the authority's directives.

Similar arguments apply to validate rules which do not derive from any authority, and to commitments. The first argument, depending on ignorance or other individual inefficiencies in attempting to comply with reasons, clearly applies to personal rules. One reason for taking decisions long in advance and for adopting personal rules is to reduce the burden of decisions on the spot, and to improve their quality by taking them in advantageous conditions when one can muster the best information available and assess it properly. Improving coordination is another ground for early decisions and for personal rules: they enable others to rely on one with, as is hoped, advantages to all.

Conventional rules and social practices can meet similar conditions, and so can conventional ways of undertaking commitments. Role-defining practices are a familiar example. These work best when they are based on a reciprocal division of labour. Parents look after the interests of their children, teachers after those of their students, doctors care for the interests of their patients, etc. In each case, when the role-defining practices are justified, they are reasons to exclude certain reasons, and not to comply with them. That explains the partiality of roles, their requirement of giving priority to one's charge over all others. The reciprocal partiality of all roles brings about the hoped-for benefits. The beneficial results are assured by following an indirect approach, improving conformity with reason (say, to promote the general good) by refraining from compliance, and relying instead on alternative reasons (i.e. the rules about acting to promote, within limits, the interests only of the people in one's charge). Where other people follow similar roles, and the system of roles is well-coordinated not to leave anyone unprotected, conformity with the protected reasons which constitute the roles can be one's best contribution to conformity with the general reason of promoting the general good.

Commitments, by creating a similar partiality in favour of the undertaken course of action, increase the chances that it will actually be undertaken and thus generate possibilities of secure reliance otherwise unobtainable. In certain situations, and within certain conditions, including again a reasonable *ex ante* chance or reciprocity, these may lead to better conformity with reason than can be attainable without commitments.

All the considerations briefly, and rather crudely, mentioned here are the common stuff of much writing. The only novel thesis this book advanced is that all of them involve recognising the validity of exclusionary reasons. This depends on the point made above about the nature of rules: Any explanation of rules has to solve the apparent dilemma which purports to show that they are either unnecessary or unjustified, and that the solution is in the indirect strategy of achieving conformity by rejecting compliance, i.e. through exclusionary reasons.

But does the indirect strategy really involve exclusionary reasons? I will deal briefly with two objections. First, could one not say that the factor one relies on, the rule, whether promulgated by authority, or embedded in social practices, or adopted as a personal policy by the agent, is reason to believe that a certain action is best supported by reason, and is not itself a reason for that action? Secondly, if there is a reason for action involved, is it not a reason not to act on *one's belief* that there are certain reasons, rather than a reason for not acting for those reasons? Both questions take us back to the conceptual analysis of rules in the previous section. But as issues of analysis and of justification are closely related, they are better treated under both aspects here. The first objection takes us back to the basic apparent dilemma of rules. That dilemma, as we saw, is resolved because the indirect strategy justifies following rules[34] even in cases in which they require action not justified by the underlying reasons, even when one knows this to be the case; the justification of such action depends on a sound argument to the effect that one should adopt an indirect strategy and not rely on attempting to comply with the underlying reasons. Thus, while in general the fact that the rule requires an action is indeed a reason to believe that the action is justified by the underlying reasons, this does not exhaust its force. It is a reason for conforming behaviour even if one knows that the action is not justified by the underlying reasons.[35] This shows that rules are reasons for action and not (merely) for belief.

The second objection requires a more complex response. In the book (p. 64) I presented an argument against this objection. It is based on holding (1) that all second-order reasons are also reasons to act or not to act on one's judgement (i.e. they are also reasons for attempting to comply with them); (2) that there is no practical difference between a reason to act on one's judgement that p and a reason to act for p (i.e. they both require the same conduct); (3) that there is no special reason to prefer the 'subjective' analysis in some cases and not in others. The first of these propositions still seems to me true. This is because (as explained above) all reasons are reasons to take sufficient steps to conform to them, and attempting to comply is such a step. The second assumption can be challenged in the following way. It is true, it can be said, from the point of view of the agent before the act, from the *ex ante* perspective. But evaluation of the action from an *ex post* point of view shows the difference. If one does not back one's judgement and happens to conform to reason, then one has done all one had reason to do if one acts for a reason not to trust one's judgement; but one acts wrongly if one had reason not to act for a reason. But by now we are familiar with the fallacy in this argument.[36] If you do not trust your judgement and do not act for the excluded reason, you conform to the exclusionary reason. If, through luck or miscalculation, you nevertheless happen also to conform with the excluded reason, you made a lucky mistake. It therefore seems to me that the second of my original propositions is also true.

The trouble starts with the third proposition. Even if true it falls short of the mark. It merely establishes that there is as much reason to support the exclusionary reason analysis as to support the subjective analysis. It does not establish the superiority of one over the other. Furthermore, consider the fact that the justification of some rules is due to one's subjective incapacity, or inferior competence: is this not reason enough to distinguish these cases from the others and give them a subjective analysis, preserving the objective one for the others? I think that defective though my argument was, it can be supplemented by three further propositions, which make it good: (4) Ultimately reasons are facts; our beliefs matter only inasmuch as and because they aim at the facts. This seems to me to suggest that the objective interpretation is true of the ordinary case. (5) Some cases are not amenable to the subjective construction. The paramount examples are all those cases in which a protected reason is justified by a reason that the agent has to change the reasons which face him, as in the Prisoner's Dilemma-type situations. Here it is clearly not one's judgement which is at fault, but the situation one faces, and one has reason to improve it, rather than simply to avoid relying on one's judgement. Improving one's situation is accomplished by avoiding compliance with certain reasons. (6) There are strong reasons to prefer a unitary interpretation. If this is so then it should be the objective one. This much follows from proposition (4). The reason for preserving a unitary interpretation (while not denying, of course, that the grounds for exclusionary reasons are sometimes in subjective incapacities, inferiority of judgement, etc.) is that the different cases shade into each other. This is clearest in the case of coordination, where expertise is required to identify cases in which coordination is needed and to settle on the best course of action for achieving it. For while in coordination problems, doing as others do is better than all alternatives, still, given that there may be several courses of action which can secure coordination, some might be better than others.

All the considerations relied upon so far to explain the role of exclusionary reasons are purely instrumental. One of the themes of the book was that rules belong to the middle and lower levels of practical reasoning and are on the whole absent from its foundations. Do intrinsic values ever constitute exclusionary reasons? Do exclusionary reasons play a non-instrumental role in practical reasoning? The preceding discussion removes the air of paradox involved in the thought that it may be instrumentally good to avoid complying with reason. But can it be intrinsically valuable to avoid being guided by (valid) reason? Here the answer that non-compliance may improve conformity is unavailable, since it is an instrumental consideration. The question—analogous to the question 'Can there be intrinsically valuable self-denying ordinances?'—is complex and requires delving deeper into the theory of value than is possible here. It requires a vindication of a certain kind of value pluralism, by which value is not entirely realisable even under ideal conditions. This means that all people have to choose between different goods, that rejection of some goods, abandonment of some reasons for action, is an inevitable part of the life of good, even of ideal people. Granted that, we can understand, in principle, how exclusionary reasons may be intrinsically valuable. This task remains to be completed.[37]

Notes and references

The main purpose of these notes is to provide bibliographical references where appropriate. (Full bibliographical details are given on the first citation only.) They also contain some further comments on points discussed in the main text of the book and a few remarks relating some of my views to those of other authors.

INTRODUCTION

1. *Moral, political and legal philosophy as branches of philosophy.* There is a growing awareness of the unity of practical philosophy. Some of the books manifesting this trend are D. P. Gauthier, *Practical Reasoning* (Oxford, 1963); G. H. von Wright, *Norm and Action* (Routledge and Kegan Paul, 1963), and *The Varieties of Goodness* (Routledge and Kegan Paul, 1963); R. Edgley, *Reason in Theory and Practice* (Hutchinson, 1969); D. A. J. Richards, *A Theory of Reasons for Action* (Oxford, 1971). There is also a growing awareness by philosophers of the relevance of the work done in theoretical economics, games and decision theory, as well as a revival of interest in philosophical problems affecting their work by economists and game and decision theorists. The best work to date which combines philosophical and economic acumen is A. K. Sen, *Collective Choice and Social Welfare* (Holden-Day Inc., San Francisco, 1970).

2. *Normative and value theories.* The works by Gauthier and Richards mentioned above cover both fields. Edgley's book belongs primarily to normative theory. Other major works in general normative theory are G. H. von Wright, *Norm and Action*, and A. Ross, *Directives and Norms* (Routledge and Kegan Paul, 1968). Von Wright's *The Varieties of Goodness*, and N. Rescher's *Introduction to Value Theory* (Prentice Hall Inc., Englewood, N.J., 1969), are among the more important recent books in value theory. I mention all these books primarily because all of them treat practical philosophy as a

unified field of study cutting across the divisions between moral, political and legal philosophy. In *The Varieties of Goodness*, pp. 6ff., von Wright suggests a classification of ethical concepts which resembles in some respects my suggested division of practical philosophy into the value theory, normative theory and the theory of ascription.

3.   *The theory of responsibility.* For a discussion of various senses of responsibility, cf. H. L. A. Hart, 'Responsibility and Retribution', in *Punishment and Responsibility* (Oxford, 1968), pp. 211–30.

4.   *The logical study of practical philosophy.* For a bibliography of modern works which preceded the revival of interest in the logic of practical reason in the 1950s, see G. H. von Wright, *An Essay in Deontic Logic and the General Theory of Action* (North Holland Publishing Company, Amsterdam, 1968), and N. Rescher, *The Logic of Commands* (Routledge and Kegan Paul, 1966).

CHAPTER 1 ON THE STRUCTURE OF REASONS

1.   *The role of reasons.* On reasons in general the following are particularly useful: Roy Edgley, 'Practical Reasons', *Mind*, 1965, p. 174, and *Reason in Theory and Practice*; Thomas Nagel, *The Possibility of Altruism* (Oxford, 1970); David A. J. Richards, *A Theory of Reasons for Action*.

2.   *Reason and the explanation of action.* The following are some of the more important recent contributions to the discussion on the relation between an action and the agent's beliefs and desires because of which it was done: G. E. M. Anscombe, *Intention* (Blackwell, Oxford, 1957); A. I. Melden, *Free Action* (Routledge and Kegan Paul, 1961); A. Kenny, *Action, Emotion and Will* (Routledge and Kegan Paul, 1963); A. I. Goldman, *A Theory of Human Action* (Prentice Hall Inc., Englewood, N.J., 1970); G. H. von Wright, *Explanation and Understanding* (Routledge and Kegan Paul, 1971); A. C. Danto, *Analytical Philosophy of Action* (Cambridge, 1973); D. Davidson, 'Actions, Reasons and Causes', *Journal of Philosophy*, **60** (1963), and 'Freedom to Act', in T. Honderich (Ed.), *Essays on Freedom of Action* (Routledge and Kegan Paul, 1973); R. Brandt and J. Kim, 'Wants as Explanations of Actions', *Journal of Philosophy.*, **60** (1963); D. Pears, 'Desires as Causes of Action', in *Royal Institute of Philosophy Lectures* (Macmillan, 1968), **1** (1966/7),

'Are Reasons for Action Causes?', in A. Stroll (Ed.), *Epistemology* (Harper & Row, New York, 1967), and 'Two Problems about Reasons for Action', in R. Binkley, R. Bronaugh, A. Marras (Eds), *Agent, Action and Reason* (University of Toronto Press, 1971).

3. *A complete reason.* Cf. J. L. Pollock, 'The Structure of Epistemic Justification', in N. Rescher (Ed.), *Studies in the Theory of Knowledge* (Blackwell, Oxford, 1970). Pollock's definition of 'a logical reason for belief' is similar in some respects to my definition of 'a complete reason for action'. But since his definition presupposes the notion of a good reason and is used to deal with different problems, it differs in several important respects from mine. I am indebted to Jesse Yoder for pointing out to me the need for the proviso.

4. *Conflicting reasons.* We require the definition of logical conflicts to be wider than that of a strict conflict in order to account for 'partial' or 'non-diametrical' conflicts. For a brief description of some partial conflicts see my 'Reasons, Requirements and Practical Conflicts' in S. Körner (Ed.), *Practical Reason* (Blackwell, Oxford, 1974), where I have described three such conflicts: (a) where ϕ-ing is compatible with ϕ'-ing on most occasions but incompatible with it in some contexts; (b) where some ways of ϕ-ing are compatible with some ways of ϕ'-ing, but certain ways of ϕ-ing are incompatible with some ways of ϕ'-ing; (c) where the two reasons are reasons to pursue certain goals which can be mutually realized to a certain degree but where the complete realization of one would come at the expense of the other.

5. *On 'overriding'.* Cf. R. Chisholm, 'The Ethics of Requirement', *Am. Phil. Quar.*, 1964, p. 147; 'Practical Reason and the Logic of Requirement', in S. Körner (Ed.), *Practical Reason*, and see also my comments in 'Reasons, Requirements and Practical Conflicts', *ibid*.

6. *'Cancelling' and 'overriding'.* There is another feature which is often associated with this distinction. Consider my promise to meet a friend at Carfax. The fact that I am unable to keep my promise because I have to take an injured man to hospital is itself a reason to explain and apologize to my friend. In the appropriate circumstances it is also a reason to compensate in some way for any inconvenience or loss he may have suffered through my failure. No such reason to compensate is created if I am released from my promise by him. We often feel that a reason which has been cancelled has been cancelled completely and is no longer a reason whereas a reason which is

'merely' overridden is somehow still there, it somehow survives. This feeling is explained by the fact that generally, but not always, if a reason is overridden (but not if it is cancelled) one has a reason to compensate. It may also be partly explained by the appropriateness of various emotions and attitudes such as regret that it has been overridden. These are extremely important considerations, which cannot be pursued here. Suffice it to say that they cannot be accounted for in terms of my distinction between cancelling and overriding alone. Other factors are also relevant to their explanation.

7. *Practical inference.* Practical inferences of the type alluded to in the text conform to the logic of satisfactoriness. Cf. A. J. P. Kenny, 'Practical Inference', *Analysis* (1966), p. 65; P. T. Geach, 'Dr Kenny on Practical Inference', *Analysis* (1966), p. 76; R. M. Hare, 'Practical Inferences', in his *Practical Inferences* (Macmillan, 1971).

8. *Conflicting 'ought' statements.* See, for an examination of some related problems, E. J. Lemmon, 'Deontic Logic and the Logic of Imperatives', *Logique et Analyse*, **29** (1965), p. 39.

9. *Belief and action.* See, for a discussion of related problems, von Wright, *Explanation and Understanding*, pp. 96–118.

10. *Interests as reasons.* For a most illuminating discussion of some of the presuppositions of regarding interests as reasons, see T. Nagel, *The Possibility of Altruism*, part ii.

11. *Desires as reasons.* There is a case for holding that, if a person did A just because he wanted to do A, he did not act for a reason. R. Edgley in his *Reason in Theory and Practice*, p. 159, maintained that a desire to perform an action is no reason to perform *that* action. Even so it is clear that even such a desire could well be a reason to perform some other action as when I go to the kitchen because I want to drink. Since desires in general are reasons and since failure to do what one desires to do raises the same problems and can be criticized on the same grounds as failure to do what one knows one has reason to do, it seems reasonable to generalize and regard the desire to do A as a reason for doing A. My view conforms to M. Black's in 'The gap between "Is" and "Should" ', *Philosophical Review* (1964), pp. 165–81. For a different approach, cf. R. M. Hare, 'Wanting: Some Pitfalls' in *Practical Inferences*, pp. 44–58.

12. *The two tests.* The argument in the text indicates the strategy adopted here and throughout the book. It is not claimed that it is

impossible to justify on the basis of a logic of first-order reasons all the practical conclusions that people wish to justify. The claim is that this is not the way we actually go about justifying our practical conclusions. Despite the indiscriminate application of the terminology of 'weight', 'strength', 'overriding', 'on balance', etc., we do in fact use different modes of reasoning to support different practical conclusions. It is this variety which the logic of exclusionary reasons helps to capture.

13.   *Conflicts between second-order reasons.* Another type of conflict which is of great importance and has not been considered here is that between two exclusionary reasons which exclude strictly conflicting reasons. Assume that p is a reason to exclude p' which is a reason for ϕ-ing and that q is a reason to exclude q' which is a reason for not ϕ-ing. We could say that p and q define conflicting points of view: consisting of all the reasons not excluded by p and all those not excluded by q, respectively. A complete theory of practical reasoning will have to explore the conditions under which such conflicts can or cannot be resolved.

14.   *Reasons of higher order.* In the present section I argued not merely that one can consistently talk of exclusionary reasons but also that some aspects of common practical discourse can be best explained as referring to exclusionary reasons. Whether or not there is any need to refer to reasons of higher orders remains to be seen. It should be noted, however, that a reason not to act on a second-order reason is itself a second-order reason (cf. the definition on p. 39 above).

15.   *Reasons for mistrusting one's judgement.* This interpretation may lead to a violation of Davidson's Principle of Continence. My principle (P 3) on the other hand does not contradict the principle of continence. Cf. D. Davidson, 'How is Weakness of the Will Possible?' in J. Feinberg (Ed.), *Moral Concepts* (Oxford, 1969).

CHAPTER 2 MANDATORY NORMS

1.   *Rules and principles.* On the distinction between them see M. G. Singer, 'Moral Rules and Principles', in A. I. Melden (Ed.), *Essays in Moral Philosophy* (University of Washington Press, Seattle and London, 1958); R. M. Dworkin, 'Is Law a System of Rules', *University of Chicago Law Review*, **35** (1967), p. 14; J. Raz, 'Legal Principles and the Limits of Law', *Yale Law Journal*, **81** (1972), p. 823.

2. *Rules and norms.* See generally on the analysis of rules, von Wright, *Norm and Action*; A. Ross, *Directives and Norms*; H. L. A. Hart, *The Concept of Law* (Oxford, 1961); D. P. Gauthier, *Practical Reasoning*; D. Lewis, *Convention* (Harvard University Press, 1969). Cf. also J. Rawls, 'Two Concepts of Rules', *Philosophical Review* (1955), pp. 3–32; B. J. Diggs, 'Rules and Utilitarianism', *American Philosophical Quarterly* (1964), pp. 32–44; M. Black, 'The Analysis of Rules', in *Models and Metaphors* (Cornell University Press, Ithaca, 1962); G. J. Warnock, *The Object of Morality* (Methuen, 1970), ch. 4.

3. *Rules and reasons.* Saying that rules are reasons is not saying that all rule statements are reason-giving statements. Similarly the fact that desires and values are reasons does not mean that whenever one states a value or that someone desires something one is engaged in giving a reason for some action.

4. *The imperative theory of rules* has been very influential in legal and political philosophy. In recent years its most subtle and determined defender has been H. Kelsen in his *The Pure Theory of Law*, 2nd ed. (University of California Press, Berkeley and Los Angeles, 1961) (English trans. 1967). For criticisms of the theory see H. L. A. Hart, *The Concept of Law* (Oxford, 1961), chs. 2–4; J. Raz, *The Concept of a Legal System* (Oxford, 1970).

5. *Hart's theory.* The analysis of Hart's theory is based on his *The Concept of Law*, pp. 54–6, 86–8, 96–107, 244.

6. *'Ought'-sentences and 'there is a rule' sentences.* The distinction between the 'ought' formulation and the 'it is a rule' formulation is of considerable importance. Hart does not, however, appear to regard it as important. On p. 56 of *The Concept of Law* he refers to expressions of the first type, whereas on p. 86 he refers to expressions of the second type.

7. *The practice theory* was criticized on grounds similar to my first and third points by R. M. Dworkin in 'Social Rules and Legal Theory', *Yale Law Journal*, 81 (1972), p. 855, and on grounds similar to my second point by G. J. Warnock in *The Object of Morality*, ch. 4.

8. *On conventional rules* cf. R. M. Dworkin, 'Social Rules and Legal Theory', *Yale Law Journal*, 81 (1972), pp. 855, 862f., and D. Lewis, *Convention*.

9.   *Decisions*. For a subtle and imaginative analysis of the first two conditions see Meiland, *The Nature of Intention* (Methuen, 1970), pp. 55–65. Meiland does not, however, recognize the importance of the other conditions.

10.   *The Promise Keeping Principle*. Cf. J. Raz, 'Voluntary Obligations and Normative Powers', *Proceedings of the Aristotelian Society*, supp. vol. **46** (1972), pp. 96–100.

11.   *Norms as exclusionary reasons*. My account of mandatory norms resembles in some important respects that of D. P. Gauthier, *Practical Reasoning*, and G. J. Warnock in *The Object of Morality*.

12.   *The application of the test*. Some may believe that statements of rules are statements of absolute reasons. To allow for such cases we should regard every fact which is an absolute reason as being also an absolute exclusionary reason with universal scope.

13.   *Orders and other prescriptions*. Cf. generally on orders and commands D. N. MacCormick, 'Legal Obligation and the Imperative Fallacy', in A. W. B. Simpson (Ed.), *Oxford Essays in Jurisprudence*, 2nd series (Oxford, 1973); A. Broadie, 'Imperatives', *Mind* (1972), p. 179.

CHAPTER 3 NON-MANDATORY NORMS

1.   *Strong permissions*. Cf. von Wright, *Norm and Action*, pp. 85–9; C. E. Alchouron and E. Bulygin, *Normative Systems* (Springer-Verlag, Vienna and New York, 1971), pp. 119–25; S. Munzer, 'Validity and Legal Conflicts', *Yale Law Journal*, **82**, pp. 1140, 1141–2. For a criticism of von Wright's distinction see also A. Ross, *Directives and Norms*, pp. 120–4. Von Wright has since explored other possibilities of distinguishing between permissions. For his most recent suggestion see 'Deontic Logic Revisited', *Rechtstheorie* (1973), p. 37.

2.   *Supererogation*. For some accounts of supererogation see J. O. Urmson, 'Saints and Heroes', in A. I. Meldon (Ed.), *Essays in Moral Philosophy*; J. Feinberg, 'Supererogation and Rules', in *Doing and Deserving* (Princeton University Press, 1970); M. Stocker, 'Supererogation and Duties', in N. Rescher (Ed.) *Stuides in Moral Philosophy* (Blackwell, Oxford, 1968); D. A. J. Richards, *A Theory of Reason for Action*, ch. 11.

3. *'Ought to φ but permitted not to φ'*. This is consistent with the principle P3, cf. p. 40, which states only what ought, all things considered, to be done. For a more detailed defence of the view defended in the text see J. Raz, 'Permissions and Supererogation', *American Philosophical Quarterly* (1975).

4. *Granting permissions*. In 'Some Alleged Differences between Imperatives and Indicatives', *Mind* (1967), R. M. Hare has argued that 'Do not do A' is the contradictory of 'Do A' on the ground that to say 'You may do A' is either to refuse to command or to state that no command was given. It seems to me, however, that the two commands are contraries because by saying 'You may do A' one can be granting a permission. Permitting and commanding are speech-acts of the same type and together they form a square of opposition in which the commands 'Do A' and 'Do not do A' are the contraries and the permissions 'You may do A' and 'You may not do A' are the sub-contraries. Therefore, *pace* Hare, the logic of commands is analogous in this respect to standard systems of deontic logic.

5. *Norms granting weak permissions*. In *The Concept of a Legal System*, pp. 170–5, I have argued on the assumption that all permissions are weak permissions, that there cannot be permissive norms.

6. *Normative Powers*. For discussion of legal powers see particularly J. Bentham, *Of Laws in General* (Ed. H. L. A. Hart, Athlone Press, 1970); H. L. A. Hart, 'Bentham on Legal Powers', *Yale Law Journal*, **81** (1972), p. 799; Hohfeld, *Fundamental Legal Conceptions* (Yale University Press, New Haven, 1919); Kelsen, *The Pure Theory of Law*, 2nd ed., pp. 145–63; C. Tapper, 'Powers and Secondary Rules of Change', in A. W. B. Simpson (Ed.), *Oxford Essays in Jurisprudence*, 2nd series. Pörn, in the second half of his *Logic of Power* (Blackwell, Oxford, 1970), offers a formalization of Hohfeld's scheme. For some instructive but on the whole unsuccessful attempts to discuss powers in a wider philosophical context, see von Wright, *Norm and Action*, ch. 10; A. Ross, *Directives and Norms*; N. D. MacCormick, 'Normative Powers and Voluntary Obligations', *Proc. Aristotelian Society*, supp. vol. **46** (1972).

7. *Power and Influence*. Many have tried to provide a reductive analysis of normative power in terms of influence. Hobbes, Spinoza and Bentham all favoured reductive analysis of powers in various forms, and the influence of their approach, particularly in political philosophy, is still considerable. In *The Concept of a Legal System*,

pp. 156–64, I have tried to analyse legal norms of all kinds as various species of O-norms which are in fact generalized influence relations. I no longer believe that norms can be analysed in terms of patterns of influence.

8.   *Power-conferring norms.* Much of the interest in power-conferring norms in recent years was stimulated by H. L. A. Hart's discussion of the subject in *The Concept of Law,* and in particular by his distinction between primary and secondary rules. I have criticized this distinction in 'On the Functions of Law' in A. W. B. Simpson (Ed.), *Oxford Essays in Jurisprudence,* 2nd series.

9.   *The analysis* propounded here is further discussed in J. Raz, 'Normative Powers and Voluntary Obligations', *Proc. Aristotelian Society,* supp. vol. **46** (1972), p. 79. The analysis presupposes a certain doctrine of the individuation of norms. For an outline of my views on this subject cf. *The Concept of a Legal System,* pp. 70–92, 140–7. I have already mentioned several times that not all rules are mandatory, permissive or power-conferring rules. There are other types of rules. In *The Concept of a Legal System,* pp. 168–86, I discussed the nature of non-normative rules, and there are many other rules as well. The reader should be warned, however, that unless otherwise indicated 'a rule' is used to refer to a rule of the kinds analysed here.

CHAPTER 4 NORMATIVE SYSTEMS

1.   *Constitutive Rules.* For ideas similar to Searle's see J. Rawls, 'Two Concepts of Rules', *The Philosophical Review,* **64** (1955), p. 3. For an attempt to construct a theory of law largely based on the distinction between constitutive and regulative rules cf. D. N. Mac-Cormick, 'Law as Institutional Fact', *Law Quarterly Review,* **90** (1974), p. 102. For effective criticism of Searle see G. J. Warnock, *The Object of Morality,* pp. 37f.

2.   *On games, rules and values* cf. Hubert Schwyzer's interesting article, 'Rules and Practices', *Philosophical Review* (1969), p. 451. It seems to me that Schwyzer is confusing two important points. Firstly, games cannot be defined in terms of their rules alone. To identify a game one must refer to its values. Secondly, some activities which are governed by the rules of a game and its values are not the playing of a game if in their social context the values of the game are not

artificial values, having acquired a systematic relationship to wider human concerns. Schwyzer describes a community in which chess is 'played' only once a year by the priests as a holy rite whose outcome is indicative of the will of the gods. In this community chess is being 'played' according to our rules and in order to 'win' (i.e. the values are the same as in our chess). The only difference is that the values are no longer artificial values. One could say that their chess is the same as ours except that theirs is not a game.

3. *Rules of games other than continuity rules.* The definition offered in the text should be narrowed by excluding rules of thumb. There are such rules the validity of which depends entirely on the values of the game, but they are not normally considered as part of the rules of the game. They are aids to the players when pressed for time, etc.

4. *The existence of institutionalized systems.* The classical jurisprudential discussions of the existence of legal systems are in J. Bentham, *A Fragment on Government* (1770), ch. 1, *Of Laws in General* (1970), ch. 1; J. Austin, *The Province of Jurisprudence Determined* (1832), lectures 2 and 6; H. Kelsen, *General Theory of Law and State* (Russell & Russell, New York, 1945), chs. 1 and 10; rnd H. L. A. Hart, *The Concept of Law* (1961), chs. 4 and 6. I have discussed some of the problems involved in ch. 9 and elsewhere *passim* in *The Concept of a Legal System* (1970) and I shall not aeturn to these here.

5. *Systems of common origin.* Hobbes, Austin and Kelsen are the most important proponents of the principle of common origin. The American Realists, J. Salmond in his *The First Principles of Jurisprudence* (1893), and H. L. A. Hart are the most important legal philosophers who emphasized the role of norm-applying institutions. I have discussed the issue at length in *The Concept of a Legal System* (1970).

6. *Unity.* Cf. Hume: 'A wheel within a wheel, such as we observe in the German empire, is considered by Lord Shaftesbury as an absurdity in politics: but what must we say to two equal wheels, which govern the same political machine, without any mutual check, control, or subordination, and yet preserve the greatest harmony and concord? To establish two distinct legislatures, each of which possesses full and absolute authority within itself, and stands in no need of the other's assistance, in order to give validity to its acts; this may appear, beforehand, altogether impracticable . . . And

should I assert, that the state I have in my eye was divided into two distinct factions, each of which predominated in a distinct legislature, and yet produced no clashing in these independent powers, the supposition may appear incredible . . . But there is no need for searching long, in order to prove the reality of the foregoing suppositions: for this was actually the case with the Roman republic', David Hume, 'Of Some Remarkable Customs', in *Essays* (Oxford, 1963), pp. 375–6.

7.   *Law-enforcing organs.* I have offered a different but related solution in *The Concept of a Legal System*, pp. 189–97. For the reasons explained on p. 134 and in section 5.2, I have opted here for a solution which is not based on the use of force or of sanctions.

8.   *Institutionalized systems and exclusionary reasons.* The views defended here were most powerfully criticized by R. M. Dworkin in his 'Is Law a System of Rules', in R. S. Summers (Ed.), *Essays in Legal Philosophy* (Blackwell, Oxford, 1968), and in 'Social Rules and Legal Theory', in *The Yale Law Journal*, **81** (1972), p. 855. I have discussed Professor Dworkin's views as they then were in 'Legal Principles and the Limits of Law', ibid., p. 823. For a characterization of ancient Athenian law which suggests that it might have been devoid of exclusionary reasons see A. M. Honoré, 'Legal Reasoning in Rome and Today', *Cambrian Law Review*, **4** (1973), p. 58.

9.   *Rules of recognition.* Cf. Hart, *The Concept of Law*, ch. 6, and his 'Kelsen's Doctrine of the Unity of Law', in H. E. Kiefer and M. K. Munitz (Eds.), *Ethics and Social Justice* (State University of New York Press, Albany, 1970). Cf. also my 'The Identity of Legal Systems , *California Law Review* (1971), p. 795, and 'Legal Principles and the Limits of Law', *Yale Law Journal*, **81** (1972), p. 823.

10.   *Conflicts of laws.* Cf. on this question R. M. Dworkin, 'Is Law a System of Rules', in R. S. Summers (Ed.), *Essays in Legal Philosophy*; J. Raz, 'Legal Principles and the Limits of Law', *Yale Law Journal*, **81** (1972), p. 823; S. Munzer, 'Validity and Legal Conflicts', *Yale Law Journal*, **82** (1973), p. 1140.

CHAPTER 5 LEGAL SYSTEMS

1.   *A sanctionless legal system.* I am much indebted to Professor H. Oberdiek for many discussions of this problem and for letting me read an unpublished paper of his on this subject.

2. *Natural law theories.* For critical evaluation of such theories see, e.g., Felix E. Oppenheim, *Moral Principles in Political Philosophy* (Random House, New York, 1968), and H. L. A. Hart, 'Positivism and the Separation of Law and Morals', *Harvard Law Review*, **71** (1958), p. 593. Lon L. Fuller's *The Morality of Law*, rev. ed. (Yale University Press, New Haven and London, 1964, 1969), is the best known contemporary example of the derivative approach. Hart's doctrine of the minimal content of natural law is explained in *The Concept of Law*, pp. 189–95.

3. *Statements of what ought to be done according to law.* Hart explains such statements by saying that they are made either from the external or from the internal point of view. He thus claims that all these statements are of one or the other basic types discussed above. My claim that many such statements belong to a third type which is logically related to the basic ones, but is not identical with them, is closely related to Kelsen's view. Kelsen's position is admittedly very obscure and much of it is wrong and confused but he was right to insist on the existence of a third class of statements. For an interpretation of his views see my 'Kelsen's Theory of the Basic Norms', *American Journal of Jurisprudence* (1974).

POSTSCRIPT TO THE SECOND EDITION:
RETHINKING EXCLUSIONARY REASONS

1. Much of my original interest in the project of the book was in an attempt to provide a foundation for a theory of law which is only part of the general theory of practical reason. From this point of view the main interest of the book is in its explanations of the systemic nature of law, of detached statements, of the relation between law and coercion, etc. Having somewhat further developed these points in subsequent writings, I will not address them here.

2. I am here disregarding the modifications required to make the above true in the face of the possibility of conflicting reasons.

3. A view which is of course compatible with holding that sometimes one has reasons for compliance as well. This was the view I took in the book.

4. But other things are not always equal. The reasons may be defeated by being overridden or excluded or cancelled.

5.   Especially since they are also reasons for belief. They are reasons to believe that one ought to perform that act (i.e. the act that one has reason to perform).

6.   Though again not because of any general fault in my attitude to it, merely because of my justified preoccupation with other matters.

7.   I consider here only cases of moral wrongs, but analogous comments apply to many cases where one has other kinds of reasons for certain omissions.

8.   Naturally I would want to qualify these observations in the way noted above to show that not every failure to act for a good reason attests to a failure in motivation or sensitivity.

9.   Rather than, that the moral law is simply a statement of what reasons are morally appropriate, so that the moral law cannot be a reason in its own right.

10.   I have discussed this kind of case in *The Morality of Freedom* (Oxford, 1986), ch. 2. This type of case is halfway between ordinary reasons and good-making characteristics which are not reasons because one cannot act for them without defeating their point. The need of students for encouragement from their teachers is such a case. They need the encouragement if it is motivated by belief in the value or promise of their work (i.e. when it is given for a belief that they deserve it). They do not need encouragement motivated by their need for it which is given without belief that they deserve it. Therefore, if I encourage a student because of his need for encouragement without believing that he deserves encouragement, my action achieves its aim only if he misunderstands my reason for encouraging him.

Properly developed, such common cases show that not all good-making characteristics are reason-giving. They therefore demonstrate that I took too simple a view of the relation between value and reason in the first edition of this book.

11.   Unless the overriding reason is excluded, on which see further below.

12.   It is crucial to remember that exclusionary reasons exclude valid reasons. One needs no special reason to exclude bad reasons. Their invalidity itself disqualifies them from being legitimate guides to action. Furthermore, exclusionary reasons do not cancel the reason they exclude. The exclusionary reason notwithstanding, the excluded reason remains a valid reason.

13.   As distinguished from, say, a medical one.

14.   Cf. pp. 37–39. See also my 'Facing Up', *Southern California Law Review*, **62** (1989), p. 1156.

15.   Though some promises, e.g., to look after his paintings until his children are old enough to appreciate them, are not so cancelled.

16.   See Ruth Marcus, 'Moral Dilemmas', *Journal of Philosophy*, **77** (1980), p. 127.

17.   I am here using the explanation I offered in 'Facing Up'.

18.   Perhaps one should say 'lead to the conclusion that the action is best done', for in ordinary language not all reasons support 'ought' conclusions. Suppose a new brand of margarine tastes better than the one I regularly use: other things being equal, it is best (or idiomatically better) to change to the new one. But ought I to do it? I will disregard such differences between reasons, important though they are, for they are immaterial to my purposes. I will use 'ought' sentences to indicate that an action is such that failure to do it, unless excused, indicates some fault, which need not be a moral one, nor a neglect of one's self-interest.
   This shows one aspect in which the explanation of 'ought' statements offered in this book is inadequate. In my introduction to J. Raz (Ed.), *Practical Reasoning* (Oxford, 1978), I retracted the suggestion in this book that 'ought to do A in circumstances C'-statements are logically equivalent to 'there is a reason to do A in circumstances C'-statements. Instead I suggested that they are logically equivalent to 'there is a reason to A in C which is not defeated by other reasons in every case of C'. Thus 'ought to A in C'-statements are justified by a reason to A in C, with a statement that other things are equal. The circumstances in which it is said that the action ought to be done determine the scope of the 'other things being equal' premise required to justify it. Other things are equal if whatever other considerations defeat the reasons for so acting in those circumstances do not defeat it in all the circumstances in which it is said to be required.

19.   There are also exceptions to what we say, and the remarks about exceptions to rules apply to them as well. If I assert that one should never deceive, I may nevertheless admit to an exception when deceit is necessary to save life. What we say expresses our judgement on all the relevant considerations we are aware of, and is subject to exceptions when the main reasons which apply to the case are overridden in particular circumstances. Sometimes we use 'there is reason' sentences to

convey not what there is a reason to do, but what there is the best reason to do, i.e. to reflect our overall judgement of the way conflicts of reasons are to be resolved. Such statements are subject to exceptions. One says, 'There is reason to go swimming every day except when the sea is rough'.

20.   They may also be competing instrumental reasons (see above p. 182). Or perhaps these should be considered as a type of cancelling conditions. I may get into this room through one door or through the other. Given that going through either is sufficient to achieve the end of getting there, I have reason to get through each of them, and I cannot do both. But then I do not have reason to do both. If I did one this cancels the reason to do the other.

21.   Under that description. If I have been released from my promise to help a friend find accommodation, doing so will no longer be keeping my word and therefore will not be desirable under that description. It may still be desirable as helping a friend in need, etc.

22.   Equally common and better studied are the cases in which both reasons secure the same good, and the question is of evaluating the relative degree to which conformity with each will secure it. Both writing to 'The Times' and appearing on TV will publicize the cause I am concerned with. If I can do one but not both, often the only question is which course of action will provide greater publicity.

23.   Colin's case is an example of a different category of exclusionary reasons. Here one feels that his promise is binding because people may sacrifice their interests, i.e. they may within bounds act against the better reason if their own interest is the only victim. The 'may' here is the exclusionary permission analysed in this book. This notion is akin to S. Sheffler's 'agent-centered prerogative' (*The Rejection of Consequentialism* [Oxford, 1982]), though exclusionary permissions need not be agent-centered. 'Agent-centered prerogatives' are permissions to give in one's reasoning some considerations more or less weight than they have. Exclusionary permissions are permissions to disregard certain reasons altogether. If one views this as giving them zero weight, then Sheffler's prerogatives are seen as a generalisation of exclusionary permissions (in the same way that S. Perry's 'weighting reasons' ('Second Order Reasons, Uncertainty and Legal Theory', *Southern California Law Review*, **62** [1989], p. 913) which require people to give certain reasons more or less weight than they have are a generalisation of exclusionary reasons). Sheffler's interest is in arguing for the permissibility of giving extra

weight to one's interest. Colin's example belongs to the other side of this coin, i.e. the permissibility of giving one's own interest less weight than it has. See M. Slote, *Common Sense Morality and Consequentialism* (Routledge and Kegan Paul, 1985).

Some people may disagree with this explanation of Colin's situation (the disagreement being on substantive moral issues). They will regard him as duty bound to make the promise he made. They may even say that he is duty bound, by his obligations as a parent, to ignore his interest in choosing his son's school. I do not share this view of parenthood, but I agree with the point of principle and will comment later on the fact that certain roles and responsibilities involve excluding certain reasons from being the basis of one's action.

24. This is compatible with certain exclusionary reasons' specifying a condition that they exclude only reasons of certain importance, etc. It is also consistent with maintaining that some reasons can never be validly excluded. Remember that an exclusionary reason succeeds in excluding only if it is valid.

25. Since the original publication of the book I have attempted to develop its central theses further. Commitments were considered in 'Promises and Obligations', in P. M. H. Hacker and J. Raz (Eds.), *Law, Society and Morality* (Oxford, 1977); rules issued by authority have been extensively discussed, especially in ch. 1 of *The Authority of Law* (Oxford, 1979) and chs. 2–4 of *The Morality of Freedom*. See also 'Facing Up', 1153.

26. 'Right' given that it will be required of everyone impartially by an effective authority. Thus the authority's intervention may make a difference. The required action may not have been the best action to take had it not been required by such an authority.

27. For an argument that this duty is independent of whatever duty of obedience one owes to a legitimate authority, see *The Morality of Freedom*, ch. 4.

28. The person who does so to escape a Prisoner's Dilemma problem has of course reason to escape the dilemma, i.e. his conformity with general reasons he has to achieve certain results leads him to seek a way to change the concrete reasons for action which confront, or may come to confront, him in certain concrete situations.

29. And they defeat all competing considerations. In the monist value theory of the Utilitarians this last condition can be omitted.

30.   In both cases the decision may be neither final nor exhaustive. Non-excluded considerations may override the reason constituted by the rule; and the rule leaves unsettled many details about the particulars, timing, and other circumstances of the action required.

31.   For the details of the argument from expertise, see *The Morality of Freedom*, ch. 3, pp. 67–69, and 'Facing Up', pp. 1194–6. For the argument about coordination, see 'Facing Up', pp. 1194–6.

32.   Ignorance may be rational, given the costs of acquiring information. So having an opportunity to rely on, say, consumer protection and environmental protection standards required by law saves me much time which otherwise would have had to be dedicated to learning about the potentially damaging properties of various products. The justification of expertise-based authority may include not only the overcoming of the limitations of existing ignorance, but the possibility of extending one's ignorance without (significant) detriment.

33.   In 'Facing Up' I analysed such cases, in much greater detail, and pointed to a range of related problems in securing coordination, in addition to the one mentioned here.

34.   When they are justified. In other words, rules are justified, valid, if this condition holds true.

35.   When following a rule in such circumstances is not justified, the rule itself is not valid as stated but subject to an exception. See my discussion of rules with an exception when the agent is confronted by a clear case of unjustified requirement in *The Morality of Freedom*, p. 68, and in 'Facing Up', p. 1195.

36.   See p. 185 above. In the case of rules and other protected reasons the argument is more complex. The complicating factor is that protected reasons are a combination of an exclusionary reason and a first-order reason. Rules, promises, decisions, and authoritative decrees affect the outcome not only by excluding certain considerations, but also by adding certain reasons to the balance of (first-order) reasons. How does that factor affect the case of luck through miscalculation?

We need to distinguish between the two ways in which the first-order reasons provided by promises, authoritative directives, rules, and decisions can be related to the reasons excluded by the exclusionary aspect of such protected reasons. The first-order reasons may be meant to reflect the excluded ones, or they may be meant to add to them. A decision is typically meant to reflect the reasons which led (or should have led) to it. An authoritative rule prohibiting the marketing of a dangerous toy is similarly meant to reflect the reasons which make the toy too dangerous for use by children. A court's decision that the plaintiff defamed the defendant and is liable to pay damages is likewise meant to reflect considerations which applied to the plaintiff prior to the decision. But a law imposing a tax on capital gains, while reflecting reasons which indicate that people who benefit from capital appreciation should contribute to financing public projects, also adds to the excluded reasons. It settles precisely how much one should pay, at what times and to what address such contributions should be made, and so on. It thus creates 'new' first-order reasons (e.g., to file reports within a certain period, to pay within a certain period, to pay a particular sum rather than a little less or a little more, etc.). When we talk of acting on the right balance of reasons, with the excluded reasons taken into account, we mean all the first-order reasons, including the 'new' first-order reason created by the promise, the law, etc., but excluding the 'dependent' first-order reasons created by them which are merely a reflection of other first-order reasons, and which should not be allowed to count twice.

37.   I have had a stab at this in *The Morality of Freedom*.

Index

Made in the USA
San Bernardino, CA
16 December 2013